THE FORGOTTEN LABRADOR

The Forgotten Labrador

Kegashka to Blanc-Sablon

CLEOPHAS BELVIN

McGill-Queen's University Press
Montreal & Kingston · London · Ithaca

© McGill-Queen's University Press 2006

ISBN-13: 978-0-7735-3151-2 ISBN-10: 0-7735-3151-3

Legal deposit fourth quarter 2006
Bibliothèque nationale du Québec

Printed in Canada on acid-free paper

McGill-Queen's University Press acknowledges the support of the
Canada Council for the Arts for our publishing program. We also
acknowledge the financial support of the Government of Canada
through the Book Publishing Industry Development Program (BPIDP)
for our publishing activities.

Library and Archives Canada Cataloguing in Publication

Belvin, Cleophas, 1959–
   The forgotten Labrador : Kegashka to Blanc-Sablon / Cleophas
Belvin.

Includes bibliographical references and index.
ISBN-13: 978-0-7735-3151-2 ISBN-10: 0-7735-3151-3

   1. Labrador and Newfoundland – History.   2. Fisheries –
Newfoundland and Labrador – History.   I. Title.

FC2193.51.B44 2006   971.8'2   C2006–903164-9

Typeset in 10½/13 Sabon by True to Type

Contents

Preface

For the past nine thousand years people of diverse cultural backgrounds have occupied the Quebec-Labrador coast, known today as the Lower North Shore, extending eastward from Kegashka, a village near the Natashquan River, to Blanc-Sablon, a community near the Newfoundland-Labrador border. These people were drawn to the region because of an abundance of aquatic creatures, including salmon, seal, and cod; the many terrestrial mammals, such as the caribou and the beaver; and a large avian population.

The Aboriginal people, the first occupants of the area, followed a seasonal round and hunted a variety of animals, such as seals and caribou; harvested different kinds of fish, including salmon and trout; and gathered berries and birds' eggs. In the sixteenth and seventeenth centuries migratory fishermen from Europe came to the region annually in the summer months, erected temporary dwellings, and pursued the cod and whale fisheries. From the middle of seventeenth century through to the first two decades of the nineteenth century, French- and English-speaking entrepreneurs from the town of Quebec established permanent fishing posts in the area, engaged in the seal and salmon fisheries and the fur trade, and maintained a monopoly in the area.

With the demise of the company known as Labrador New Concern in 1820, French-speaking migrants from places such as Quebec and the surrounding area and the Îles de la Madeleine (Magdalen

Islands) and English-speaking migrants from various localities, including the British Isles and Newfoundland, arrived on the coast. They built permanent residences and became involved in the seal fishery, the salmon fishery, the cod fishery, and the fur trade. With the settlers came missionaries, schools, medical facilities, and eventually communication and transportation links with the outside world. Throughout the years the French- and English-speaking residents developed a culture, a lifestyle, an identity, and an economy that were particular to that part of Canada.

Recently, however, because of the demise of the fisheries and modernization, this distinctive culture, lifestyle, identity, and economy have undergone many changes, and much of what was has disappeared. As well, many of the people living in the region, especially the younger generation, have little or no sense of what life was like prior to the 1970s. Unfortunately, very little has been done by historians to document the history and culture of the region.

This book outlines the history of the Quebec-Labrador coast between Kegashka and Blanc-Sablon. It provides details about the occupation of the area by the different groups at various times. Emphasis, however, has been placed on the lifestyle, living conditions, and activities of the French- and English-speaking residents. Special attention has been given to the development of the fisheries – the seal and cod fisheries in particular – because they were essential to the occupation and development of the region.

Most of the information for this book was garnered from archival documents, many of which have been used for the first time. This publication is intended for people with little or no knowledge of the history of the Quebec-Labrador coast. If it leads to further attempts to expand our knowledge of the region, so much the better. For much, far too much, remains to be discovered.

Acknowledgments

I am very grateful to a number of people. John Bell encouraged me from the onset and made a number of wonderful suggestions, including the title of my book. Antonio Lechasseur also provided some interesting insights. I am indebted to Elizabeth Hulse, a superb editor, who did an excellent job in tightening up the manuscript, verifying and correcting errors, and removing duplication.

I am also extremely grateful to many coasters past and present for their input: Nathaniel and Philip Lloyd, Samuel Robertson, John Goddard, Martin Parent, James Belvin, Michael Kenty, Benjamin Reed, James McKinnon, Francois Michael, Laurent Gallibois, Charles Bilodeau, Louis Lessard, Matthew and Andrew Kennedy, Robert Shattler, Samuel Robin, John Fequet, Louis Chevalier, James Buckle, Darius Choaker, Sam Keats, Randall Jones, Michael Lavallee, Richard Burke, Louis Labadie, Daniel Monger, Charles Dicker, and J.B. Dumas.

I am deeply indebted to the staff at Library and Archives Canada, the Archives nationales du Québec, the Archives Deschâtelets, the Coasters' Association, Louise Abbot and Kent Benson for their annotated stills, and Stephen Engle for the map.

I would also like to thank Helen, who has been extremely supportive for the past twenty-five years.

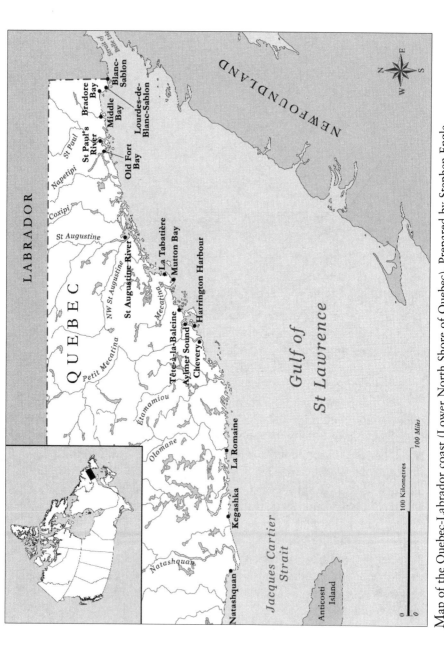

Map of the Quebec-Labrador coast (Lower North Shore of Quebec). Prepared by Stephen Engle

Jacques Cartier's sailing ship (LAC C5933)

Itinerant trading schooner (LAC PA48310)

Summer house – sod hut (LAC PA187171)

Winter house (LAC P178348)

Itinerant trader Captain Narcisse Blais and his descendants (ANQ, Côte-Nord, 1948, SHCN Coll. no. 243)

Reverend Charles Carpenter, Congregational Church minister (LAC 187167)

Summer house and garden (LAC P179230)

Trapboats tied up at the wharf (LAC PA196627)

Congregational Church at Bonne-Espérance Harbour (LAC C133725)

Tête-à-la-Baleine Harbour (LAC C142365)

Petit Mecatina Harbour (LAC C133724)

Lower North Shore Economic Council, Bishop Lionel Scheffer and Father Gabriel Dionne in front row (ANQ, Côte-Nord, no. 135, CEDAG Coll.)

Harrington Harbour (LAC PA196627)

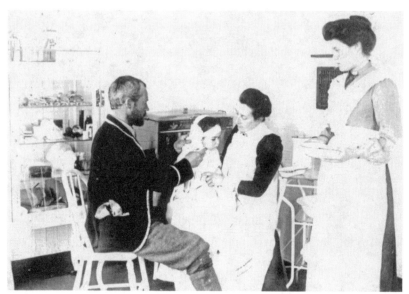

Dr Wilfred Grenfell attending to a patient at Harrington Harbour Hospital
(LAC PA178342)

Dr Donald G. Hodd (PANL, IGA Coll., 16A 22–42, no. 140)

Grenfell Mission Hospital at Harrington Harbour (LAC PA194898)

Hospital at Lourdes-de-Blanc-Sablon (ANQ, Côte-Nord, no. 101, CEDAG Coll. no. 300)

Fishermen off-loading cod (LAC PA193577)

Men returning from a duck-hunting expedition (LAC PA193550)

Men collecting dried cod (LAC PA193552)

Hauling a cod trap (LAC PA193548)

Winter mail run (LAC PA193603)

Seals stored in pen (LAC PA179232)

A Norseman airplane (ANQ, Côte-Nord, no. 125, CEDAG Coll. no. 302)

The ss *North Shore* was a Clarke Steamship that transported passengers, mail, and cargo along the coast (ANQ, Côte-Nord, no. 1922, SHCN Coll. no. 264)

Mailman Jos Hébert (LAC PA194901)

William Henry Whiteley's fishing establishment at Bonne-Espérance (LAC 187168)

THE FORGOTTEN LABRADOR

I

Forgotten Labrador

Geographically, the term "Labrador" refers to the entire northeastern peninsula of North America. This vast region, bounded on the northwest by Ungava Bay, on the north by Hudson Strait, on the east by the Atlantic Ocean, and on the south by the Gulf of St Lawrence, has an area of some 1,620,000 square kilometres.

For several centuries, however, mariners and geographers commonly used the name Labrador to identify the coastal area of the Labrador Peninsula, from Pointe-des-Monts in the Gulf of St Lawrence eastward to the Hudson Strait. In 1825 the boundary for the Labrador coast was redrawn, and the coast lying westward of a line running due north and south from the bay or harbour of Ance Sablon (Blanc-Sablon) as far as fifty-second degrees north latitude was made part of the province of Lower Canada (Quebec). The western boundary, however, was never clearly defined, and for the next century or so both Canada and the colony of Newfoundland (present-day province of Newfoundland and Labrador) laid claim to Blanc-Sablon. Canada maintained that the boundary line was at the eastern headland of the Bay of Blanc-Sablon and therefore included Blanc-Sablon. The colony of Newfoundland claimed that the boundary passed through Lazy Point, a little headland a short distance west of Blanc-Sablon and Île au Bois. The situation was resolved in 1927 by the Judicial Committee of the Privy Council of Great Britain, which declared that Blanc-Sablon and Île au Bois belonged to the province of Quebec.[1]

Since 1825 the Quebec portion of the Labrador coast has undergone various name changes. For a number of years the coast in the province of Quebec west of Kegashka was referred to as the North Shore, and that portion extending from Kegashka to Blanc-Sablon was typically called either the Canadian–Labrador coast or the Quebec-Labrador coast. When Newfoundland and Labrador joined Canada in 1949, the terms Canadian Labrador coast and Quebec-Labrador coast fell into disuse, and the Quebec portion was renamed. The terms Upper North Shore, Middle North Shore, and Lower North Shore were used to designate those parts of the Labrador coast in the province of Quebec.

That portion of the Quebec-Labrador coast known today as the Lower North Shore extends eastwards from Kegashka to Blanc-Sablon. It is bounded to the north and east by the Newfoundland-Labrador border, to the west by the Natashquan River, and to the south by the Gulf of St Lawrence. It consists of an area approximately 400 kilometres long and 80 kilometres wide. Most local residents, however, rarely use the name Lower North Shore when referring to the region. Instead, they prefer "the coast," and they call themselves "coasters."

LANDSCAPE

Geologically, the Quebec-Labrador coast between Kegashka and Blanc-Sablon, with the exception of Bradore Bay, which consists mainly of red and brown sandstone and minor grey shale, is part of the Canadian Shield and is largely made up of plutonic and metamorphic rock, some of which is several billion years old. For several hundred million years erosion dominated the geology of the coast. Rivers stripped rock from the land surface, carrying it to the oceans to be deposited offshore. Long periods of fluvial erosion led to the development of extensive plains, the remnants of which are the upland surfaces of the area.

Some two million years ago, great ice sheets advanced and retreated many times across the Labrador Peninsula, including that portion extending from Kegashka to Blanc-Sablon. The continual movement of the glaciers smoothed and polished wide areas, eroded lake basins, and carved deep valleys through mountainous areas. Along the coast, the sea flooded these valleys, creating deep fjords. This type of activity reached its peak approximately twelve thousand years ago. Slowly, over the following six millennia, the ice cap receded, and around six thousand years ago it disappeared. As the ice moved back from the shore, the coastline was revealed in its now familiar terrain.

Currently, the mainland portion of the Quebec-Labrador coast consists primarily of a succession of hills extending inland from the sea. Indented by numerous inlets, bays, and rivers, the coast is very low in most places, seldom exceeding 150 metres above sea level. The only portion of the mainland that does not conform to this description is the Bradore Hills, three contiguous round-backed mountains situated seven or eight kilometres inland, north east-ward from the head of Bradore Bay.[2] The Northwest Summit, the highest point of land along the coast, is 385 metres above sea level. Those seemingly barren hills bear a variety of flowers, plants, and berries including the famed bakeapple (cloudberry) and red-berry (partridge berry). In the sheltered bays and along the streams and rivers, there is a fairly dense growth of underbrush and trees, such as balsam, black spruce, and birch.

The sea near the mainland of this portion of the Quebec-Labrador coast is replete with numerous isles and islets composed of granite. Some of these are entirely bare. Others are covered with moss, scrubby spruce bushes, a few birch trees, and numerous ponds of dark bog water. All the islands except for Gros Mecatina Island, sit-uated opposite the present-day village of La Tabatière, and Petit Mecatina Island, located near the mouth of the Petit Mecatina River, are at or below sea level. These two large islands tower above the rest, the high land of Gros Mecatina Island reaching 210 metres above sea level.[3]

CLIMATE

Along the Quebec-Labrador coast, the climate is highly variable and harsh, often with short-term changes in the weather patterns that can be difficult to predict. James McKenzie, an employee with the North West Company in the early nineteenth century, described the climate of the region as possibly the least favoured by nature of the inhabited globe.[4]

The Labrador Current, a cold surface current that flows down from the islands of the Canadian Arctic, has a great impact on the climate of the region. It travels along the coast of Labrador, where it is split into two streams by the northwest projection of New-foundland. The lesser stream passes through the Strait of Belle Isle into the Gulf of St Lawrence, skirts Anticosti Island, and emerges past Cape Breton Island to join the parent stream. The portion of the Labrador Current that goes through the Strait of Belle Isle transports icebergs and pack ice from the Arctic, which clog the harbours and bays along the Quebec-Labrador coast from Blanc-Sablon to Kegashka from December to May. The cold current also chills the coast.

As a result, winters along this section of the Quebec-Labrador coast tend to be brutally cold, stormy, and long, lasting anywhere from seven to eight months. The cold weather usually sets in during the second half of November and lasts until the middle of May, with snow still visible in some areas until late June. The temperature throughout the winter months varies considerably, ranging anywhere from o to –40 degrees Celsius. The Reverend Charles Carpenter, a Canada Foreign Missionary Society minister stationed at the present-day village of St. Paul's River,5 in his annual report for 1863, describes the arrival of winter in the following manner: "Cold weather now rapidly comes on. The river and its large bays above us, suddenly freezing. Storm followed storm till the average depth of snow in the woods, when settled down was six feet. Farther inside it was nine feet, while the wind piled it in walls around some of our houses so high that staircases were cut down to the doors, and avenues to the windows. Although we have experienced no such terrible drift storms as in the previous winters, the cold was steadily and almost uninterruptedly severe."6

The summers, on the other hand, are usually very short and cool; they begin during the first week of July and end about the middle of August. Along the shoreline and among the islands, summer temperatures rarely exceed 15 to 18 degrees Celsius. Twenty-five to thirty kilometres inland, however, it is considerably warmer, with the thermometer hovering around 20 to 22 degrees Celsius. Fog and strong southerly winds are common at this time of the year, especially by the seashore and among the islands. John James Audubon, the pre-eminent American naturalist and artist, on 4 August 1833 observed, "The fruits are now ripe, yet six weeks ago the whole country was a sheet of snow, the bays locked in ice, the air a constant storm. Now and then an appearance of summer does exist, but in thirty days all is over; the dark northern clouds will enwrap the mountain summits; the rivulets, the ponds, the rivers, the bays themselves will begin to freeze; heavy snowfalls will cover all these shores, and nature will resume her sleeping state of deso-lation and death."[7]

The short summers are punctuated by hordes of black flies and mosquitoes. A.S. Packard, an American naturalist who visited St Paul's River in the summer of 1860, commented, "Here we met the black flies in full force, and although we had been fearfully annoyed by them in rambling over Caribou Island, here they were more astounding, both for numbers and voracity ... The armies of black flies were supported by light brigades of mosquitoes."[8]

FAUNAL RESOURCES

The Labrador Current also provides a productive habitat for many aquatic creatures along the Quebec-Labrador coast between Kegashka and Blanc-Sablon. Nutrients required for the production of microscopic plant plankton are found in high concentrations in the Hudson Strait Outflow. In the spring the increasing light and warming effects of the sun combine with this rich nutrient source to create the conditions necessary for an extensive plant plankton bloom along the comparatively shallow continental shelf of Labrador. The water temperature of the Labrador Current during the bloom slows down the growth of bacteria, which in warmer waters destroy many of the tiny plant plankton that forms the base of all food chains in the sea.

For many years, two species of whale frequented the waters in this region at different times of the year to feed on the plankton. Augustin Le Gardeur de Courtemanche, owner of a post at Bradore Bay in the early eighteenth century, reported that there were numer-ous right and bowhead whales along the Quebec-Labrador coast.[9] The right whales migrated northward during the spring and early summer and arrived in the region sometime in July. They remained there until the onset of cooler conditions signalled the time to return south, probably in late August, or early September. Bowhead whales, an Arctic species, travelled southward ahead of the pack ice and probably arrived in late October in the area, where they remained for several months. Both right and bowhead whales move relatively slowly. They also produced oil and baleen in large quan-tities. But more importantly, the bowhead and right whales float after death; so they were ideal prey for individuals involved in the whale fishery. Successive years of overfishing, however, eventually resulted in the disappearance of the bowhead and right whales from the region.

Several species of seals, including the harp seal (1.5 to 2 metres in length) and the hooded seal (2.5 to 3 metres in length), were also found in abundance among the coastal islands and in the estuaries of various rivers.[10] In late fall, both species leave the Arctic and Greenland waters, where they have been feeding since the month of July. The seals migrate southwards along the Labrador coast in December; there they separate into two herds near the Strait of Belle Isle. One herd stays along the coasts of southern Labrador and northern Newfoundland. The other passes through the Strait of Belle Isle, follows the Quebec-Labrador coast westward, and stops at Anticosti Island. From January onwards, both herds stay on pack ice. The females give birth between the end of February and the middle of March, after which the young are milked for a month or more. In May the seal herd residing in the Gulf of St Lawrence starts to move towards the Atlantic, going directly towards the Strait of Belle Isle. There it meets up with the southern Labrador and northern Newfoundland herds, and both start their June migration back to the Arctic waters.

Numerous cod visited these waters on a regular basis as well. The cod follow a pronounced seasonal migration. In the winter and spring, sea life withdraws to deep waters, but with the retreat of the ice the cod follow the capelin and the herring, their main food source, and come to spawn from May to September in the gulfs and fjords and the shallow layer of water that covers the banks. Cod making for the Quebec portion of the Labrador coast strike the land at Natashquan, one-half keeping to the westward, along the north shore as far as Pointe-des-Monts, and the other half going eastward to the Strait of Belle Isle. Cod generally appear along the coast east of the Natashquan River around mid-June. They were most abundant at Blanc-Sablon, Bradore Bay, Salmon Bay, Dog Islands, and Mutton Bay.[11] Today, the cod, overfished by foreign trawlers and local fishermen for many years, have all but disappeared from the region.

The rivers along the Quebec-Labrador coast between Kegashka and Blanc-Sablon were once replete with salmon. Louis Jolliet, who explored the area during the latter part of the seventeenth century, reported seeing many salmon in the St Augustine River, and Courtemanche in his memoir of 1705, states that all the rivers along the coast were teeming with salmon.[12] Salmon usually begin showing up in this area in late June or the beginning of July. They spawn in the upper reaches of the rivers in the fall. The eggs hatch the following spring, after which the young salmon spend from one to six years in freshwater river mouths and estuaries. The adult salmon then disappear to sea, making seasonal migrations to the inshore regions during the spring and early summer, in pursuit of the smaller spawning fish. Much like the cod, the salmon, because of overfishing by local fishermen for many years, have diminished considerably, and many of the rivers in the region now carry very few.

In addition to the many aquatic creatures, numerous species of terrestrial mammals roamed along the Quebec-Labrador coast. James McKenzie in 1808 noted that caribou in some years browsed in great herds on the plains and hills.[13] Known as woodland caribou, these animals, which are found in small groups, spend the summer months on alpine and windy slopes and the winter months in the forest. They breed in early to mid-October, and the calves are usually born between late May and early June. A cow does not mate or breed until she is two-and-a-half years old and will usually produce one calf a year. The woodland caribou once roamed the region in herds several thousand strong, especially in the St Augustine River and Gros Mecatina River regions. Today they are rarely seen in the area. Their decline has been mainly the result of disease and over-hunting.

Beavers occupied many of the brooks, ponds, and lakes throughout the region. The adult beaver weighs from 16 to 32 kilograms and is approximately 114 centimetres in length including the tail. Its coat is composed of fur and hair; the fur grows to about 1.9 centimetres in length, and the hair to about 5 to 6.3 centimetres. A colony of beavers usually consists of an adult pair and a number of yearlings and kits (the young per litter average two or three). The carrying capacity for a beaver habitat is about one active lodge per square kilometre. There were also numerous bears, otters, rabbits, porcupines, lynxes, muskrats, foxes, martens, and minks.

Along with the aquatic and terrestrial animals, a large avian population was found in the area. Seabirds of all kinds were plentiful, especially on the outer islands. The sixteenth-century explorer

Jacques Cartier and others reported seeing numerous auks, murres, and gulls.[14] Some birds, such as gulls, common murres, and eider ducks, are part of a year-round resident population. Others, such as the common loon, the Canada goose, and the cormorant, come to the coast in the spring to nest. Many migratory birds, including the mallard, the passenger pigeon, and the Eskimo curlew, stopped over on their annual spring and fall migration. Both the partridge and the ptarmigan were found in abundance as well. James McKenzie in 1808 reported, "In the spring and fall, the coasts swarms with wild fowls, in such variety as would require the knowledge and skill of the naturalist to classify and describe."[15] Compared to former years, the avian population has decreased considerably. Its decline has been due in part to the destructive egging practices carried on for many years by outsiders and local residents alike, and in part to over-hunting by local inhabitants.

Jacques Cartier, one of the first Europeans to visit that portion of the Quebec-Labrador coast extending from Kegashka to Blanc-Sablon, was not overly impressed with what he saw. In his journal for 1534 he reports that the region had little or nothing whatsoever to offer humankind. "It was broken and rocky, having no soil nor timber except in some of the valleys. In truth, it could scarcely be termed, 'the New Lande,' being composed of stones and horrible rugged rocks; for along the whole of the north shore of the Gulf, I did not see one cartload of earth and yet I landed in many places. Except at Blanc-Sablon there is nothing but moss and short, stunted shrub. I am rather inclined to believe that this is the land God gave to Cain."[16] Nevertheless, there had been a continuous migration of people to the region long before Jacques Cartier arrived.

2

The First Inhabitants

The original inhabitants of North America left no direct written account of their history prior to sustained European contact, which began in the sixteenth century. Archaeological evidence suggests they migrated from Siberia to Alaska via a land bridge approximately twelve to fifteen thousand years ago. Once they arrived in North America, the newcomers gradually spread across the continent in search of favourable hunting and fishing sites. Some took up residence along what is now the Quebec-Labrador coast between Kegashka and Blanc-Sablon.

THE MARITIME ARCHAIC PEOPLE

The first inhabitants of the area were the Maritime Archaic people, who arrived some seven or eight thousand years ago. Evidence of their presence has been unearthed along the Quebec-Labrador coast at places such as Blanc-Sablon, Bradore Bay, Middle Bay, St Paul's River, Old Fort Bay, St Augustine River, La Tabatière, Mutton Bay, and the Mecatina islands.[1]

The Maritime Archaic people were probably the descendants of the Palaeo-Indians of the present-day Maritime provinces and New England states. Some may have arrived in the area by crossing the St Lawrence River by boat during the summer. Others possibly wandered far enough up the St Lawrence to cross by foot during the winter. They probably came to the region because of its abundance of animals, particularly seals, cod, salmon, birds, and caribou.[2]

Archaeological artifacts unearthed at Belles Amours, Petit Mecatina Island, Gros Mecatina Island, and elsewhere in the region suggest that the Maritime Archaic people along the Quebec-Labrador coast attained a certain level of sophistication. They lived in moderate-sized rectangular houses, which had several internal partitions or multi-segmented rooms (three to five rooms) and hearths, and probably housed more than one family. The houses were usually erected in outer coast areas and had food caches that were undoubtedly used to store seals and other marine animals. The artifacts that suvive include triangular points and lanceolate spears or knives made of local quartz or quartzite, small round skin scrapers of the same types of material, and ground stone axes and gouges made of slate and diorite.[3]

Archaeological sites farther eastward in the Strait of Belle Isle and elsewhere indicate that the Maritime Archaic people practised a variety of magic and religious rituals, including honouring their dead and belief in an afterlife, which are confirmed by the discovery of cemeteries containing up to a hundred or so burials accompanied by many funeral offerings. In exceptional cases, they built burial mounds comprised of several layers of sand and stone. Maritime Archaic people usually covered the bodies of the deceased with ochre and wrapped them in bark or skins. In order to facilitate the deceased's life in the next world, offerings of polished stone tools, birds, flutes, amulets, pendants, and various animal parts were placed near the dead person's body. These acted as charms for good hunting or endowed their owners with the qualities and powers of the animal represented.[4]

The Maritime Archaic people probably followed a seasonal round. In the spring they would have hunted marine mammals such as seals with toggle harpoons. At this time of year they in all probability killed sea and migratory birds and collected their eggs. Throughout the summer months these people likely fished for salmon, cod, trout, and other freshwater and saltwater fish with nets and harpoons. As well, they probably collected a variety of wild berries, some of which may have been preserved for the upcoming winter. In the fall they turned in all likelihood their attention to the seal hunt and later moved farther inland to take advantage of the migrating caribou and to pursue other fur-bearing animals, including bears, beavers, and hares.

These people disappeared from the region some two thousand years ago or later. Very little is known about their departure, but it may have been due to a number of factors including environmental change, migration, and the arrival of the Palaeo-Eskimos.

THE PALAEO-ESKIMOS

The Paleo-Eskimos were descendants of the immigrants who had had established themselves throughout the Arctic from Alaska to Greenland. They migrated to northern Labrador approximately four thousand years ago and made their way along the coast and eventually travelled westward through the Strait of Belle Isle some twenty-five hundred years ago, taking up residence at various places along the Quebec-Labrador coast between present-day Blanc-Sablon and Cape Whittle and possibly farther westwards.[5]

Various artifacts, including harpoon points, notched knives, ground stone axes, large "eared" skin scrapers, and small razor-like microblades, have been found throughout the region. The harpoons were probably used to hunt seals, and the knives and the microblades for cutting.

Little is known about the dress, art, or religious beliefs of the Palaeo-Eskimos, though they may have resembled today's Inuit people in appearance. The Palaeo-Eskimos were maritime-oriented and, like their predecessors, probably followed a seasonal round hunting marine mammals in the spring with toggle harpoons and killing sea and migratory birds and collecting their eggs. Throughout the summer months these people likely fished for salmon, cod, trout, and other freshwater and saltwater fish. They undoubtedly also collected various wild berries, took advantage of the migrating caribou, and pursued other fur-bearing animals.

Archaeological evidence suggests that there was some contact between the Maritime Archaic people and the Palaeo-Eskimos. The nature of any relationships that existed between these peoples, however, has not been determined. The Palaeo-Eskimos disappeared from the region around two thousand years ago and possibly earlier. Their disappearance is as mysterious as that of their predecessors. One probable reason was the arrival of the Dorset people.

THE DORSET PEOPLE

The Dorset people arrived on the Quebec-Labrador coast some two thousand years ago. It is not known whether these people came from the Arctic following the pattern of the Palaeo-Eskimos or whether there was an evolutionary link between the two groups. Evidence of the Dorset people's presence has been found in the Strait of Belle Isle region and westward along the Quebec-Labrador at places such as Blanc-Sablon, Bradore Bay, Middle Bay, St Paul's River, and Old Fort Bay.[6] But little excavation to date has been carried out with respect to Dorset sites in the area.

Excavation of Dorset sites east of Blanc-Sablon indicates these people lived in stone houses in the winter. These dwellings had a square or rectangular central living area, surrounded by low walls of earth and rock, and a raised sleeping platform at the rear. The kitchen, a paved trench bordered by vertically placed flat stones, was situated in the centre of the dwelling. Within the trench were a series of soapstone lamps that were used for heating, lighting, and cooking. Igloos may have been used as well. In the summer the Dorset people lived in semi-subterranean tents. These structures did not have hearths, and all the cooking appears to have been done outside.

The Dorset people also practised magical and religious rituals. However, very little is known about these ceremonies. It does appear that they, like the Maritime Archaic people, believed in an afterlife. In an attempt to facilitate life in some other world, their dead were usually supplied with weapons, tools, lamps, and other objects. Finely carved birds and animals, as well as more abstract carved objects, may have served as charms and amulets. These maritime-oriented people migrated to the coast mainly because of the abundance of seals, which they depended on for subsistence. They undoubtedly followed the familiar seasonal round and pursued salmon, cod, trout, sea birds, migratory birds, and caribou.[7]

Archaeological evidence suggests that there was some contact between the Palaeo-Eskimos and the Dorset people. The nature of any relationships that existed between these peoples, however, has not been determined. The Dorset people disappeared from the region fifteen hundred years ago and possibly earlier; but as with their predecessors, the cause of their disappearance is unknown. Competition with resident or newly arrived populations; changes in climate, weather, and sea-ice conditions; natural disasters; and disease all have been suggested as contributing factors.

THE INTERMEDIATE INDIANS

Very little is known about the people known as Intermediate Indians. Archaeological evidence suggests these people probably lived in southern Labrador and along the Quebec-Labrador coast between thirty-five hundred and two thousand years ago. The artifacts that have survived consist of notched points, leaf-shaped knives, large end-scrapers, and chipped preform blades made of Ramah chert. The leaf-shaped knives were likely used for cutting, while the large end-scrapers were probably used to dress hides and shape wood.

While it is difficult to determine the origins of these people, the styles of their stone tools and their choice of raw materials for tool manufacture indicate that the Intermediate Indians were likely the descendants of earlier Maritime Archaic people. Remains of early settlements have been found near river mouths, on the coast, and inland near lakes. Like those who had come to the coast earlier, they undoubtedly followed the familiar seasonal round, spending the spring, summer, and fall near river mouths and on the coast, hunting sea and land mammals and birds, catching various types of fresh and saltwater fish, and collecting wild berries. The Intermediate Indians probably spent the winter inland, where they would have hunted land animals such as caribou and beaver.

THE INUIT

The Inuit, formerly known as Eskimos, were the last migrants from Alaska into the Canadian Arctic. About seven hundred years ago they moved southward in the eastern Arctic and are believed to have crossed to the Labrador Peninsula from the east coast of Baffin Island. This culture, called Thule by archaeologists, quickly adapted to the mixed arctic and subarctic conditions found in the Labrador region. They would have migrated to the Labrador because of the availability of whales, seals, fish, and caribou.

Like their many predecessors, the Inuit derived most of their livelihood from the sea. Throughout the spring, the men hunted seals from kayaks. In the summer they caught salmon, trout, and cod and hunted for birds and eggs. The Inuit also gathered berries in their season. In the fall they pursued the giant Greenland whale from open, skin-covered umiaks. Throughout the winter months they killed seals and caribou. The Inuit used an assortment of tools and weaponry, including bows and arrows, spears, darts and three-pronged leisters. They also introduced the dog team and the komatik to the coast.

By the late fifteenth or early sixteenth century, Inuit families from the Atlantic coast of southern Labrador were making trips to the Strait of Belle Isle region and westward along the Quebec-Labrador coast to Kegashka. Some of these people were following the migration of the seals and whales in the area. Later, others came in the winter to scavenge for iron tools, fishing equipment, and other European goods left behind at seal and whale fishing stations. Still others came to work at the European-owned posts. For example, a Captain A. Crofton, based at Temple Bay in the Strait of Belle Isle in 1798, reported that eighteen Inuit were on their way to Bradore Bay to spend the winter with the European fishermen and to seek employment in the seal fishery.[8] These trips to the Quebec-Labrador coast continued well into the first half of the nineteenth century. Admiral Henry Wolsey Bayfield, who visited the region in the early 1830s, observed that "a family or two of half-civilized Esquimaux occasionally visit the coast from the northward."[9]

Some of these Inuit eventually took up permanent residence in the region. The Reverend Edward Cusack, an Anglican minister who visited the area in the summer of 1840, mentions that he called on an Inuit family living at Bonne-Espérance and another at Five Leagues.[10] Charles Carpenter, who visited the region in the following decade, noted that there was an Inuit family living in the St Augustine River archipelago as well. He wrote, "There was another family of Esquimaux, whose residence was at St. Augustine; I cannot recall the surname. I used to see one, Louis the Esquimaux."[11] Noel H. Bowen, who visited the area in the 1850s, reported that the Inuit living on this part of the Quebec-Labrador coast had adopted the dress and habits of the fishermen, and the only original articles seen in their possession were kayaks or seal-skin boats.[12]

The offspring of these Inuit families eventually married some of the coast's early European settlers. As a result, today there are many residents of mixed Inuit-European descent on the Quebec-Labrador coast especially in the present-day villages of St Paul's River and St Augustine River. The Inuit, however, were not the only Aboriginal people to occupy the area at this time.

THE BOETHUKS

The Boethuks appear to have been descendants of the Maritime Archaic people. Their ancestors may have arrived on the Quebec-Labrador coast as early as a thousand years ago, and the Boethuks may have remained in the area until about four hundred years ago. Evidence of their presence has been unearthed at the Blanc-Sablon and Lourdes-de-Blanc-Sablon areas.[13]

In the cold weather the Beothuks wore a caribou-skin mantle with moccasins, leggings, mittens, and arm coverings. They also used skins and bark to make a variety of containers. In the winter months they wore snowshoes. When the ice melted, the Beothuks employed a variety of canoes, some of which were capable of making trips of considerable distance across the open sea. Their homes appear to have varied considerably. Their prehistoric ancestors seem to have constructed only lightly built, temporary structures, perhaps resembling the conical wigwams consisting of a framework of saplings covered with sheets of bark that the historic Beothuks used.

In all likelihood the Beothuks, like other migrants to the coast, followed a seasonal round, hunting marine mammals and sea and migratory birds in the spring, fishing for salmon, cod, trout, and other freshwater and saltwater fish and collecting and preserving wild berries in the summer, and hunting seals, caribou, bears, beavers, and hares in the fall.

Given that the Beothuk remained in the area until about four hundred years ago, it is quite probable that there was some interaction between them and the Europeans involved in the coastal fishery.

THE INNU

Another group of Aboriginal people, the Innu, formerly known as Montagnais, gradually began to make their presence known on the Quebec-Labrador coast between Kegashka and Blanc-Sablon. They, like others before them, migrated to the region because of the abundance of caribou, beavers, salmon, trout, and birds. Initially, the Innu spent most of their time inland in the forest and near bodies of fresh water. Led by a chief who directed their activities and movements, they travelled in small parties. Each multi-family group exploited the resources of a territory, which they considered their own. The group would establish a base camp, where the women and children stayed, while the men hunted beaver, caribou, or other big game for several days. In early summer the groups would gather together on the coast, at river mouths, or in the interior on the shore of a river or a lake abounding with fish. There they fished and collected wild berries. With the coming of fall, the hunting groups formed, and everyone returned to the interior to spend another winter.

Much of the Innu culture focused on their relationship to the game animals, a relationship that had both pragmatic and spiritual aspects. It was, in fact, the focus of their philosophical and religious beliefs. While shamans foretold the future hunting success for a whole band of hunters, great emphasis was also placed on each individual's ability to achieve religious power through dreams, through songs, and by observing the correct rituals and feasts, which were held in conjunction with hunting activities.

Although they were experts at killing game, the Innu saw this relationship with animals, not in terms of violent conquest over their prey, but as one of love and respect. Animals were seen to have so much spiritual power that hunters would have never been able to kill them were it not that they gave themselves willingly. The Innu believed that the animals did so only for those hunters who respected them, would treat their corpses with the proper rituals, and, more importantly, would dispose of their bones in the proper ritual manner. The caribou played an important role in the lives of the Innu, who celebrated the caribou at a special feast, called a *mokushan*, where they consumed quantities of caribou fat and bone marrow. After the feast, the Innu beat the drum and sang songs to the animal spirits.

The lodgings of the Innu varied, depending on the season. In the summer months they lived in conical tents covered with birchbark or caribou hides whose hair had been scraped off. Their winter dwellings were more substantial and could include a partially excavated snow or earth-covered conical lodge with a rectangular porch. The Innu hunted with snares, bows and arrows, and lances.

These were eventually replaced with guns purchased from the Europeans. They used nets and spears to catch fish. In the summer they travelled in birchbark canoes. During the winter months the Innu used snowshoes, sleds, or toboggans.

During the sixteenth century, the Innu began travelling to the Strait of Belle Isle and westward along the Quebec-Labrador coast, visiting the European fishermen at their cod and whaling stations. These trips became more frequent after French entrepreneurs from the town of Quebec and missionaries in the seventeenth and eighteenth centuries persuaded the Innu to come to their coastal locations at places such as Bradore Bay, St Paul's River, and Mecatina. The Innu exchanged furs for food, cloth, tools, guns, and various other goods that were useful for life in the forest. Today they reside principally near St Augustine River and La Romaine River, where they maintain a semi-nomadic lifestyle.

3

The Arrival of the Europeans

Europeans began visiting to the Labrador coast, including that portion extending from Kegashka to Blanc-Sablon, on a regular basis from the sixteenth century on. Some of these people came to search for commodities such as wood and gold. Others came to exploit the cod and whale fisheries and to trade with the Aboriginal peoples. No matter what their specific motives, the principal force was an economic one.

THE NORSE

The first Europeans to explore North America were undoubtedly the Norse, who came from Scandinavia, including the present-day countries of Sweden, Denmark, and Norway. These Norse voyagers, best known as pirates and raiders, looters of monasteries and spoilers of towns, appeared around the coasts and along the rivers of western Europe in the eighth and ninth centuries. Traders who, with their swift ships, built a commercial empire ranging eastward from the Baltic to the Black Sea and from the Baltic northwestward to the Shetland Islands, often followed the raiders. The Norse also crossed the North Atlantic and established themselves in Iceland. From there they moved still farther westward, and by the end of the tenth century they had turned their attention to North America.

According to the Icelandic sagas, in 981 Eric the Red, a recent settler in Iceland, left its shores because of trouble with his neighbours to search out land reported to the westward. He found that land and named it Greenland, and established a settlement there. In that same year, Bjarni Herjoldsson, after a long absence on the high seas, returned home to Iceland to find that his father had just left with Eric the Red. Bjarni weighed anchor and set out after them. On the way he encountered foggy weather, and he sailed on for many days without seeing either sun or stars. Eventually he sighted land, "a shore without mountains, showing small heights and covered with dense woods." Many believe that the land Bjarni sighted was the Labrador coast.

While Bjarni apparently had no desire to explore the land he sighted, his reports about its dense forest generated some interest in Greenland, where wood was in short supply. Around 1001 Leif Ericsson, son of Eric the Red, set out to investigate land observed by Bjarni. After many days of sailing, he landed at a place that he named Helluland (flat stoned land), now believed to be either the southern coast of Baffin Island or the northern coast of Labrador. He then sailed southward, landing at a place he called Markland, or "woodland," probably the central or southern coast of Labrador. The third landfall was named Vinland, which means wine land. Historians and geographers have variously located Vinland from Labrador to Florida. After wintering in Vinland for a year, Ericsson and his crew returned to Greenland with a cargo of timber and vines.

Leif Ericsson never returned to Vinland, but the Norse launched several expeditions from Greenland to establish settlements in the newly discovered lands. In the process, according to the Icelandic sagas, they explored various regions in North America, including possibly the coastal areas of Canada and the Gulf of St Lawrence. Farley Mowat, a Canadian author and historian, maintains that a party commanded by Thorvald Ericsson in the spring of 1005, set sail from L'Anse aux Meadows, crossed the Strait of Belle Isle near Cape Norman, and travelled in a southwestward direction along the Labrador coast to Blanc-Sablon. From there they proceeded up the coast, passing St Paul's River through the Grand Rigolet to the Mecatina region onwards to Sept-Îles. In the fall of 1006, however, the Norse abandoned their settlement in Newfoundland and returned to Greenland.[1] Some historians maintain that the Native people drove the Norse settlers from Newfoundland.

As to whether Mowat's account of a Norse voyage along the Labrador coast west of the Strait of Belle Isle is accurate or not is difficult to say. To date, no concrete evidence has been found in the region to substantiate his claims. A Norse settlement, has, however, been unearthed at L'Anse aux Meadows, on the northern tip of Newfoundland, a hundred or so kilometres east of Blanc-Sablon. Given the close proximity of this settlement and the Norse penchant for exploring, it is conceivable, if not probable, that the Norse explored the bays and shoreline of the Labrador coast between Blanc-Sablon and Kegashka. Nevertheless, it is safe to say that over the next few centuries, there were no voyages of discovery by Europeans to North America.

FIFTEENTH- AND SIXTEENTH-CENTURY EXPLORERS

During the late fifteenth century, various European nations desirous of finding a sea route to Asia, a land of spices and precious gems, once again became involved in voyages of discovery. One of those at the forefront of exploration was John Cabot, a Venetian who was familiar with Christopher Columbus's explorations in the New World.

During the last decade of the fifteenth century, Cabot moved to Bristol, England, with his family. Shortly thereafter, he approached the merchants of that port and the king of England about his scheme to reach Asia by sailing west across the North Atlantic. Cabot estimated that this route would be shorter and quicker than Columbus's southerly route. Both the Bristol merchants and the king agreed to Cabot's proposal. On 5 March 1496 Henry VII issued letters patent to Cabot and his sons authorizing them to sail to the eastern, western, and northern sea, to discover and investigate islands, countries, regions, or provinces that were unknown to Christians. Very little is known about Cabot's first voyage of exploration, except that he left England with one ship, had a disagreement with the crew, was short of food, ran into bad weather, and decided to turn back.

The following year Cabot, supported by the Bristol merchants, received another commission from the king of England to explore the "New Found Land" and to seek a passage to Asia. In May 1497 he sailed from Bristol in the *Matthew*, a 50-ton vessel, with twenty or so people on board, including a Genoese barber (surgeon), a Burgundian, two Bristol merchants, and sailors from Bristol. Little is known about Cabot's 1497 voyage. Some historians maintain that on this particular voyage he coasted the shores of Newfoundland and probably those of Nova Scotia and New England. Others claim that he explored the coast of Greenland and Labrador and that he travelled as far south as the Strait of Belle Isle, which he mistook for a bay.

Three years later the king of Portugal gave Gaspar Corte-Real, a Portuguese from the island of Terceira, a commission to find islands and a mainland across the Atlantic, with the promise of possible hereditary rights of governorship on any of the lands he might discover. In the summer of 1500, Corte-Real sailed for the Azores, explored the coast of Greenland, and returned to Lisbon with news of his voyage. The following year with the assistance of the crown, he fitted out two vessels and made another voyage, in which he sailed northwards towards Greenland. He resighted this island and then proceeded in a southward direction along the coast of Labrador, exploring the various bays and inlets along the way. Supposedly, he, like John Cabot, mistook the Strait of Belle Isle for a bay.

The notion that the Strait of Belle Isle was a closed bay remained current among geographers and explorers alike until the explorations of Jacques Cartier. The only thing, it seems, that these individuals could agree upon was the nature of the land they had sighted:

on this dim verge of the known world there were other perils than those of the waves. The rocks and shores of those sequestered seas had, so thought the voyagers, other tenants than seal, the walrus, and the screaming sea-fowl, the bears which stole away their fish before their eyes, and the wild natives dressed in seal skins. Griffins infested the mountains of Labrador, ... devils rampart, with wings, horns, and tail, [and one] heard in the air, on the tops and about the masts, a great clamour of men's voices, confused and inarticulate – the din of their infernal orgies, and woe to the sailor or the fisherman who ventured alone into the haunted woods."[2]

In 1533 François 1, king of France, selected Jacques Cartier, an experienced French sailor, "to travel to that kingdom in New Land to discover certain islands and countries where it is said must be found much gold and other riches."[3] On 20 April 1534 Cartier set out from Saint-Malo, a port on the coast of Brittany, with two ships and sixty-one men to explore the New World. Twenty days later he arrived at Catalina, a well-protected port in Trinity Bay, Newfoundland. Following a ten-day stay at Catalina, he sailed northward, arriving at Chateau Bay on the Labrador coast on 27 May. An overabundance of ice in the harbour forced Cartier to return to Qurpon, Newfoundland, where he was icebound for nine days. After leaving that harbour, he returned to Chateau Bay, and from there he sailed westward through the Strait of Belle Isle, anchoring on 9 June at Blanc-Sablon. Cartier then proceeded onwards to Woody Island, Greenly Island, and Bradore Bay. On 10 June, he harboured at Brest (possibly the present-day village of Old Fort Bay)[4] to take on wood and water and to prepare for the exploration of the new region.

On the following day he continued his explorations for some distance to the westward, exploring, in his longboats, harbour after harbour, the excellence of which impressed him. First, he and his men made their way amongst islands so numerous that they were unable to count them. Cartier called these islands "Toutes Isles" (all isles). Today they are known as Eskimo Island, Old Fort Island, and Dog Islands. Cartier, it seems, spent an evening on one of these islands. The following day he continued on his way through the islands and stopped at Rocky Bay. From there he sailed on to Lobster Bay,[5] where he erected a cross. He then visited Checatica Bay and Cumberland Harbour, which he claimed to be "one of the best harbours in the world."[6]

Cartier returned on 13 June to Brest, where his ships had been making preparations to enter the unknown regions beyond. From there he sailed to Newfoundland, along which he coasted south, crossed over to Cape Breton and then sailed in a northerly direction until he had made a complete circuit of the gulf and returned to Blanc-Sablon. On 15 August he left Blanc-Sablon and returned to Saint-Malo.

In the summer of 1535 Cartier returned to the New World and carried on with his explorations. He entered the Gulf of St Lawrence by the Strait of Belle Isle, harbouring at Blanc-Sablon on 8 July to await the arrival of his consorts. While there, he had his vessels refitted and replenished with wood, fresh water, and other necessities. Following the arrival of the other vessels, on the morning of 29 July he sailed from Blanc-Sablon westward along the Labrador coast. That evening he anchored opposite Dukes and Shagg islands, near Cumberland Harbour. The following day he sailed past Ha Ha Bay and a number of islands, including Gros Mecatina, Treble Hill, Flat, Dukes, Petit Mecatina, and Harrington. Finally, on 31 July he arrived at Kegashka Bay. A day or two later he sailed up the St Lawrence River all the way to the island of Montreal.[7]

Some of these explorers returned from the New World with incredible tales about fish, cod in particular. Sebastian Cabot, John Cabot's son, claimed that the shoals of codfish were so numerous "they sumtymes stayed his shippes." Soncino, a historian, writes that "practically all English, and from Bristol ... affirmed that the sea there is swarming with fish, which can be taken not only with the net but in baskets let down with a stone, so that it sinks in the water."[8]

THE BRETON FISHERMEN

By the time Jacques Cartier had arrived in the New World, French fishermen from Brittany, a province in northern France near the English Channel, were already fishing for cod in the Strait of Belle Isle and westward along the Labrador coast from Blanc-Sablon to Kegashka.

Various individuals intimate that fishermen from Brittany began making regular trips to that region as early as 1504. S.E. Dawson, a geographer, claims that "both Brest and Blanc-Sablon were being frequented by Breton fishermen long before the arrival of Cartier, who, doubtless named them at some time between 1504 and 1534 from places in their own country."[9] This notion is reinforced by observations made by Jacques Cartier. In his journal of 1534, when describing Bradore Bay, Cartier notes that "there great fishing is done."[10]

The Breton fishermen typically left their home province in April or May, arriving in the Strait of Belle Isle and westward along the Labrador coast at the beginning of June. Usually, the first vessel to arrive took the best site, the next vessel the second next best, and so on. Since the first vessels to arrive on the coast could choose the best harbours and could rule over disputes arising between ships operating in the same harbour, some captains did not wait for the shore ice to melt. They sent a shallop from as far as 190 kilometres from the coast, manned by the best members of the crew. The shallop sailed in open water and was pushed over the ice up to the coast, where a harbour was selected, thus ensuring the possession of a suitable haven.

Once the fishermen had selected a fishing site, they anchored their vessel and removed its rigging. Fishing gear, provisions, and salt were brought ashore, and cabins erected near the shoreline to house the men and store the supplies. The fishermen also built stages or wharves out from the shoreline, as well as flakes on which to dry their fish after it was salted.

They then turned their attention to the pursuit of the cod. The crew was divided into two groups, the shoremen, who specialized in shore activities, and the launchmen, who did the cod fishing. Very early each morning, the shoremen would stretch their nets across the mouths of bays to collect bait with which to catch the cod. They gave the bait to the launchmen, who left early each morning in groups of three in a shallop, rowing or sailing to their destination. The launchmen baited their lines, threw them overboard, and drew up the cod, taking the fish from the hook and piling the catch in the bottom of the boat. This process was repeated until the boat was loaded. Afterwards, the fishermen returned to the fishing station and unloaded their cod catch onto the wharf, where the fish were cleaned and salted.

The cleaning and salting process was quite elaborate. A fish was placed on the splitting table before the "cutthroat," who cut the throat and made a horizontal slit down the belly of the fish. He then passed the fish to the header, who reached into the fish and removed the liver, which was reserved to make cod-liver oil. Then the header would gut the fish, removing the entrails and discarding these (often through a hole in the stage floor). The header then removed the head of the fish in one quick motion, and slid the body across the table to a splitter. The splitter opened the fish down to its tail along its backbone, removing a large portion of the bone; but the section down to the tail was left in place to hold the fish together. The cod livers were put into a tub and left to condense into oil. The fishermen then salted the cod and piled and left it to lose its water for two or three days. Afterwards the cod was left to dry under the sun for as long as fifteen days.[11]

When the cod was dried and the cod livers melted, the fishermen placed the product of the fishery on board the fishing vessel. They then sailed back to Europe to sell their catch on the European markets. The cod-fishing season lasted to the end of August, but the drying and melting operations often forced the fishermen to stay on the coast until the middle or end of September. The French fishermen continued to pursue the cod fishery in this area well into the nineteenth century.

The time spent waiting on the shore for the fish to dry permitted sustained contacts with the Natives. As a result, trade with the Natives came to have a considerable economic importance as the market for furs increased in Europe. A major factor was the demand for wide-brimmed felt hats. The best material for the felt was the soft under-fur of the beaver, since each strand had tiny barbs that caused the felt to mat securely and gave a lustrous finish. The supply of European beaver was by this time exhausted; thus beaver pelts brought to France by the fishing fleets fetched high prices, particularly since they were of far better quality than the European variety. The coastal Natives were eager to obtain the European metal goods. The only goods they had to offer in exchange were furs. Hence the shore-based dry fishermen managed a brisk trade. They paid for the costs of the voyage with the cargo of fish, and the furs provided a tidy profit.

THE BASQUE WHALERS

French fishermen from the province of Brittany were not the only ones to exploit the fisheries in the Strait of Belle Isle and westward along the Labrador coast from Blanc-Sablon to Kegashka. Numerous Basque fishermen from the western Pyrenees regions of France and Spain were involved in the coastal fishery.

Some historians maintain that Basque fishermen began showing up in the area during the 1480s. Others claim that they became active in the region between 1525 and 1545. Nevertheless, it was most likely the cod that drew Basques to the locality. Harry Thurston writes, "It was the search for cod, not whales that probably brought the Basque ships into the Strait of Belle Isle."[12] These fishermen, shrewd in money matters, quickly realized, however, the commercial potential of the numerous whales along the Labrador coast and in the Gulf of St Lawrence.

The Basque whaling ships (called galleons) normally left for the Strait of Belle Isle and the surrounding area in early June. Usually, after two months of arduous travel, they arrived at their destination. The captain's first task was to find a well-protected harbour where a whaling station could be set up. Most harbours selected had at least one island in the middle of the bay. This was probably chosen because of considerations of safety and security. The crew generally used the same harbour for several consecutive years.

Once the crew had moored the vessel, they set about establishing onshore facilities. The carpenters constructed shelters for rendering the blubber into oil and residences for the coopers and other crew members. The coopers assembled the barrels, and the crew members installed the cauldrons in the ovens and cut firewood. After they erected the onshore facilities, the crew members turned their attention towards the whale hunt.

A vessel, manned by several men, was sent from the harbour to patrol. When they sighted a whale, several boats would set out in pursuit, as quietly as possible, under sail or oar. After the whalers had selected a whale, they positioned a boat between the whale and the open sea so as to force the animal towards the shore. The whalers then approached the whale from the rear, and when they were within eight to ten metres, the helmsman would order the harpooner to harpoon the whale. Once hit, the whale would dive or swim away quickly, dragging the vessel for several kilometres. By now the whale would have grown tired. The men would then pull on the line, bringing themselves in a position where they could use a lance to finish off the whale.[13]

The whalers then towed the whale ashore for flensing. Men wielding long knives minced the strips of whale blubber for rendering in copper cauldrons set atop fieldstone fireboxes or ovens, also called tryworks. A man stood on a platform erected at the back of this primitive processing plant. Occasionally, he skewered a piece of whale fatback and forked it into the fire, to a crackling explosion as the fat burned. Behind the tryworks, a labourer ladled the finished oil into half-barrels of water, where it was purified. The dross sank to the bottom, and the whale oil rose to the top. This oil was used to light much of Europe in the sixteenth century, including Southampton, London, and towns in Flanders. Archaeologist James Tuck compares the whale-oil industry of four hundred years ago with the imminent oil boom in today's Newfoundland. "They were over here for the main chance, like people who go on the offshore today," he says. "It was an oil boom. Maybe the world's first oil boom."[14]

Initially, the Basque whalers limited their activities along the Labrador coast to the area between Cape St Charles and St Paul's River. Bradore Bay seems to have been one of their favourite regions. For instance, Courtemanche, in his memoir of 1705, reports that the Spaniards formerly had fisheries at Bradore Bay.[15] Eventually the Basque whalers extended their activities farther westwards along the Labrador coast, establishing whaling stations at various places such as Middle Bay, St Augustine Harbour, the Mecatina region, and Mingan.

The opening up of the whale fishery in the Strait of Belle Isle and westward along the Labrador coast brought new wealth to the Basque region and gave an extra boost to the Basque shipbuilding industry. Within a short period this fishery became a popular endeavour, involving numerous merchants and fishermen. Selma Barkham reports there was a heavy concentration of Basque whalers in the area from the early 1540s to the mid-1580s – so many that they created a monopoly over the Straits area, where no outsider dared to intervene for nearly half a century or possibly more. She writes, "At times there were well over a thousand Basques living and working for at least six months of the year in various ports."[16]

They, like their Breton counterparts, also traded with the Natives. Robert Lefant declared that "the people trade in marten skins and other skins, and those who go there take all kinds of iron whare."[17] Moreover, Odelica mentions that the Natives had given his fellow crew members deer and old skins in exchange for axes and knives and other trifles.[18] The Basques, it seems, even included some of these Natives in various activities associated with the whaling industry itself. According to Barkham, the Innu, who had learned some Basque, helped to prepare the fish on shore in exchange for a little bread, biscuit, and cider.[19]

The Basque whalers carried on their fishery with a great deal of vigour in the Strait of Belle Isle and westward along the Labrador coast from Blanc-Sablon to Kegashka and beyond until the end of the sixteenth century. Shortly thereafter, the Basque whaling fishery fell into decline. The demise of the fishery appears to have resulted from a combination of factors, including the embargo of Basque ships for the Spanish navy, strong Dutch and English competition, continual conflict with the Inuit, overfishing of the whales, and the growing strength of New France.

TRADING COMPANIES

During the latter part of the sixteenth century, the French government decided to exclude Breton and Basque fishermen from carrying on the fur trade with the Natives in the Strait of Belle Isle area and westward. They were officially prohibited from such trading after 1598, when France began to send governors and viceroys to its newly created colonies in the Gulf of St Lawrence region and the St Lawrence valley.

Henry IV, the newly crowned king of France, in an attempt to control the individual and wildly competitive trading in the new colonies, allotted monopolies to various trading companies. In 1598 he commissioned the Marquis de La Roche as lieutenant general of the king in the lands claimed by France, namely, Hochelaga, Newfoundland, Labrador, the Gulf of St Lawrence, and Acadia. La Roche was permitted to build forts, grant lands, and make new laws, and what was more significant, he was given a monopoly on the trade on these lands.

La Roche granted New France to a Huguenot merchant mariner of Honfleur, Pierre de Chauvin de Tonnetuit, for a ten-year period. To protect his monopoly against the fierce opposition of the Breton and Basque fishermen, Chauvin in 1600 established what he intended to be a permanent year-round base at Tadoussac, where the Saguenay flows into the St Lawrence from the north, but the cruel winter proved to be too much, and the notion of a permanent trading post at Tadoussac was abandoned. In any event, the majority of the French traders had no inclination to invest capital in permanent posts. They preferred to send ships to Tadoussac each summer to meet the hundreds of northern Natives who foregathered for the trade and then return to France in the fall when the Natives departed for the hunt.

In 1603 a trader by the name of Pierre du Gua de Monts was granted a ten-year monopoly over the fur trade of the St Lawrence valley and Acadia. De Monts and his associates again attempted a post at Tadoussac, and again the venture was a disaster. After several more failures, the French, lead by Samuel de Champlain, in

1608 established a permanent post at present-day Quebec City. Over the next few years Champlain gradually gained control of the trade in the St Lawrence valley. By 1610 he had managed to exclude his main trade rivals, the Bretons and the Basques, who made their way up the St Lawrence almost to Quebec every summer. Champlain, however, was less fortunate when it came to developing and exploiting the resources of the new colony and attracting new settlers. As a result, the colony of New France expanded very little over the next two decades.

Frustrated with Champlain's failure to develop and attract settlers to the region, the government of France embarked upon yet another scheme. Cardinal Richelieu, grand master and superintendent of navigation and commerce, founded a new company in 1627, the Compagnie des Cent-Associés (Company of One Hundred Associates), later known as the Company of New France. The enterprise was formed to develop and exploit the resources of New France, establish self-sufficient agricultural settlements, and foster missionary activity. More than a hundred persons, including officeholders, merchants, noblemen, and clergy, invested 3,000 livres each to provide working capital. The company became seignieur of the lands claimed by France in North America, with a monopoly on all trade, except fishing and the right to concede land in seignieurial tenure to settlers.

The Compagnie des Cent-Associés, dependent on commercial profits in a very risky enterprise, was loath to sink the profits it did make in establishing settlers (at a cost of some 1,000 livres each) in significant numbers. But the danger remained that the Crown would revoke the company's title if it did not discharge this obligation. It therefore granted subfiefs in New France to seignieurs, requiring them to bring settlers, which the company deducted from the number of people it was required to establish in the colony. The company conceded land to seignieurs in the hope that they would bring in settlers, clear the land, strengthen the fur-trading base, and discharge the company's obligation to the Crown. In the ensuing decades, the company granted numerous seignieuries throughout the colony of New France, including several along the Labrador coast west of the Strait of Belle Isle between Blanc-Sablon and Kegashka.

4

French Entrepreneurs from Quebec

Between 1660 and 1760 various individuals from the town of Quebec received land grants in the form of seigneuries and concessions along the Labrador coast from Kegashka eastward to Blanc-Sablon. They established posts throughout the region and engaged in the seal and the salmon fisheries and the fur trade. Most of the grantees operated their enterprises from Quebec, with variable results.

FRANÇOIS BISSOT AND HIS HEIRS

One of the first people to receive a land grant in the region was Sieur François Bissot (Byssot) de la Rivière, an enterprising Norman immigrant who had settled at Quebec in 1646. Several years after his arrival, Bissot, an experienced fisherman and judge provost, received a lease from a M. d'Avaugon for two years, allowing him to hunt seals and trade with the Native people in the Saguenay River region.

Eventually, however, Bissot's lease was broken. Realizing that the Saguenay River region was closed to him, he turned his attention eastward. On 25 February 1661, the Compagnie des Cent-Associés awarded Bissot the Terre Ferme de Mingan seigneury with the right to form establishments on the mainland from Eggs Island eastward to Bradore Bay for the purpose of seal, whale, and porpoise fishing and other trades.[1]

Shortly after, Bissot set about establishing posts at various places on the Terre Ferme de Mingan seignieury. According to historian J.E. Roy, Bissot built his first post on Eggs Island, a small island east of Tadoussac near the Montpelles. "In the depth of the granite rocks were installed the fishermen's huts. Nothing was more primitive than these shoreline encampments. The undersized pines and the cypress of the neighbouring coast were the only expenses. Large furnaces made from dried stones served to boil the oils."[2] Supposedly, Bissot had established himself there to avoid the Inuit. Later he abandoned the post on Eggs Island and built a little stone fort on the mainland at the present-day village of Mingan, approximately 1,000 kilometres east of the town of Quebec. He also established a number of posts throughout the Mingan archipelago. Bissot appears to have spent little time at his posts on the Labrador coast, preferring to direct the operations from Quebec.

Each spring he dispatched a vessel laden with fishing gear, trade goods, and employees from Quebec to the posts on the Labrador coast. The employees, upon their arrival, would unload the vessels and make preparations for the seal hunt. Sealing at that time was carried on mainly along the mainland, where seals would go to warm themselves in the sun. The methods the sealers employed to kill the seals varied. Sometimes they trapped them in coves and clubbed them. "The entrances to these coves were closed off with nets and stones except for an opening where the seals would slide in. As soon as the tide was high the opening would be closed and the animals in the cove would be trapped inside, and when the tide fell it would leave fish there. All we had left to do was to club them. One club on the nose with a stick was enough to kill them."[3] On other occasions the sealers shot the seals with guns. According to historian Pierre-François-Xavier de Charlevoix, dogs were trained to retrieve the seals. These faithful animals supposedly fetched up seal carcasses from a depth of seven or eight fathoms.[3]

After the seal hunt was concluded, the fishermen turned their attention to the salmon fishery. Nets were used to procure salmon in the nearby rivers. The fishermen also carried on the fur trade with the Natives in the area. In the fall the vessel returned to Quebec with the employees and the catch for that season. The salmon were disposed off at Quebec, whereas the sealskins and seal oil were exported to France and the West Indies.

Sieur François Bissot de la Rivière benefited considerably from the trade along the Labrador coast. According to historian E.T.D. Chambers, Bissot carried on fishing, trading, and sealing with great success. "Between his farm, his tannery at Lévis, and his posts on the Labrador coast, it was not long before he made his fortune."[4] Bissot maintained his enterprise along the Labrador coast until his death in 1673.

Following Bissot's death, his possessions on the Labrador coast were passed on to his numerous heirs. Among the inheritors were the famous explorer Louis Jolliet, discoverer of the Mississippi River, and Jacques de Lalande, a merchant from Quebec. Both men received shares in Bissot's Labrador possessions because of their marriage into the Bissot family; Jolliet by his marriage in 1673 to Claire-Françoise Bissot, daughter of François Bissot de la Rivière; and Jacques de Lalande, through his marriage in 1675 to Marie Couillard, Bissot's widow.

Jolliet and Lalande, aware of the abundance of seals and salmon along the Labrador coast, after their marriage into the Bissot family petitioned the government of New France for additional seig-nieuries in the region. In March 1679 Jacques Duchesneau, the intendant of New France, awarded them the seigneury of the Isles and Islets of Mingan, consisting of all the islands along the Labrador coast from Mingan to Bradore Bay.[5] A year later Intendent Duchesneau awarded Jolliet the Anticosti Island seigneury. Both Jolliet and Lalande were given the right to conduct the cod and seal fisheries wherever they deemed fit. Furthermore, the land grants were to be enjoyed by them and their heirs forever.[6] Shortly after, they established posts on the Anticosti seigneury and on various islands in the Mingan archipelago.

Bissot's heirs, including Jolliet and Lalande, carried on the Labrador business in the same manner as their predecessor. In the spring a vessel filled with trade goods, employees, and fishing gear travelled from Quebec to the posts on the Labrador coast. After arriving at their destination, the men would set about hunting seals. Following the completion of the seal hunt, they turned their attention to the salmon fishery. Furs were also procured from the Native people. In the fall the vessel returned to Quebec with the employees and the returns for that season.

Throughout the 1680s some of Bissot's heirs experienced considerable success with their posts on the Labrador coast. For example, in the fall of 1680 Jolliet and Lalande, two of the more active co-owners, returned from their Mingan Island and Sept-Îles posts with a barque full of pelts and other merchandise.[7] E.T.D. Chambers, in his study of the Quebec fisheries, also reports that it was not uncommon for Jolliet to take five to six thousand salmon from various rivers along the Labrador coast. In 1685 Jolliet requested that the king of France lend him a large ship for a period of four years. He intended to use the vessel to increase the output from his fisheries, while employing as sailors a number of young Canadians who otherwise, he urged, would become libertines through the temptations that awaited them in the woods. His industry proved so successful that he was able to provide both the town of Quebec and its soldiers with all the fish that was needed.[8]

In 1690, however, a British fleet, commanded by Commander William Phips, attacked the posts along the Labrador coast, destroying many of them in the process. Louis Jolliet, in particular, suffered greatly from the forays. He lost a barge and 10,000 to 12,000 livres in merchandise. The British invaders also captured his wife and his mother-in-law, but later released them unharmed.[9] Two years later, the British once again attacked Jolliet's establishment on Anticosti Island and another one belonging to him on one of the Mingan islands. As a result of that invasion, the grantees for a time were forced to abandon their Labrador possessions. Nonetheless, with the help of various individuals, they were eventually able to re-establish their posts. In 1711 the British again attacked and burned the post at Mingan.[10] And once again the Mingan post was re-established by the heirs of Bissot.

Jolliet, however, died in 1700, and the seigneuries of the Isles and Islets of Mingan and Anticosti Island were passed on to his heirs, who continued to exploit the resources of the Mingan archipelago with varying results until the middle of the eighteenth century.

EASTWARD EXPANSION

At the time of Jolliet's death, Augustin Le Gardeur de Courtemanche, a lieutenant in New France, became involved in the trade along the Labrador coast. Like Jolliet and Lalande before him, he was drawn into the Labrador business because of his marriage into the Bissot family. A widower, on 20 July 1697 he married Marie-Charlotte Charest, a granddaughter of François Bissot de la Rivière.

Courtemanche in 1700 hired Sieur Pierre Constantin, a voyageur residing at Sillery, to explore the possibilities of fishing and trapping on the Labrador coast east of the Mingan archipelago.[11] A year later Constantin, on Courtemanche's behalf, erected a trading post in a bay a short distance west of St Paul's River, which he called Fort Courtemanche. Courtemanche in his memoir of 1705 described the area as follows: "This bay is bordered with islands where food of all kinds can be found in abundance and the islands are so rich in game that one could easily feed with it all the Frenchmen and savages. Above the fort, at the head of the bay, are three pretty hills, on the summits of which are small lakes in which trout and salmon abound to such a degree that, with two or three hand lines or a common net, one might catch enough to feed a considerable garrison, and half a league down is the Eskimos river, rich in salmon of extraordinary size."[12]

In 1702 Courtemanche sent a petition to François de Beauharnois, intendant of New France, requesting that he be granted a concession at the place called Labrador, "commencing from the river called Kegashka to that called Kessessakiou [Hamilton River], which rivers shall be the two boundaries."[13] In October of that year, intendant Beauharnois awarded Courtemanche the Kegashka-Kessessakiou concession for ten years with the exclusive right to trade with the Natives and to fish for seals, whales, and cod.[14] Two years later Courtemanche took up residence at his post near St Paul's River and took control of the business. In 1705, however, he transferred his headquarters forty kilometres eastward to Bradore Bay, to the newly constructed Fort Pontchartrain. He established himself there because it was convenient for carrying on the fishery. Courtemanche commented, "Bradore Bay was a very advantageous place, a good harbour with an abundance of seals and codfish and also whales. There are a prodigious number of birds called 'Moyeis' which furnish quantities of eider-down, and of which the eggs are good to eat."[15] A short while later Courtemanche also established a seal fishery five kilometres below Bradore Bay at a place called Passe des Loups-Marins Brasseurs.

Courtemanche also developed a salmon fishery and pursued the fur trade. For a time he involved himself with the cod fishery as well. In his memoir of 1705 he observed, "At Bradore Bay there is an abundance of cod. In a word the cod are so numerous that a line has not even time to reach the bottom ... the three men, whom I have fishing there, caught thirteen hundred of them in a single day."[16] Despite his success with the cod fishery, it was never fully developed. One of the probable reasons was because the returns from the seal and salmon fisheries were considerably better.

Under Courtemanche's aegis the establishments in the Bradore Bay area continued to grow. In a letter to the king of France in the summer of 1706, he stated that his enterprise on the Labrador coast was growing in importance every day and that he was doing well with the seal and salmon fisheries.[17] Over the next few years Courtemanche carried on his business with a great deal of vigour, and as a result, he continued to have success with the trade at his posts.

Seven years after the establishment of Fort Pontchartrain, however, the lease on the Kegashka-Kessassakiou concession expired. Courtemanche, eager to maintain his establishment on the Labrador coast, in 1714 travelled to France with the intention of persuading the king to renew his rights to the concession. The king, wishing to treat Courtemanche favourably because of his involvement in the Labrador trade, granted him the Baie de Phélypeaux (Bradore Bay) concession.

The new concession was considerably smaller than Courtemanche's previous one. It consisted of "the Bay of Phelypeau and four leagues [19 kilometres] of frontage on the coast, two leagues [9.6 kilometres] above and two leagues [9.6 kilometres] below the bay, by four leagues [19 kilometres] in depth."[18] Also included in the new concession were the islands opposite the mainland. As with the former concession, Courtemanche was given the right to take seals, trade with the Natives, and carry on the cod fishery concurrently with French vessels coming to the bay.[19] Furthermore, he was granted this concession for life.

With the awarding of the new concession, Courtemanche returned to his establishment at Bradore Bay and continued to pursue the seal and salmon fisheries and the fur trade. Under his supervision, his enterprise continued to prosper. A visitor to the area in 1715 commented, "Courtemanche is well established there, fortified and furnished. The seal fishery is the principal industry, and quantities of oil and skins are obtained. He has a large garden and grows all sorts of vegetables including beans, peas, barley and oats. He also keeps horses, cows, sheep and pigs."[20] Three years after receiving the Baie de Phélypeaux concession, however, Courtemanche died.

Following his death, the king of France in 1718 awarded the Baie des Phélypeaux concession, with its privileges, to Courtemanche's widow, his stepson, Sieur François Martel de Brouague, and Courtemanche's three daughters, to be enjoyed by them so long as they continued to develop the concession.[21] Courtemanche's widow was granted one-quarter of the concession, Brouague one-quarter, and the three daughters the other half, each of them getting one-third of the half. Brouague took on the management of the post at Bradore Bay in the name of his mother and half-sisters and conducted the business in the same manner as his predecessor. Later, a royal commission ensured him and his wife the succession rights to the concession. Brouague carried on the seal and salmon fisheries and fur trade at the Baie des Phélypeaux concession, with varying results, until the fall of New France to the British in 1759.

Several years after Brouague took over the operations of the Baie des Phélypeaux concession, François Margane de Lavaltrie, a relative and former employee of Augustin Le Gardeur de Courtemanche, also became involved in the trade along the Labrador coast east of the Mingan archipelago. Like Jolliet, Lalande, and Courtemanche before him, Margane was brought into the Labrador business because of his relationship to the Bissot family.

On 26 May 1720, Margane de Lavaltrie received from the government of New France the St Augustine River concession, which consisted of "the harbour of the St Augustine River, together with two leagues [9.6 kilometres] east of the river and two leagues [9.6 kilometres] west by four leagues [19 kilometres] in depth inland and also the islands and islets adjacent to the harbour."[22] He was granted the sole right to hunt seals and trade with the Natives, and to carry on any other fishery in conjunction with any vessel that came to his concession. Like Courtemanche, he was awarded the concession for life.[23] Shortly thereafter Margane established a post on his concession.

He carried on the Labrador business in the same manner as Bissot's heirs. In the spring he sent a vessel filled with trade goods, employees, and fishing gear from Quebec to his post at the St Augustine River concession. After arriving at their destination, the men would set about hunting seals. Following the completion of the seal hunt, they turned their attention to the salmon fishery. Furs were also procured from the Native people. In the fall the vessel returned to Quebec with the men and the catches for that season. Margane de Lavaltrie maintained his business on the coast until his death in 1750.

Following the awarding of the St Augustine concession to Margane de Lavaltrie, no new concessions were granted along the Labrador coast west of the Strait of Belle Isle for a decade or so because the French government viewed new establishments as "prejudicial to the development of the cod fisheries." Cod fishermen coming to the region from France had to rely on the local wood to construct flakes upon which to dry their fish. More enterprises would mean a greater demand for wood, which was already in short supply along the coast. Because of the French government's concerns about the development of the cod fishery, the Bissot family maintained its hegemony over the Labrador coast west of the Strait of Belle Isle throughout the 1720s without any major disruptions.

THE DEMISE OF THE BISSOT EMPIRE

The ensuing decade, however, proved to be one of considerable difficulty for the heirs of François Bissot de la Rivière. Pierre Carlier, who held the post of "adjudicataire général des fermes unies de France et du Domaine d'Occident," on behalf of the French government, in 1732 initiated a lawsuit against the owners of the Terre Ferme de Mingan seignieury. He demanded that they produce the title by which they had taken possession of the north shore of the St Lawrence from the Moisie River to Bradore Bay. The adjudicataire général did not dispute the title of Jolliet's heirs to the seignieury of the Isles and Islets of Mingan; he only required the title claimed to anything on the mainland.

Bissot's descendants responded to the adjudicataire général's request by referring to the grant of 1661, under which they claimed they had formed establishments and had continuous possession for seventy-one years. Carlier, while admitting that the grant of 1661 and the declaration of 1668 were valid title deeds, declared they gave no propriety title except on Eggs Island. "On the mainland it conferred no right of ownership, but only the right to establish there sedentary fisheries from Eggs Island to Spaniards Bay (Bradore Bay). A right which it would have been useless to express if the intention of the concession had been to give a right of property, and which by its expression positively excludes a right of property."[24]

The adjudicatire général insisted that the French government be maintained in its right, to the exclusion of all others, to carry out trading, hunting, fishing, and commerce in the tract of the Domaine du Roi from Eggs Island to the Moisie River. The heirs responded by declaring that they did not use that portion of the mainland and that they were wiling to abandon it, in order to avoid any problems with the Domaine.

A year later, Gilles Hocquart, the intendant of New France, passed an ordinance stipulating that land from Eggs Island to the Moisie River belonged to the Crown and was to be reunited with the Domaine. The ordinance also prohibited the defendants and others from trading, hunting, and fishing in the reunited territory. In consideration of their loss, Hocquart discharged Bissot's heirs from any arrears that might be due from them, and "as to the new title of concession required by them for the establishment made by them and their predecessor at Mingan, the parties shall have to apply to the King to obtain the same, with such frontage and depth and on payment on such dues as His Majesty shall be pleased to grant."[25]

Shortly after, François-Joseph Bissot, son of the deceased François Bissot de la Rivière, addressed a lengthy petition to Jean-Frédéric Phélypeaux, Comte de Maurepas, the French secretary of state for the Marine, requesting that the family be granted a new title. He declared that Hocquart had fixed the limits of the Domaine at Cormorant Point, which is approximately ten kilometres below the Moisie River, and he prayed that he might continue in the remainder of his possessions from that point eastward.[26] Bissot stated he would be satisfied, even if, in granting the new title, the king should restrict his property to the Itamamiou River. He summed up his representations in the following manner: "It is very sad that after a possession of seventy years ... to see it disappear little by little. The act of faith and homage of which he has the honour to attach a collated copy, proves that this land was conceded to his father ... and he begs ... that in his old age he will taste the tranquillity that this work in similar areas could permit him."[27]

Maurepas, in a letter to Hocquart, stated that he would recommend the concession be limited to the Labrador coast from Cormorant River eastward to the Itamamiou River. There is no indication, however, that his recommendation was ever conveyed to the owners of the Terre Ferme de Mingan seignieury. Nevertheless, the heirs of François Bissot de la Rivière maintained their possessions along the Labrador coast from the Cormorant River eastward to the Itamamiou River until the middle of the eighteenth century.

NEW CONCESSION OWNERS

While François-Joseph Bissot was petitioning the French government on behalf of his father's heirs, various individuals from Quebec, well aware of the abundance of seals and salmon along that part of the Labrador coast, approached the government of New France about the possibility of establishing fishing posts along the coast from the Itamamiou River eastward to the Bradore Bay concession. The government agreed to their solicitations.

In the fall of 1733, Jacques de Lafontaine, a government official, was assigned the Montagamiou concession, which extended from the Itamamiou River to the Montagamiou River. Five years later the government of New France granted the Checatica concession, consisting of the frontage between the concessions of François Margane de Lavaltrie at St Augustine and François Martel de Brouague at Bradore Bay, to Sieurs François Foucault, member of the Conseil Supérieur of New France, and Nicolas-Gaspard Boucault, lieutenant general of the Admiralty court at Quebec. On 2 May 1738 the Gros Mecatina concession, stretching from Cap Gros Mecatina to the Thekapoin River, was given to Sieur Jean-Baptist Pommereau, a clerk with the government of New France. Two years later Henri Albert, an officer in the French army, received from the government of New France the Petit Mecatina concession, a tract of land situated between the concessions of de Lafontaine and Pommereau. In November 1748 Jacques Bréard, comptroller of the Marine, and Guillaume Estèbe, a Quebec merchant, were awarded the Kecarpoui concession, which began at the Thekapoin River, near Pommereau's concession and extended all the way to the boundary of that of Margane de Lavaltrie.[28] These individuals like Courtemanche and Margane, established posts at various points throughout their concessions.

The new concessions in some respects resembled the ones granted to Courtemanche and Margane. They were typically four leagues in length (19 kilometres) and four to five leagues (19 to 24 kilometres) in depth and included the islands opposite the mainland. The new grantees were also given a monopoly over the sealing and the Native trade and the right to fish for cod concurrently with fishing vessels that came from France.

The government's decision to grant the islands opposite the mainland, however, proved to be a cause for concern for Jolliet's heirs, owners of the Isles and Islets of Mingan seignieury. They immediately approached the government of New France and demanded compensation for the loss of the islands between Itamamiou and Bradore Bay. In 1739, the Government of New France passed an ordinance declaring that individuals with concessions on the coast containing a portion of the Isles and Islets Mingan seignieury would pay Jolliet's heirs a fixed rent of 25 livres per league.

Four years later the government issued another ordinance declaring that the concession grantees pay half a per cent of the annual produce of the fisheries in oil and sealskins to the heirs of Jolliet and de Lalande. The rent was to be paid to the owners of the Isles and Islets of Mingan seignieury on the arrival of the vessel at Quebec from the fishing grounds. Moreover, the ordinance provided the owners of the seignieury with the right to hunt seals with guns concurrently with the concessionaires. They were, however, not allowed to establish any sedentary seal fishery in the region.[29]

Furthermore, the new concessions, unlike the ones granted to Courtemanche and Margane de Lavaltrie, were not given in perpetuity or for the lifetime of the concessionaire. One of the reasons that the government abandoned that policy was because such grants often gave rise to disputes. Another was because it wanted to ensure that grantees would fully develop their land. Therefore the government awarded new concessions for a period of six to ten years. If, at the end of that time, the concessionaire showed that he had suitably developed it, his grant was renewed. Otherwise it was granted to someone who was capable of developing the land grant to its fullest potential. Hence the government's policy was "to make grants only to those in a position to use them, to revoke concessions which were being neglected, to locate posts so as not to interfere with one another, to protect those with posts in successful operation for damage from newcomers setting up in too close proximity and to limit the number of posts so as to avoid total destruction of the seals."[30]

The methods employed by the newcomers to take seals also varied considerably from those used in former years. Men from the town of Quebec were hired to work at the post, usually for a share in the proceeds. In September a vessel laden with food, fishing gear, and a crew of experienced fishermen would depart from Quebec and sail down the St Lawrence to its destination on the Labrador coast. Once the ship arrived, the fishermen transported the provisions and other necessities ashore and placed them in storage. "The fishermen employed in this business must be there at their station in the course of the month of September and cannot get away from there before the end of May. Thus besides the fishing implements and materials, a sufficient stock of provisions and other necessities must be laid up."[31]

The men then set about preparing for the fall seal fishery, which usually took place during the first week of December, when the seals were migrating in an easterly direction, and continued for a period of about two to six weeks. The sealers set a series of nets that were fitted to the depth of the water and the width of the respective passes. The nets were attached to strong cables or hawsers and placed in the pass at certain distances, with one end secured on a rock or island by anchors and the other on the mainland by capstans. The lowermost nets were sunk to the bottom, and the others were kept at full stretch across the pass. The sealers then watched for the appearance of the seals as they approached the pass, either coming up or going down the St Lawrence River. As soon as the majority of the seals passed over the outermost or end nets, all hands set to work heaving these nets to the surface of the water by which means the seals were enclosed. The seals entangled in the nets were caught. Then, hemmed in on every side, they were, with dogs, guns, and shouting, frightened into the nets and drawn ashore. "They were no sooner dead, than they were frozen as stiff as board where they are thrown into a heap where they remain until June, when the oil is extracted from their fat."[32] In May or June of the following spring, when the seals were migrating in the opposite direction, the nets were once again strung out at various passes. Once the seal fishery was over, the sealers set about extracting the blubber and trying out the oil. The blubber was fried in large kettles slung over fires or spread on platforms made of planks, where it melted in the sun and the oil collected in a barrel underneath.

Eventually, when the St Lawrence River became free of ice, many of the sealers and their catch were transported by vessel to Quebec, where the skins were tanned and used chiefly for covering chests and furniture and also for waterproof boots and shoes. The whole product of the seal fisheries was exported to France except for a little amount of oil, which was used in the colony for lighting.

The men who remained at the various posts occupied themselves with the salmon fishery, which was pursued with nets at the mouths of rivers during the months of July and August. Occasionally the concessionaires had some difficulty in getting rid of their salmon catch. De Lafontaine, lessee of the Montagamiou concession, for example, in the summer of 1739 undertook to fish for salmon at the urging of a certain Lambert, a ship's captain from Dunkirk, who promised to buy up the entire catch. Lambert failed to return to the coast, however, and de Lafontaine had some difficulty in disposing of his catch. In the winter months some of the employees hunted in the hinterland and cut wood and engaged in the fur trade with the Native people. Both the fur trade and the salmon fishery, however, was of secondary importance.

A few of the new concessionaires for a time also engaged in the manufacturing of glue. The glue was made by boiling the flippers and bones of the seals with water, straining the mixture through a cloth, boiling it again, and turning it into paper moulds to cool and harden. In 1745 Foucault, the lessee of the Checatica concession, generated one hundred pounds of glue. But owing to its cost, the glue industry was eventually abandoned.[33]

The revenue generated by the sealing industry along the Labrador coast from the 1730s onwards was substantial. The posts produced 10,000 to 18,000 skins and 1,500 to 2,500 hogsheads of oil annually. The sealskins brought in about 30,000 to 40,000 livres a year. The average annual income for oil all along the Labrador coast was probably at least 150,000 livres, perhaps more.[34]

The French entrepreneurs from the town of Quebec managed to pursue their endeavours along the Labrador coast throughout the better part of the 1730s and 1740s without any major disruptions. With the onset of the war between the British and the French in North America in the 1750s, however, the situation changed considerably. British warships frequently interfered with the French grantees' activities along the coast, destroying a number of the posts in the process. Finally, in 1758, the seigniers and concession holders were forced to abandon their property along the coast.

The fall of Montreal in 1760 to the British forces brought an end to French hegemony in North America. Many of the French entrepreneurs from the town of Quebec who had operated sealing posts along the Labrador coast between Kegashka and Blanc-Sablon returned to France. Their departure opened up the region to newly arrived English-speaking merchants based at Quebec.

5

English Merchants from Quebec

Following the conquest of New France, various English-speaking merchants from the town of Quebec took possession of the seigneuries and concessions along the Labrador coast between Kegashka and Blanc-Sablon. The newcomers had to contend with the policies of Governor Hugh Palliser in Newfoundland, wars, American interlopers, and ever-dwindling returns from their fishing and trading activities.

THE RE-ESTABLISHMENT OF THE POSTS

With the capitulation of the government of New France in Montreal on 8 September 1760, the new colony of Quebec was placed under British military rule. James Murray, a British military officer who had commanded a battalion in the 1758 siege of Louisbourg and served under General James Wolfe at the Battle of the Plains of Abraham, was made governor of the town of Quebec in 1760. Four years later he became the first civil governor of the colony of Quebec.

Murray immediately began to search for ways of improving the prosperity of the people under his jurisdiction. He was well aware of the successful winter and spring sedentary seal fishery that some of the French settlers had established along the Labrador coast at places such as Bradore Bay and Gros Mecatina. Murray, like his

French predecessors, realized that the holders of private property were the only ones that could carry on a successful seal fishery. A net made to fit a particular pass could not be used elsewhere. He also knew that if the sealers were not to lose much time and money annually in procuring new equipment, a guarantee that they would be allowed to use the same posts year after year was essential. As well, Murray was aware that the rivers on the Labrador coast contained an abundance of salmon.[1] These fish could be caught in nets during the summer as they passed along the coast towards the river mouths.

After the defeat of the French, several merchants from Great Britain with large quantities of merchandise moved to the town of Quebec. The products of the new colony and its dependencies were soon discovered to be smaller than imagined. Finding it difficult to make their returns to Britain and seeing that the seal fishery was abandoned because of the war, various merchants approached Murray for permission to pursue the Labrador seal fishery.[2] He agreed to their solicitations. He saw this as an opportunity to revive the seal-fishing industry, which he believed had unlimited potential. He also realized that if the seal-fishing industry along the Labrador coast between Kegashka and Blanc-Sablon were revived, many of the French-speaking settlers in the town of Quebec who were presently unemployed would be put to work. Thus Murray, like his predecessors, began allotting concessions along the coast to various English-speaking merchants residing at Quebec.

One of the first to receive a concession from Murray was John Lymburner, a native of Kilmarnock, Scotland, who arrived at Quebec around 1760 as a result of his mercantile association with Robert Hunter, a London merchant with connections in the Quebec trade. That same year Murray granted the Baie de Phélypeaux concession to Lymburner.[3] Lymburner also obtained access to the Montagamiou and Petit Mecatina concessions.[4] The following year Murray awarded the St Augustine River concession to a man by the name of Mofisseaux, who in turn leased it to William Grant. A Scotsman from Blairfindy, Grant had come to Quebec in the fall of 1759 as an agent for the company of Alexander, Robert, and William Grant, which was owned and operated by his cousin. Murray also granted the Checatica (Apety) concession to Thomas Dunn, a migrant from Durham, England, who arrived at Quebec soon after the general capitulation in September 1760, undoubtedly to take advantage of the various possibilities for economic development afforded by this newly conquered territory. Furthermore, Murray leased the Gros Mecatina concession to John Gray, an associate and friend of William Grant and an agent for the company of Alexander, Robert, and William Grant.[v]

Murray, however, was unwilling to allow the heirs of François Bissot and Louis Jolliet to re-establish themselves at their old posts. One of the purported reasons was because the heirs did not have enough money to rebuild the seal fishery. Another was that Murray did not trust them. He wrote to the secretary for the colonies, "Our situation made it necessary to allow none to establish themselves in or frequent those parts but such as we could confide in."[6] Murray did not object to the heirs of Bissot and Jolliet leasing their Labrador possessions to English-speaking merchants. For instance, on Murray's recommendation, the co-proprietors of the Terre Ferme de Mingan seignieury leased that property to Joseph Isbister, an incomer from Stromness in the Orkney Islands and a one-time governor of the Hudson's Bay Company, who immigrated to Quebec in 1760 with his wife and family.

Having obtained the right to fish for seals on the Labrador coast, the English-speaking merchants from Quebec immediately went to work reviving the seal fishery, which had been destroyed by the war. They purchased supplies, repaired ruined posts, and outfitted ships. Investors in this way laid out £3,000 to re-establish the seal fishery at one post or pass.[7] The fishing posts were established on the Terre Ferme de Mingan seignieury and eastward at various places, including La Romaine, Menicoute, Gros Mecatina, Checatica, Belles Amours, and Bradore Bay.

The English-speaking merchants from Quebec, like their French-speaking predecessors, would fit out a vessel at Quebec sometime in September. With a crew of francophone seal hunters and laden with food and fishing gear, the vessel would sail down the St Lawrence to its destination on the Labrador coast. When the crew arrived, they would make preparations for the upcoming winter seal fishery. Early in December the sealers set their seal-fishing nets when the seals were travelling in an easterly direction, and most of the seals caught were taken over the next two to six weeks. In May or June of the following year the seal nets would be strung out once again, when the seals were migrating in a westerly direction. In the spring came the task of extracting the blubber and trying out the oil by heating it in large boilers. It was then sealed in large wooden casks. Eventually, when the St Lawrence became free of ice, most of the crew would depart for Quebec, and the seal oil would eventually be shipped to Europe.[8]

A few men were left to watch over the posts during the summer months and to pursue the salmon fishery. The employees also traded goods for furs with the Native people. Both the fur trade and the salmon fishery, as in the time of the French, were of secondary importance.

Throughout the first half of the 1760s the English- speaking merchants from the town of Quebec managed to pursue their activities along the Labrador coast without any difficulties. For that matter, they had considerable success with their endeavours, especially the seal fishery. The number of seals taken and the volume of oil produced during the early years, of course, varied from post to post. In 1765, for example, the La Romaine post produced 640 sealskins and 80 weight in seal oil; the Menicoute post, 800 sealskins and 100 seal-oil weight; the St Augustine post, 800 sealskins and 100 seal-oil weight; and Gros Mecatina post, 3,200 sealskins and 400 seal-oil weight.[9]

THE STRUGGLE WITH
GOVERNOR HUGH PALLISER

Once peace was restored, the British government began making arrangements for the administration of its newly acquired territories in North America. One of the first tasks undertaken by the British was to assert their dominance in the valuable North American fisheries. Of particular concern were the whale fishery in the Strait of Belle Isle, the salmon and seal fisheries on the southern coast of Labrador, and the cod fishery in the Gulf of St Lawrence, and the general fishery of Newfoundland.[10]

The issue at the moment appeared to be how best to secure the exclusive possession of the fisheries for the British subjects. The Board of Trade in London was anxious that the French should not derive any benefits other than those set out in the Treaty of Paris of 1763. The king's decision that year to extend the jurisdiction of the governor of Newfoundland to the Labrador coast resolved the board's dilemma. The king "judged it proper that all the coast of Labradore, from the entrance of Hudson's Straights, to the River St. John, which discharged itself into the sea nearly opposite that island, with any other small islands on the said coast of Labradore, and also on the islands of Madeleines in the Gulf of St Lawrence should be included in the Government of Newfoundland."[11] Shortly after, the British government issued a proclamation declaring that a free fishery was to be carried on along the Labrador coast, including that portion extending from Kegashka to Blanc-Sablon.

The news that the British government intended to extend the Newfoundland free fisheries system to the Labrador coast created quite a stir at Quebec. Various English-speaking merchants from the town of Quebec with interests in the Labrador seal fishery in February 1764 presented a memorial to Governor James Murray, begging that he inform the board of the actual state of affairs. Murray forwarded the memorial to London, with a note in which he expressed his confidence that the board would procure the petitioners every benefit they could reasonably wish or desire. The petitioners informed the British government that the grants issued by Murray were considered valid in the colony and that leases had been purchased and many ruined posts had been repaired. They declared that they were apprehensive that the invalidation of these grants would not only injure the present occupiers but also ruin the seal fishery. Furthermore, they asserted that the carrying on of the seal fishery did not conflict with the freedom of the British fishery: "The seal fishery is carried on so early or very late in the year as not to interfere with the cod fishery. Nor is it detrimental to these settlements that the freedom of fishing and curing should prevail all over the coast as long as navigation is practicable."[12]

The petitioners' entreaties proved to be to no avail. Hugh Palliser, a long-time British naval officer who was appointed governor of Newfoundland, Labrador, and the Îles de la Madeleine in 1764, had already decided that encouragement of the ship fishery along the Labrador coast merited further attention. In accordance with his commission and instructions, he pursued the traditional policy of the British government with regard to the Newfoundland fishery and endeavoured to extend that policy to the Labrador coast.

Palliser, however, was confronted with two obstacles on the Labrador coast that prohibited him from pursuing this policy. One revolved around the hostility of the Inuit inhabiting the Atlantic seaboard northward from the Strait of Belle Isle. The other emanated from residents of the town of Quebec who claimed, under either French titles or leases granted by Murray, the right to exclusive possession and permanent occupation of certain tracts of the seacoast with the adjacent islands, for carrying on the sedentary seal fishery. It was essential to Palliser that the seacoast should remain open to British adventurers to enjoy their privilege of first choice of places on the shore for the fishery each year. Before this practice could be achieved, Palliser realized, something had to be done about the grants from Quebec. He hit upon a rather simple plan.

In the spring of 1765, Palliser issued a series of regulations for the Labrador, Îles de la Madeleine, and Gulf of St Lawrence fisheries. One of the first things he did was to relieve all private landowners on the Labrador coast of their property. He managed to do so by declaring that all land on the territories which had been added to Newfoundland "is in the Crown," and "since the conquest thereof no part of it has been lawfully given or granted away, and no power being vested in me to give or grant to any persons whatever."[13]

In his bid to get the British adventurers involved in the trade along the Labrador coast, he ordered that this extensive field for fishing and trade be public and for all the king's British subjects in preference to all others. The Statute of King William of 1690 was to be strictly observed, except for the proviso that for any person who since the 25th day of March 1685 had built there the statute was not to be enforced regarding the coast and islands. Furthermore, Palliser eliminated all North American fishermen from participating in the Labrador fishery by declaring that no vessel was a British fishing ship except those that came from Britain in the same season, carried men to be employed in the fishery, and returned to Britain when the fishing season was over.[14] He also declared that no person from any of the colonies would be allowed to go to the Labrador coast, except whale fishers within the Gulf of St Lawrence. Anyone found there would be corporally punished for the first offence, and the second time his boat would be seized for the public use of British shippers on the coast. Palliser also declared that no one could come to Labrador to fish or trade except on British vessels arriving annually from Britain and lawfully cleared as ship fishers and carrying at least twenty-five men, all engaged to return home after the season was over.[15]

In an attempt to attract fishermen from Britain to the Labrador, Palliser proposed that the first arrivals to any harbour be given the privilege of leaving one small vessel, with a crew of not more than 12 men and nets, to carry on a winter whale and seal fishery. The second arrivals to any harbour were given exclusive rights to the salmon fishery of their districts. The third to arrive, along with the first and second arrivals, were given exclusive rights to trade with any Natives within the limits of their harbour.[16] Palliser, during the latter part of August 1765, sent a copy of these orders to Murray, with the request that he make them publicly known, in order to put a stop to people from the colony of Quebec resorting to the coast.

By the time Palliser's regulations had reached Murray, vessels from the town of Quebec had already been fitted out for the Labrador trade and were well under way. Some of them had reached Mingan, opposite the western end of Anticosti, before news of Palliser's regulations was received. When the crews heard of his threats of corporal punishment, they could not be persuaded to continue their voyage, and the ships returned to Quebec. The English-speaking concession grantees and the French-speaking seignieury owners at Quebec, frustrated with Palliser's regulations, decided to take up the issue with the Lords of Trade in London.

The English-speaking merchants from Quebec, led by John Lymburner, sent a petition to the Lords of Trade on 1 November 1765, expressing their displeasure with Palliser's regulations. They stated that "we the merchants of Quebec, being largely in advance for the different seal fishery posts upon the Labrador coast, can hardly express the consternation we are thrown into by his excellency the Governor of Newfoundland's order dated the 28 August last ... the purport of which seems entirely to deprive us and the great number of people we employ of the fruits which we hoped would accrue from the labour, industry and expense we have bestowed on these settlements."[17] They further declared that they were mortified to see that not only were their labour and expense in the last outfit totally lost, but also many of their settlements were left deserted and their buildings, fixtures, fishery materials, provisions, and merchandise totally exposed to destruction.[18] About that time, the heirs of Bissot and Jolliet also signed a notary's declaration stating that they were the owners of the Anticosti, Terre de Ferme de Mingan, and the Isles and Islets of Mingan seigneuries and that they had, for time immemorial, enjoyed peaceable and continuous possession of these properties.

In March of the following year, the board called upon Palliser to provide answers to some questions concerning the Labrador coast. He informed the board that cod fishing was carried on to a considerable degree by fishing vessels from France and that the seal and salmon fisheries and the Native trade were being pursued under exclusive grants from the governor of Quebec. He wrote, "For that matter, the whole coast was divided into districts or posts and granted in monopoly. Governor James Murray of Quebec had taken upon himself in imitation of the maxims of the French government to make exclusive grants of the Coast from St. John [River] to Cape Charles and as a result no British adventurers have offered to go there."[19]

Palliser indicated that the annulment of Murray's grants should be approved and that he knew of no titles derived from the crown of France to monopolies in fishery and trade that was binding on the British government. The board expressed its disappointment with the limited amount of information provided by Palliser. Nevertheless, it drew up a new representation to the king, in which it noted that the greatest commercial benefit to be derived from the Labrador coast was that of a cod fishery.

Towards the end of March 1766, fifteen merchants from the town of Quebec presented a memorial to the Lords Commissioners for Trade and Plantations. In it they complained of the manner in which they had been dispossessed of their property on the Labrador coast. Those who derived their titles from French grants pointed out that when New France had surrendered, the British king had promised that the possessions of his new subjects would be safeguarded. Those who had acquired their rights from the concessions granted by Murray declared that the decisions made by Murray, who was a British governor, ought also to be respected. The merchants noted that if Palliser's regulations were enforced, three hundred French Canadian families would be reduced to conditions of great distress.[20] Palliser replied that his rules had been made to prevent lawless murdering crews resorting to that coast from the colonies. According to him, the Labrador post owners had carried on an illicit trade with the French and slaughtered the Natives. He therefore hoped that his plan would be given a trial equal in length to that which had been allowed to Murray's.

The Board of Trade in May 1766 drew up a report on the memorial of the Quebec merchants. The commissioners stated that they believed Palliser to have mistaken the meaning of the Statute of King William in taking it to imply the exclusion of Americans from the Newfoundland fisheries. If this was so, he had no authority to exclude New Englanders from the Labrador coast. The board concluded by declaring that a free fishery was to be carried on the coast and that the part of the regulations which excluded a section of the king's subjects from the Labrador fishery should also be continued.[21]

In January of the following year, the heirs of Bissot and Jolliet presented a petition to Sir Guy Carleton, the newly appointed governor of the colony of Quebec, in which they declared that they were the rightful owners of the Terre Ferme de Mingan, Anticosti, and Isles and Islets of Mingan seignieuries. They complained that, although they had peaceable possession of these seignieuries for 104 years, the government of Newfoundland had disturbed them in their possession. Furthermore, that the government had compelled their lessee to take refuge within the limits of the colony of Quebec and that such action destroyed the value of their seignieuries and fisheries.[22] Carleton passed the petition on to the Board of Trade. With it was an enclosing letter in which Carleton pointed out that "the Canadians of all men seem to be best calculated for carrying on the winter seal fishery, the season extending from the middle to the end of December, a time when the inclemency of the weather necessitates permanent establishments to house and protect the fishermen; that the winter fishery would not interfere with the cod fishery or the taking of whales."[23] He feared that barring Canadians from it would result in total loss of that valuable branch of commerce to Britain.

By now even vessel owners from Britain began to join the seigneury and concession holders from Quebec in their complaints against Palliser's Labrador regulations. In August 1767 vessel owners from Bristol, Dartmouth, Teignmouth, Exeter, Poole, and

London presented a petition to the governor. They requested that fishing ships which had established a new place and fishing conveniences be allowed to enjoy them, so long as they continued to occupy and use the same with fishing ships every year.[24] Palliser immediately granted this request, and ships within the limits of each principal harbour were allowed to leave a crew of twelve men to pursue the winter seal fishery and protect the property from invaders.

Shortly after, the English-speaking concession holders and the French-speaking proprietors from the town of Quebec submitted a very clear statement of their case. The English-speaking merchants stated that they had valid title to the posts and wanted Labrador reannexed to the colony of Quebec. They asserted that Labrador was chiefly for seals and that seal fishing could not be carried on successfully under the Newfoundland fishing rules, which were designed essentially for the summer cod fishery. Each sealing locality was unique and required a heavy investment in specially constructed nets and gear that would not be justified if the following year the post could legally be taken over by some other merchant whose ship happened to arrive first.[25]

The continual petitioning by the French-speaking seigneurs and English-speaking merchants from Quebec eventually produced the desired results. In the summer of 1772 the board reported to the king that regulations designed to encourage the fisheries for cod and whales by laying the coast open to the first people to arrive had been found incompatible with the principles upon which the seal fishery was conducted. To subject the seal fishery to those regulations was, in effect, to destroy it. The board suggested that the policy be reversed and parts of the Labrador coast between the St John River and Bradore Bay, together with Anticosti and the Îles de la Madeleine should be reannexed to the colony of Quebec.[26] His Majesty in council on 22 April 1773 approved the report of the Lords of Trade, recommending that the Labrador coast between St John River and Bradore Bay be reannexed to the colony of Quebec.

Others, however, thought that the Labrador coast was best administered from Newfoundland, although with some modification of the Newfoundland fishing laws. Lieutenant John Cartwright, the younger brother of entrepreneur George Cartwright and a property owner on the Labrador coast east of the Strait of

Belle Isle, argued that the Newfoundland governor should be empowered to grant land in Labrador for fishing posts. Cartwright, in a letter to Lord Dartmouth, secretary of state for the American colonies, explained why Labrador should remain united with Newfoundland. The various businesses of Labrador were almost entirely carried on by English and Newfoundland merchants and fishermen, with ships going back and forth from spring until winter, while there were only a few Canadians in sealing posts in the Strait of Belle Isle, totally ignorant of what was happening at Chateau Bay and other heavily travelled parts of the coast. The merchants in Labrador could easily contact the Newfoundland governor and his naval officers, stationed all the way from Chateau Bay to St John's, whereas merchants having to apply to Quebec for redress would undergo a long voyage through dangerous waters.[27]

The British government was anxious to please the Canadians in every possible way. The ministers also trusted Governor Carleton, who favoured a restoration of the entire coast. Carleton believed that since the sedentary fisheries were the principle ones on the coast and were carried on with the use of special equipment prepared at great expense for particular spots, if the Labrador coast was not kept separate from the Newfoundland migratory fishing, disturbances of any kind would scare the seals and walruses and they would be frightened away from the nets. This was also the view of the English-speaking merchants from the town of Quebec. They argued that if the colony of Quebec was not restored to its former limits, the fur trade and the winter seal fishery would be "forever lost not only to this Colony but to great Britain, as neither can be carried on to advantage, by the inhabitants of Canada."[28] Consequently, when a new bill governing Quebec was finally drafted, it declared that all the territories, islands, and countries which had, since 10 February 1763, been made part of the government of Newfoundland were to be returned to the colony of Quebec.

When the Quebec Bill was introduced into the House of Lords in 1774, the preamble stated that certain posts of Canada, where sedentary fisheries had been established, had been annexed to the government of Newfoundland and thereby subjected to regulations inconsistent with the nature of those fisheries. Clause 1 of the bill simply annexed to Quebec, besides the isolated French Canadian settlements of the Ohio country, all the territories, islands, and countries which had, since 10 February 1763, been made part of the colony of Newfoundland. The clause relating to Newfoundland passed without changes before the Committee of the House on 6 June 1774,[29] and a few weeks later the Quebec Act received royal assent and soon afterwards became law.

After passage of the Quebec Act, Carleton, whose authority as governor of the colony of Quebec now included the Labrador coast and Anticosti Island, was informed by a British government official that the fisheries on the coast of Labrador were of the greatest importance, not only because of the commodities they produce but also as a nursery of seamen, on which the strength and security of the kingdom of Great Britain depended. Further, justice and equity demanded that the property and possession of the Canadian subjects on the coast should be preserved entirely, and that they should not be molested or hindered in the exercise of any sedentary fisheries they might have established there.[30] Thus Palliser's policy had been reversed, and the English-speaking merchants from Quebec were once again allowed to carry on the seal fishery along the Labrador coast between Kegashka and Blanc-Sablon, as they had done formerly.

CONFLICT WITH THE AMERICANS

While soliciting the British government to reannex Labrador to the colony of Quebec, Grant, Dunn, and Peter Stuart, an associate and friend of Grant and Dunn, had convinced the heirs of Bissot and Jolliet to provide them with a fifteen-year trading lease to the Terre Ferme de Mingan, Anticosti, and Isles and Islets of Mingan seignieuries.[31] Furthermore, an association was formed among Grant, Dunn, Stuart, and Adam Lymburner, who had arrived in Quebec to take over the business of his brother, John Lymburner, who had disappeared at sea in 1772. This would give them control over the seal fishery along the coast.

During the summer of 1775, however, war broke out between the United States and Britain. Shortly after, American privateers from the New England area expanded their activities into the Gulf of St Lawrence and along the shores of the Labrador coast, and slowly but surely, the American presence in the region began to have an impact on the seal fishery. Grant, Dunn, Stuart, and Lymburner, concerned about the turn of events, in December 1777 sent a petition to Lord George Germain, who had succeeded Lord Dartmouth as secretary of state for the American colonies, expressing their indignation with the Quebec government's failure to protect the coastal seal fishery. They informed Germain that since the Labrador coast had been put under the jurisdiction of the government of Quebec, no steps had been taken to ensure the safety and protection of the seal fisheries; "That for the want of a superintendent or some person with proper powers for the above purposes and to prevent or settle disputes that naturally arise and which are more frequent when there is no legal authority, the produce of those fisheries has been gradually reduced and is now only about one-third of what it was some years ago."[32] These individuals also told Germain that any person vested with proper powers to reside for two months in the summer on the Labrador coast would sufficiently answer the purposes they had in mind. They hoped that the colonial secretary would take the same view and recommend an appointment that would prove the most effectual means of promoting and extending the fisheries on the Labrador coast.

Nicholas Cox, lieutenant-governor and superintendent of the fisheries at Gaspé, on the southern shore of the St Lawrence, wrote to Germain in the spring of 1778 declaring that should His Majesty think it expedient to annex the coast to the district of Gaspé, he would have a vessel of 60 to 70 tons built. This vessel, properly manned, would go to the Labrador coast for six weeks to two months every summer, settle disputes among the settlers and adventurers, and implement rules that would encourage the development of the valuable seal fisheries. Cox informed Germain that he was willing to purchase or build a vessel at his own expense. All that he expected the British government to do was to man and supply the ship.[33] Both King George III and Lord Germain supported the idea, and Cox, while still superintendent of Gaspé, was appointed superintendent of the trade and fishery of Labrador. His authority was extended to the Labrador fishery within the colony of Quebec only, and he was to follow the directions of the Newfoundland and Quebec governments.[34] It is doubtful, however, that Cox ever exercised effective authority on the Labrador coast.

Attacks on posts along the Labrador coast by American privateers by now had become common. For instance, during the summer of 1778, Collin Jones, commander of the rebel privateer *Cumberland*, destroyed Grant's posts at Gros Mecatina, Little Bradore, Mutton Bay, and Netagamiou and Lymburner's posts at St Augustine.[35] A privateer named Samuel Hobbs, from Boston, had sailed to Mingan and plundered that post, taking away all the fishing gear. Hobbs also commandeered the sloop *Loup Marin*, a vessel owned by Adam Lymburner, and the sloop *Garrick,* a vessel owned by Peter Stuart. The owners of the posts estimated that privateers in 1778 had destroyed or taken away property and vessels valued at £15,000.[36]

In November 1778 Frederick Haldimand, who had succeeded Sir Guy Carleton as governor of Quebec, wrote to Germain, informing him that he had received word that a privateer had destroyed the houses, utensils, nets, and belongings of several fishing posts on the Labrador coast fitted out and carried on by several of His Majesty's British and Canadian subjects residing at Quebec. He noted, "The proprietors have thereby not only lost the profits for the winter fishery, but most of the establishments that was made for carrying on the trade which had been the work of twice. This will lay them under the necessity of beginning these anew and put them to considerable expense before the business can be executed there as before."[37] He also informed Germain that he hoped that it was the intention of the British government to do something about the situation.[38]

In spite of Haldimand's representations, not a single warship showed up in the spring and summer of 1779 to protect the fisheries on the Labrador coast from marauding privateers. As a result, privateers roamed at will during that summer, raiding and plundering the shores of the St Lawrence River and the Labrador coast. Grant, Dunn, Stewart, and Lymburner reported that in 1779 privateers took several of their vessels coming from the fisheries and destroyed effects to the amount of £7,000.[39] Haldimand wrote to Lord Germain again in the fall of that year and informed him that "for the want of a naval force rebel privateers were very considerable in strength and, have this spring pushed up the St Lawrence River, plundered the North Shore, the Gulf and the Labrador Coast, destroying the fisheries in every part within that extant so that these are almost totally annihilated and the people engaged there are everywhere returning to Quebec."[40] He further stated that if the colony was left as bare next year, the fisheries could possibly be abandoned.

A short while later, the Admiralty despatched Captain Thomas Young in the frigate *Hind* to winter at Quebec. In the spring of the following year Haldimand placed two armed brigs, the *Poly* and the *Liberty*, as well as other warships, under Captain Young's command for the protection of the posts and trade in the lower parts of the colony. Despite these precautions, the privateers continued to plunder the posts owned by the English-speaking merchants from Quebec.[41]

Grant, Lymburner, Stuart, and Dunn in the fall of 1782, frustrated with the ineffectiveness of the Admiralty's measures, addressed a lengthy petition to the Admiralty Board through Haldimand. They informed the board that their successive losses and the risks of bad returns and indifference to the fisheries were very hard to bear. "The warships coming out with the fleet arrived so late here, that the privateers had lots of time to burn, take and destroy their property long before the frigates arrived at their stations."[42] What they proposed was that the Admiralty order the vessels that were intended for the coast to leave England earlier, so that they would arrive in the gulf in May.

A year later, however, the English-speaking merchants' problems with American privateers along the Labrador coast were resolved. In 1783 the United States and Great Britain signed the Treaty of Paris, bringing to an end the American War of Independence. Peace, however, created new problems for the English-speaking merchants from the town of Quebec involved in the Labrador seal fishery. The Treaty of Paris allowed the citizens of the United States the right to take fish of every kind on the Grand Banks and on all the other banks of Newfoundland, also in the Gulf of St Lawrence and at all other places in the sea where the inhabitants of both countries used at any time to fish.[43] They were also given the liberty to dry and cure fish in any of the unsettled bays, harbours, and creeks of Nova Scotia, the Îles de la Madeleine, and along the Labrador coast, so long as the areas remained unsettled.

It was not long before American fishermen became a problem for the English-speaking merchants from Quebec. With the peace, a great number of vessels from the United States began frequenting the bays, harbours, and rivers in the Gulf of St Lawrence and along the Labrador coast. The American fishermen, being more numerous than the fishermen involved in the seal fishery, in many places committed the most wanton assaults and greatly injured the fisheries and trade carried on there, despite the presence of Admiralty ships. John Ross, one of Lymburner's employees, reported that the seal fishery at Blanc-Sablon was lost in 1784 as a result of the evil disposition of some American whalers, who fired upon the seals at that post and chased them out of their right course. The Americans had also landed at Peter Stuart's posts, laid their nets above his, and carried away many tierces of salmon.[44] William Grant reported that the seal fisheries on the Labrador coast in 1784 had been absolutely the worst that he had ever experienced.

In February 1785 David Alexander Grant, nephew of William Grant, met with John Campbell, governor and commander-in-chief in Newfoundland, in London to discuss the need for protection of the seal fisheries along the Labrador coast. Campbell agreed to station a warship there in the ensuing season. Despite this promise, no warships were sent, and the English-speaking merchants again suffered as a consequence. Grant, Lymburner, and Dunn in September 1785 sent a petition to Henry Hamilton, lieutenant-governor of Quebec, in which they complained that much of the depredation along the Labrador coast was being carried on within twenty-four kilometres of the men-of-war without their being aware of it. To remedy these evils, the merchants recommended that one or two schooners of an easy draught of water, equipped with four guns and twenty-five to thirty men, be placed under the direction of the Governor of Quebec and be employed to navigate during the summer months along the coasts. They believed that these vessels would contribute more to the security of the trade and fisheries of the gulf than the frigates or sloops of war, which by their great draught of water dared not approach many of the harbours where the American sloops and schooners concealed themselves.[45] In the spring of the ensuing year, the Admiralty sent the sloop *Echo* to cruise for the protection of the seal fisheries around Bradore Bay and she remained in the area until 4 September.[46] From that time onwards, the Admiralty sent a vessel to patrol the Labrador coast between Bradore Bay, and Chateau Bay only. The vessel did not meet the needs of the post owners, however, and consequently the American fishermen continued to interfere with the seal fishery.

A NEW PARTNERSHIP

Following the resolution of the war between the British and the Americans, the English-speaking merchants from the town of Quebec set about consolidating their business interests along the Labrador coast west of the Strait of Belle Isle. Dunn, Grant, Stuart, and Lymburner, having throughout the years purchased all the shares from the co-owners of the Terre Ferme de Mingan and Isles and Islets of Mingan seigneuries, created a new partnership under the name of Lymburner and Crawford.[47] Shortly after, the management of the company was placed under Mathew Lymburner, Adam's brother and their nephew, John Crawford, who was also brought into the business.

An area of the Labrador coast west of the Strait of Belle Isle that Lymburner and Crawford did not have access to was the St Paul's River seigneury, which was partially owned by Nathaniel and Philip Lloyd. The Lloyd brothers, traders from the town of Quebec, had purchased part ownership of the seigneury from some of the descendants of Jean-Amador Godefroy de Saint-Paul in 1781. Neither Godefroy de Saint-Paul, who had been granted the St Paul's River seigneury in 1706, nor his heirs had exploited it. In 1792 Lymburner and Crawford bought from one John Young a debt of £545 owed to him by rival traders Nathaniel and Philip Lloyd, along with Young's mortgage on the St Paul's River seigneury. After acquiring Young's debt, Lymburner and Crawford bought out the shares owned by James McCullum and Joseph Jutras, the heirs to the St Paul's River seigneury. Thus Lymburner and Crawford now had control of the coast from Mingan eastward to Blanc-Sablon. They managed to carry on the seal fishery until the end of the eighteenth century without any major disruptions, except for the occasional run-in with American fishermen.

At the turn of the nineteenth century, however, Lymburner and Crawford experienced a series of difficulties. In 1803 the Lloyd brothers filed a lawsuit against Lymburner and Crawford claiming £10,000 in damages for fish, fur, and timber taken within the limits of their seignieury. That lawsuit was eventually dropped, with neither party getting any compensation. In the same year John Crawford, one of the principal owners of Lymburner and Crawford, died and the company went into receivership. Strapped for funds, it leased the Terre Ferme de Mingan seignieury to the firm of McTavish, Frobisher and Company, which later became a part of the North West Company. The latter firm was eventually amalgamated with the Hudson's Bay Company, which maintained control of the Terre Ferme de Mingan seignieury until the middle of the nineteenth century.

The heirs of John Crawford in 1804 renounced their rights of succession to their father's estate on the grounds that it was more burdensome than profitable, and consequently the seal and salmon fishery establishments on the Labrador coast between Itamamiou and Blanc-Sablon were put up for sale. Included in the sale were the posts at Itamamiou, Petit Mecatina, Mutton Bay, Gros Mecatina, Kekapoui, St Augustine River, Lake Sally, Grosse Île, Kakassippi, Checatica, Bonne-Espérance, Post Stewart, Bradore, Blanc-Sablon, and L'Anse des Dunes, together with buildings, houses, sheds, store houses, and two schooners, the *Quebec* and the *Dorchester*.[48] Over the next few years, however, the owners of Lymburner and Crawford were involved in a series of lawsuits and the sale of the property was delayed. Finally, in the spring of 1808, English-speaking merchants Patrick Langan, William Burns, John William Woolsey, and Mathew Lymburner purchased the property along the Labrador coast. The partners formed a new company, Labrador New Concern, and Mathew Lymburner was appointed the agent and manager.[49]

About this time, various British government officials were discussing the possibility of returning the Labrador coast to the government of Newfoundland. The desire to reannex the Labrador coast to Newfoundland stemmed from the illicit activities that was being carried on by American fishermen fishing on the Labrador. John Holloway, a former British naval officer who was appointed governor of Newfoundland in 1807, suggested that the Labrador coast be reannexed to his command as the most effectual way of suppressing this illicit trade, which otherwise would prove a great evil to the trade of Great Britain.[50] Two years later, the British government decided to act on Governor Holloway's advice, and that portion of the Labrador coast which had been returned to Quebec in 1775 was placed under the auspices of the government of Newfoundland. The reannexation proved to be a cause for concern for the English-speaking merchants from the town of Quebec who operated posts along the Labrador coast. Governor Holloway, well aware of the seal-fishing activities of the English-speaking merchants from Quebec, wrote to the governor-general of British North America and assured him the grant holders would not be interrupted by the change.[51] They were thus able to manage their enterprises along the Labrador coast between Kegashka and Blanc-Sablon without any interference from the government of Newfoundland.

In 1812 Great Britain and its dependencies once again went to war with the United States. This war, like the one in the years 1775–83, had an impact on the English-speaking merchants from Quebec involved in the Labrador seal fishery. The British government imposed an embargo on the exportation of wheat, flour, meal of every kind, oats, potatoes, salted pork, and beef from any port in Lower Canada to any domain outside of the province.[52] Consequently, for a time, the English-speaking merchants from Quebec were unable to provide their posts along the Labrador coast with the supplies necessary to maintain their activities. The British government, made aware that enterprises such as the Labrador New Concern could not maintain their fisheries without these supplies, eventually made an exception for them.[53] As a result of the hostilities, Britain also placed an embargo on American vessels, prohibiting them from entering British territory. Therefore American fishermen were excluded from fishing off the coast of Labrador.[54] This embargo was maintained until 1817, three years after the cessation of the war. As a result, the English-speaking merchants from Quebec were able to conduct trade along the Labrador coast without any interference from American fishermen for a number of years.

In 1817, however, the Americans were given temporary permission, for one season only, to pursue the fisheries in any unoccupied harbours or bays of the British territories. Encouraged by this concession, a considerable number of American vessels visited the Labrador coast that season. The temporary permission granted in 1817 was renewed for the following season. In 1818 no fewer than four hundred American vessels visited the coast during the season, and the visitors continually exceeded the privileges given them by trespassing in occupied bays and harbours.[55]

In the fall of 1818, an agreement was signed between Great Britain and the United States, and American fishermen were given the right to fish on the southern coast of Newfoundland, on the shores of the Îles de la Madeleine, and from Mon-Joli, on the southern coast of Labrador, to and through the Strait of Belle Isle.[56] They were also allowed to dry and cure fish in any of the unsettled bays, harbours, and creeks on the southern coast of Newfoundland and on the coast of Labrador.[57] Immediately thereafter, American vessels began once again to flock to the Labrador coast.[58] Again, they became a problem for the English-speaking merchants from Quebec involved in the seal fishery along the coast.

REDEFINING THE BOUNDARY

The return of Americans to the Labrador coast in such large numbers, with unlimited access to the fisheries, proved to be a cause of concern for the government of Lower Canada and Canadian citizens with a vested interest in the seal and salmon fishery on the coast. As a result, they began to demand that it be returned to Lower Canada.

James Irvine, a member of the Executive Council for Lower Canada, in 1821 wrote to Henry Goulburn, secretary of state for the colonies, and informed him that the act which had annexed the Labrador coast to the government of Newfoundland had declared that all crimes and misdemeanours originating on the coast were recognizable in the courts of Newfoundland. Further, the legislation had originated from an application made on behalf of the merchants of Newfoundland, stating that the courts there could take cognizance of any crime or misdemeanour committed by people employed in the fisheries upon the coast of Labrador. He went on to declare, "It must be manifest how much greater and more serious injury had been created by the enactment, that followed that application, to the proprietors and lessees on the coast living in the Province of Lower Canada, and from where they carry on their trade and fisheries in those parts than could possibly give rise to application from Newfoundland."[59] He concluded by demanding that the Labrador coast be returned to Lower Canada.

James McTavish, a politician from the Gaspé, also raised concerns about the Labrador fishery before the Legislative Council of Lower Canada. He informed the council that the Treaty of Ghent allowed Americans to fish within five kilometres of the shore in the Gulf of St Lawrence, including the banks as far as Mont-Joli on the North Shore and Fox River on the South Shore. "But they go beyond these limits as far as the St. John River on the North Shore, to the injury of the lessees of the Mingan seigniory."[60] McTavish asked that regulations be made to prevent the Americans from anchoring and fishing on the banks of the principal rivers on the Terre Ferme de Mingan seigneury, because by doing so, they prevented the salmon from entering these rivers.

Members of the Legislative Assembly of Lower Canada in February 1824 presented Lord Dalhousie, governor-in-chief of British North America, with an address praying that the coast of Labrador be reannexed to Lower Canada. They informed Dalhousie that the terms of the act establishing courts of judicature on the island of Newfoundland and reannexing part of the coast of Labrador to the government of Newfoundland were such that the proprietors, most of whom were living in Lower Canada, were subjected to laws and regulations incompatible with their tenures and usages, which amounted in certain cases to a denial of justice.[61] These protestations appear to have had the desired effect. On 22 June 1825 the British government passed a bill returning that portion of the Labrador coast from Blanc-Sablon north to the fifty-second parallel and along that parallel to the St John River to the province of Lower Canada.[62]

The decision to return that portion of the Labrador coast to Lower Canada was of no consequence to the Labrador New Concern. Samuel Robertson, an employee with the company, reported that the company from about 1805 onwards experienced one bad seal-fishing season after another. The Labrador posts, once capable of generating 30,000 pounds annually, by 1820 were producing no more than 2,000 pounds a year.[63] As a result of the consecutive years of poor seal-fishing seasons and the return of Americans to the Labrador coast in 1817, the Labrador New Concern was forced to declare bankruptcy in 1820. Two years later the posts east of the Terre Ferme de Mingan seignieury were put up for sale once again.[64] This sale brought to an end the presence of English-speaking merchants from the town of Quebec along the Labrador coast between Kegashka and Blanc-Sablon, paving the way for permanent settlement.

6

The Pioneer Settlers

Between 1820 and 1850 people from various parts of North America, the British Isles, and France settled along the Quebec-Labrador coast from the Itamamiou River eastward to Blanc-Sablon. The newcomers established permanent residences and developed a distinctive lifestyle. Like their predecessors, they engaged in the seal and salmon fisheries and the fur trade. These early pioneers had to contend with numerous hardships and much privation, and want was not uncommon.

IMMIGRATION AND SETTLEMENT

Following the bankruptcy of the Labrador New Concern in 1820 the land along the Quebec-Labrador coast east of the Terre Ferme de Mingan seigneury, from the Itamamiou River to Blanc-Sablon, became available for settlement. Over the next few decades there was a steady trickle of newcomers to the area. Samuel Robertson, one of the region's first settlers, in February 1826 reported that there were some twenty families living along the Labrador coast east of the Terre Ferme de Mingan seigneury and that they possessed separate establishments and resided there in every meaning of the word.[1] Fifteen years later, Robertson, in a paper presented to the Literary and Historical Society of Quebec, stated that the number of permanent inhabitants in the area had increased to more than 250.[2] By the middle of the nineteenth century there were approximately 360 permanent residents living along the coast.[3]

Many of the people who migrated to this portion of the Labrador coast at this time were English-speaking. Some of them came from what are now the Atlantic provinces and from the New England states. Others arrived from countries such as England, Scotland, and Ireland. What attracted these people to this locality? Most came to the region because of its unlimited freedom, its abundance of resources, and the possibility of making a fortune from the seal and salmon fisheries. For instance, Samuel Robertson informed John James Audubon, the pre-eminent American naturalist, in 1833, "The country around is all my own, much farther than you can see. No fees, no lawyers, no taxes are here. I do pretty much as I choose. My means are ample through my own industry. These vessels come for sealskins, seal oil, and salmon, and give me in return all the necessities, and indeed comforts, of the life I love to follow."[4]

How did these English-speaking settlers get to the region? Some came initially as employees of the Labrador New Concern. Following the bankruptcy of the company in 1820, they purchased the posts where they were once employed. Samuel Robertson arrived on the coast in that manner. A native of Stromness in the Orkney Islands, he was hired by the Labrador New Concern early in the nineteenth century and sent to work on the coast. Following the bankruptcy of the company, he, with the help of Adam Lymburner, bought both the La Tabatière and Bradore Bay posts for £500 in 1823 and established himself at Sparr Point.[5] Robertson married Irene Boulay, who died shortly after. He then took a second wife, Mary Anne Chevalier, daughter of Louis Chevalier, owner of the post in the St Paul's River area. Robertson, while raising seven children, managed to develop a large, successful sealing enterprise at Sparr Point. He sold his enterprise at Bradore Bay to his brother-in-law, Captain William Randall Jones, an entrepreneur from Nova Scotia.

A few of the English-speaking settlers arrived on the coast while working for one of the various English firms trading on the Labrador. For instance, William Buckle and his son, also William, came from England to the Labrador in the last quarter of the eighteenth century, probably as employees of Slade and Company, a West of England firm based in Poole. It was the practice of the English fish firms to recruit workers in the spring under contract to stay on the

Labrador for the summer and the following winter until the close of fishing in the fall of the second year. Instead of returning to England at the conclusion of their contracts, the Buckles crossed the Strait of Belle Isle to Anchor Point on the west coast of Newfoundland, where they fished for an independent fisherman by the name of Abram Genge. Following the death of William Buckle the elder, the son returned to Labrador and was sent by Slade and Company to the Strait of Belle Isle to trap fur-bearing animals. In 1792 William Buckle junior married Mary Watts, a resident of Anchor Point, and moved to Forteau, where they were the first permanent settlers. Some time prior to 1832, Buckle and his six sons settled at the present-day village of Middle Bay, fifteen kilometres east of St Paul's River.[6]

Other English-speaking settlers came to the region originally as employees of Philip and Nathaniel Lloyd, part owners of the St Paul's River seigneury. For example, John Goddard, a resident of Salisbury, England, arrived on the Labrador coast as an employee of the Lloyd brothers in 1810 and worked for them at St Paul's River for several years. In 1813 he struck out on his own, and he established a home for himself at the present-day village of Old Fort Bay, ten kilometres west of St Paul's River.[7] Eventually Goddard abandoned his home in Old Fort Bay and moved back to St Paul's River, where he married Patty Dukes, an Inuk from Belles Amours. Still others came to fish, and finding the fishing good, remained.

The English-speaking incomers, however, were not the only ones to settle in this locality. Many French-speaking immigrants also took up permanent residence along the Labrador coast from the Itamamiou River to Blanc-Sablon. These settlers came from a variety of places. Some arrived from communities in the present-day province of Quebec, such as Berthier, Bellechasse, and Saint-Thomas. Others emigrated from France or from Jersey, an island in the English Channel off the coast of France belonging to the British crown. Why did they choose to come to the area? Most of the French-speaking settlers, like their English-speaking counterparts, were drawn to the region because of its unlimited freedom, its abundant resources, the dream of becoming their own masters, and the possibility of earning a good living from the fishery.

How did these French-speaking settlers get to the coast? Some, like their English-speaking counterparts, arrived originally as employees of the Labrador New Concern. Following the bankruptcy of the company in 1820, they too bought the posts where they were once employed. For instance, Michael Blais and Édouard Hamel, residents of Berthier, a small town near Quebec City and former employees of the New Labrador Concern, bought the post at Itamamiou River from the their employer in 1823 for £250 and settled there.

A few French-speaking settlers came to the coast as fishermen on French vessels involved in the Labrador cod fishery. Jean-Baptiste Michaud, one of the region's first French-speaking settlers, arrived there in this manner in the summer of 1823. That same year he abandoned the French fishing vessel on which he had come and established himself at Gros Mecatina Harbour, on the island of Gros Mecatina, opposite the present-day village of La Tabatière.[8]

Still other French-speaking settlers were brought to the region as employees of various Jersey firms, including those of De Quetteville and Le Bouthilier, who had established large fishing rooms in the Blanc-Sablon Bay region and who carried on the fishery, the cod fishery in particular, until the early 1880s.[9] The number of employees engaged by some of these firms was quite large. The Reverend Edward Cusack, a minister with the Church of England who had been to the coast in 1840, reported that "the Dequitteville firm, which owned an establishment at Blanc-Sablon, alone brings out 300 men every year."[10] Some workers were recruited from the island of Jersey; others were hired from the Gaspé Peninsula, the Îles de la Madeleine, or Lévis and Montmagny, two riverine parishes in Quebec. The hired hands were brought to the coast in the spring, and most returned home in the fall after the fishing season was over. "These come and go yearly with the vessels to which they belong, and have no permanent habitation on the coast."[11] Cusack, upon his return voyage to Quebec City in the fall of 1840, noted that the vessel in which he was travelling was carrying many French Canadians who had spent the past summer working for various Jersey houses at Blanc-Sablon.

The employees who remained at the posts during the winter months stayed to carry on the seal fishery, take care of the buildings, and prepare for the upcoming fishing season.[12] These individuals were not allowed to have their families with them. Nevertheless, many of the men who came first simply to work for the Jersey firms, after saving some money and discovering good locations for hunting and fishing, eventually built themselves homes in the area and began working for themselves. The women and children followed soon after to take care of the homes and the main family duties.

Octave Letemplier appears to have arrived on the coast in this manner. According to anthropologist Yvan Breton, Letemplier, who was born on the island of Jersey, emigrated to the Gaspé at the beginning of the nineteenth century. During the summer of 1840 he came to Blanc-Sablon to fish, and after several visits, he decided to stay there. By the time he had settled at Blanc-Sablon in 1845, he was the thirtieth resident.[13]

The English- and French-speaking settlers, however, seldom inhabited the same territory. The English-speaking residents generally settled along the Quebec-Labrador coast east of the St Augustine River archipelago, principally in the St Paul's River archipelago and Bradore Bay region. The French-speaking settlers, on the other hand, established themselves mainly in the St Augustine River archipelago and westward along the coast to the Itamamiou River. Some French-speaking settlers also took up residence in the Blanc-Sablon Bay area. As a result, the French language was spoken mainly in these areas. The English language, on the other hand, was spoken primarily in the St Paul's River archipelago and the Bradore Bay area. Many of the early pioneers, however, spoke both languages.

LIFESTYLE

Although the English- and French-speaking settlers occupied different areas of the coast, they had similar lifestyles. The majority owned both a summer and a winter dwelling. The summer house or fishing post was usually situated on some open and elevated spot along the shore near the sea or on the islands skirting it near the fishery. The winter quarters were typically located inland in more sheltered positions up the rivers or bays, where wood was more easily obtained and some protection was afforded from the severe winter storms and the cold. The closest neighbour, whether it be a summer home or winter dwelling, would have been a kilometre or two away, if not farther.

In mid-April the settlers gathered their belongings and moved from the winter quarters to the summer house by komatik, a sled pulled by a team of huskies, to be near their fishery. While waiting for the ice to melt and the seals to return to the coast, the settlers prepared for the upcoming fishery, gathered firewood, went ducking (for ducks, gulls, and geese), and collected gulls' eggs. Some of the eggs were stored for consumption for the remainder of the year. Noel Bowen, a mid-nineteenth-century visitor who sampled the eggs, noted that they had a slight fishy taste and that when beaten the yolks formed an excellent substitute for cream in tea.[14]

With the arrival of the seals in mid-May, the local residents turned their attention to the spring seal fishery, which they pursued, depending on the location of the seal-fishing station, until the third or fourth week of June. The local residents consumed some of the seal meat. It was usually cut into small strips, sprinkled with salt and pepper, roasted on the top of the stove, and eaten with biscuits. The Reverend Charles Carpenter, having sampled this type of cooking, commented that it was very tasty.[15] The seal meat was also used to feed the dogs, and some of the sealskins were used to make clothing, including mittens, hats, and boots.

During the latter part of June, the salmon would start running, and for the next month or two the men busied themselves with the salmon fishery. About this time of the year some of the settlers, the women in particular, turned their attention towards the garden. Turnips, cabbages, potatoes, and onions were grown wherever fertile soil was available. Both the turnips and the potatoes were rather small but good, and the cabbages were used to flavour the occasional soup.

From mid-August to October the settlers went berry picking and collected a variety of berries, including wild currants, blackberries, raspberries, bakeapples (cloudberrys), and red-berries (partridge-berries). Both bakeapples and red-berries were highly valued. Carpenter reported that "the bake apple is particularly noticeable for its delicious flavour, and the partridge berry for the ease with which it is preserved for winter use."[16] At this time of the year various types of fish, including trout and cod, were harvested, salted, and cured for the upcoming winter months.

In November the settlers busied themselves with the fall seal fishery, which was carried on for several weeks. Waterfowl such as the Labrador curlew were also killed at this time of the year and salted and packed away for the winter months. As well, about this time the settlers purchased supplies such as beef, pork, flour, and potatoes from trading schooners from Quebec City and Halifax for the upcoming winter months. Bowen observed, "Like the ant or the honey-bee they must lay up their store of luxuries during the summer season, impenetrable barriers of ice excluding communication with the outer world during about seven months in the year."[17]

After the fall seal fishery, the settlers collected their belongings and returned to their winter quarters, where the men set about gathering firewood for the upcoming winter. According to A.S. Packard, a mid-nineteenth-century visitor, "They spend a month in cutting wood, a family burning through the winter about thirty cords." Once the wood was collected, the men turned their attention to hunting. Caribou, porcupines, partridges, and rabbits, which were available in the interior, were taken. "A good hunter was capable of securing from sixty to seventy partridges a day in favourable seasons," Packard reported. "At any rate fresh meat was obtained for each family two or three times weekly."[18]

In addition to gathering wood and hunting, the residents engaged in a number of recreational activities throughout the winter months. A popular way of passing the time was to visit distant friends and relatives. Dog teams and the komatik were used to transport the families to their destinations. For the conveyance of women and young children, a coach box was used. The interior of the coach box was fitted out with pillows and sealskin rugs for the safety of the passengers, and it was fastened to the komatik with sealskin cords. According to Audubon, the parties travelled with ease. Most visiting was done during the holiday seasons, around Christmas, New Year's, and Easter, and sometimes lasted for a few weeks. Charles Carpenter in his diary entry for 25 December 1863, records, "People are astir as usual for the holidays. There was a great dance at Chalkers last night. People playing the fiddle and dancing. I suppose for many years there has been every Christmas a dance."[19] Such gatherings usually lasted until morning, and it was not unusual for the men to drink too much. Many, it seems, did not restrict their alcohol consumption to the holiday season. Ephraim Tucker, a visitor to the region in the latter part of the 1830s, commented that "the vice of intemperance prevailed everywhere among the European settlers on the coast. Scarcely a family can be found among them who do not habitually use intoxicating liquors. Men, women and children alike fall under the curse."[20] Some of the alcohol was supplied by local stills. A favourite was spruce beer, a fermented drink made from boiling black spruce boughs and molasses. Itinerant traders also brought liquor, rum in particular, to the coast in the summer months. This lifestyle, with minor changes, persisted well into the twentieth century.

RELIGION, EDUCATION,
AND MEDICAL SERVICES

Neither the French- nor the English-speaking settlers had access to a place of worship at this time. Bowen, who visited the area in the summer of 1854, observed, "No church or chapel rears its tall spire towards Heaven, no consecrated building invites the fishermen to assemble for the worship of God."[21]

Nevertheless, many of the early settlers received some form of religious instruction from the Church of England or Roman Catholic missionaries who visited the coast occasionally in the summer months. For example, Edward Cusack, an Anglican missionary from Gaspé, arrived at Salmon Bay on 3 July 1840 and remained in the area until October. He visited with the settlers, holding services and performing marriages, baptisms, and funerals. Cusack recorded that he had managed to perform twenty-five infant baptisms and services for those who had died.[22]

The lack of a place of worship and a permanent clergyman did not prevent the early settlers from practising their religious beliefs. Religious ceremonies such as baptisms, marriages, and funerals were conducted according to the custom of the coast – a civil ceremony presided over by several local residents, which was later consecrated by an itinerant minister or priest. According to Charles Carpenter, however, the early pioneers were not overly vigilant about their Christian faith. He reported that the original emigrants usually brought with them from their several homelands an indistinct knowledge of and external attachment to some name and form of religion. "This adherence was merely nominal and in most instances unconnected with anything of the spirit or practice. Profanity and intemperance was very common and the Sabbath was undistinguished from other days, except by discontinuance from Labour; and the spending of its hours in recreation and visiting. The most flagrant violations of the seventh commandment went unpunished and unrebuked."[23] Tucker also reported that the early pioneers' standard of morals was exceedingly low, that intemperance was a vice almost as common among females as males, and that little value was placed upon the virtues of chastity or morality.[24]

Nor were there any schools or teachers on the Quebec-Labrador coast between Itamamiou and Blanc-Sablon. The little schooling that was provided was left in the hands of the parents. Samuel Robertson, owner of the La Tabatière post, who had received a liberal education, when asked by Audubon in 1833 about the education of his children, replied, "My wife and I teach them all that is useful for them to know."[25] Guillaume-Louis Labadie, owner of the post at L'Anse des Dunes, near Blanc-Sablon, on the other hand, hired Pierre Petitclair, a resident of Saint-Augustin-de-Desmaures, in 1837 to tutor his twelve children. Petitclair, a notary's clerk, poet, and writer, served in that capacity until his death in 1860. Most of the early pioneers were not as fortunate as Robertson or Labadie. According to Tucker, "there are none among them who can read or write save the few traders on the coast, and these are in general sadly deficient in mercantile knowledge and honour."[26]

Furthermore, there were no hospitals, physicians, or nurses to be found anywhere in the region. As a result, the inhabitants were required to rely principally on folk remedies, especially poultices made of various concoctions, and on "old women" for cures. For example, Winfrid Stearns, an American naturalist, in 1880 reported that for several days one of the men had been suffering intensely with a felon on his thumb. "Poultices and applications were tried to cure it, but nothing was as effective as the soft, outer rind of the common larch, that had been boiled in hot water, and then kneaded into a poultice. It healed the sore with wonderful rapidity."[27] Some of these old women continued to apply their remedies, well into the first half of the twentieth century. Furthermore, babies were born at home with only the help of a family member or a midwife.

MODES OF TRANSPORTATION

Many of the English- and French-speaking pioneers along the coast between Itamamiou River and Blanc-Sablon owned a komatik and six or eight dogs. These animals, a mixture of wolf and husky, were half-wild and to be feared at all times. According to Bowen, the dogs plunged into the icy seas as readily as though it were their native element, and they were invaluable to their owners in hunting and shooting excursions no less than in travelling across the snowy deserts.[28]

In good weather and favourable sledding conditions, the dog

team and komatik were a relatively quick means of travel, covering distances of up to a hundred kilometres in a day. The komatik, which ranged anywhere from 2.7 to 4.3 metres in length and from .6 to .9 metres in width, was shod with whalebone. To it the dogs were harnessed with sealskin traces in twos in teams of six or eight, with one as the leader. Some lead dogs were twelve metres from the sled, but not too far away to be reached by the long sealskin whip. No reins were used, and the animals were guided simply by words of command. According to Captain Randall Jones, owner of the Bradore Bay post, the dogs were so well acquainted with the courses and places in the neighbourhood that they never failed to take their master and sled to their destination. He states, "It was always safer to leave one's fate to the instinct which these fine animals possess than to trust human judgement, for it has been proved more than once that men who have made their dogs change their course have been lost, and sometimes died, in consequence."[29] These animals were also used to haul wood from the interior in the winter months. The dog teams and komatik continued to be the inhabitants' main means of winter transportation well into the twentieth century.

Throughout the summer months, however, the settlers travelled from one destination to another along the coast by whaleboat. These vessels were pointed at either end, with a 4.8 metre keel and two small poles or masts. The inhabitants purchased the whaleboats from itinerant American fishermen for £9. The boats apparently sailed swiftly and weathered a storm better than any other type of vessel.[30] The whaleboats were also used to pursue the fishery. This type of sailing vessel continued to be used by many of the coastal residents until the first decades of the twentieth century.

The early pioneers' principal link to the outside world was the trading schooners that came from Quebec City and Halifax. The first trading vessels normally arrived in the area during the latter part of May or early June, when most of the ice had disappeared from along the coast. They continued to visit the region at irregular intervals until the latter part of November, when the presence of ice made it impossible for them to stay any longer. These vessels transported passengers, mail, and supplies. More importantly, the itinerant traders purchased the settlers' surplus of seal oil, sealskins, and salmon, their principal sources of revenue.

ECONOMIC ACTIVITIES

Admiral Henry Wolsey Bayfield, an officer in the British navy, in 1833 reported that along the Quebec-Labrador coast the seal and salmon fisheries were carried on by the resident inhabitants at fishing posts that were spaced several kilometres apart.[31]

As explained earlier, the summer house or fishing post was usually located on some open and elevated spot along the shore near the sea or on the islands skirting it near the fishery. A good post contained several buildings, including a house, a stage, and a shop. According to Samuel Robertson, owner of the fishing post at La Tabatière, a post, with tools, utensils, and provisions, cost several hundred pounds, sometimes thousands.[32] A good fishery was ranked as one of the most valuable species of property, was transmitted from one family member to another, and was sometimes sold for a good price. According to Tucker, the early settlers guarded their fishing posts with a great deal of vigilance. He writes, "He who pitches upon a tract, holds it by virtue of possession, and no subsequent interference disturbed his right thus acquired. Trespassers upon one of these posts would be severely punished."[33]

The resident fishermen, like their predecessors, engaged in both the fall and spring seal fishery. The fall fishery, the larger of the two, depending on the locality, took place in November or December, when the seals were migrating in an easterly direction. The spring fishery, depending on ice conditions, was carried on in the latter part of May or early June, when the seals were migrating in a westerly direction.

Knowing when the seals passed near the shore, the local fishermen positioned their nets at the various passes a few days before. A sentry, perched on a rock in front of the fishery, gave notice of the approaching seal herds. When the seals entered the fishery, the fishermen lifted the net, sunken with leaden weights at the entrance of the fishery, with a capstan, which closed the opening through which the seals made their ingress. As soon as the seals were in the fishery, the fishermen jumped into their boats, entered the fishery, shouting and beating the water with their paddles and sometimes firing guns. The frightened seals, trying to escape, dove and ran their heads into the meshes of the net, kept open by cables around the borders of the net, which were held taut by capstans. The fishermen clubbed the seals that were not strangled, loaded them into their boats, rowed ashore, and put the seals in storage. In the spring, seals taken during the fall and spring fishery were skinned, and the seal fat was melted in large wooden tubs. Bradore Bay and La Tabatière were the best places for pursuing the sedentary seal fishery.

Once the local fishermen were finished with the spring seal fishery, they turned their attention to the salmon fishery, which was usually pursued from the end of June to August. Salmon were either taken in rivers or near river mouths in 137-to-275-metre-long nets with a 15.9 centimetre mesh. The salmon catch was stored in barrels filled with pickle. The St Augustine River and St Paul's River archipelagos were the best places for conducting the salmon fishery.

Some of the men during the winter months also were involved in trapping fur-bearing animals. Audubon, in his diary for the summer of 1833, reports that in the winter men hunted foxes, martens, sables, and black bears; but neither deer nor other game was to be found without going a great distance into the interior.[34] The trapping of fur-bearing animals was typically carried on some twenty to twenty-five kilometres inland or farther. The trapper usually walked to his hunting grounds and stayed for extended periods in log cabins, which were the common property of the hunters.

The hunters relied on the gun and the trap to take down their quarry. They used traps to catch foxes, martens, otters, and sables, whereas bears, wolves, and deer were shot. St Paul's River, St Augustine River, and Mecatina River were the best places for trapping fur-bearing animals. According to Samuel Robertson, the fur trade was pursued on a limited scale because of the lifecycle of the animals. It seems that the animals appeared in abundance along the coast only every four years.[35] Trapping on a small scale has continued to the present.

As recorded earlier the settlers traded their surplus of seal oil, sealskins, salmon, and furs to itinerant traders from Quebec City and Halifax, who came to the coast in the summer months.[36] The itinerant traders brought all sorts of valuable items, including provisions, fishing gear, clothing, and liquor, and the trade was done either in the form of barter or for cash.[37] The fishermen usually received their fishing gear on credit at the beginning of the season, on the understanding that they would pay for it in sealskins, seal oil, and salmon once the season was over. The rest of the catch would be used to obtain winter provisions. The ability to pay off one's debt and to procure winter supplies depended to a great extent on the success of the seal and salmon fishery, the primary activities of the early settlers.

The traders from Halifax, laden with duty-free provisions from the United States, sold their goods to the settlers at a better price than their counterparts from Quebec City, who were required to pay a tariff on their merchandise. Some of the Halifax merchants managed to make a great deal of money from the trade. For example, Daniel Cronan, one of Halifax's richest merchants, who had been trading on the Quebec-Labrador coast since 1840, left an inheritance of $720,000 to his heirs following his death in 1892.[38]

LIVING CONDITIONS

Cronan was not the only one to benefit from the trade. Throughout much of the 1820s and 1830s many settlers living on the Quebec-Labrador coast from the Itamamiou River eastward to Blanc-Sablon earned a good living from the seal and salmon fisheries. Visitors to the region at this time in fact describe some of the settlers as living the life of lords and seigneurs.

Admiral Bayfield, who visited with Samuel Robertson, owner of the La Tabatière fishing post, in the summer of 1834, reports that Robertson carried on an extensive seal fishery and that he took several thousands of these animals in a year, whose skins and oils were worth a large sum.[39] According to Audubon, "Robertson a lord of these parts lived in a neat and comfortable mansion and that for lunch they were served bread, cheese and a good port of wine. He received the newspaper and he had a personal library."[40] Robertson also employed a number of men to help carry on his business.

Another individual who was doing quite well was Captain William Randall Jones, owner of the post at Bradore Bay. Born and raised in Liverpool, Nova Scotia, he had arrived on the coast during the early 1820s. Shortly thereafter, he married Mary Sophia Chevalier, daughter of Louis David Chevalier and sister of Mary Ann Chevalier, who was the wife of Samuel Robertson. Captain Jones purchased the Bradore post from Robertson. And like his brother-in-law, he owned a very large fishing establishment. It was not unusual for Jones to take several thousand seals during a seal-fishing season. Audubon, who visited Captain Jones in the summer of 1833, notes that he had 1,500 seal carcasses stacked near the house.[41] The Jones family lived in a luxurious home constructed of materials imported from Quebec City. The walls of the house were graced with elegant Italian pictures, for which they had paid a shilling sterling each. The carpet on the stairs leading to the second storey was held down on each side with a big silver dollar, kept bright and polished. The furniture, some of which came from France, was handmade and beautiful. The huge kitchen was stocked with copper and brass pots and pans. The Joneses also owned a hand organ, a schooner, a horse, and several cows.[42]

Admiral Bayfield, in the summer of 1834, also met Louis Chevalier, who had inherited the posts in the St Paul's River area from Nathaniel and Philip Lloyd. Chevalier appears to have arrived in the St. Paul's River area during the late 1790s. He married Mary Anne Vane, who bore him at least two daughters: Mary Sophia Chevalier, wife of Captain Jones, and Mary Ann Chevalier, wife of Samuel Robertson. According to Bayfield, Chevalier was running a very successful business at St Paul's River. Bayfield notes, "Chevalier was seignior of the country for several leagues on either side of the Eskimo River. He is married has a grown up family and has furnished wives to several other persons who live in a similar manner on this coast."[43] He goes on to state that Chevalier had a good house and that he had made much money from the salmon and seal fisheries. Chevalier, for instance, managed to catch 5,365 salmon in 1823. In the ensuing year he caught 6,091.[44]

Bayfield also notes that John Goddard, owner of the post at Stick Island, was a steady, sober man and a good hunter and that he had saved a considerable sum of money from the seal and salmon fisheries. Bayfield writes, "He has a good house at Stick Island which he occupies in the summer and a very comfortable cottage in Old Fort Bay which he occupies during the winter."[45] Carpenter, on the other hand, claims that Goddard made considerable sums of money from bootlegging. According to Bayfield, only a few of the families that he visited were "very poor people who just seem able to make out an indifferent livelihood by hunting and fishing."[46]

By the end of the following decade, however, the living conditions of many settlers along the coast between the Itamamiou River and Blanc-Sablon had declined considerably. Étienne Labadie, owner of the post at Itamamiou, in 1849 noted that "the inhabitants live in a state of poverty."[47] Mr Justice J.S.N. Bossé, a lawyer from Quebec City, also reported that "the inhabitants along the whole coast are in a state of great poverty, while they have at their doors an inexhaustible source of riches."[48] Seal-fishing stations, such as the ones owned by Captain Jones at Bradore Bay, once capable of taking several thousand seals in one fall or one spring, by 1850 were fetching only eight hundred seals annually. The Chevalier salmon fishery at St Paul's River, once capable of producing 1,400 barrels of salmon annually, by 1850 was producing only 80 barrels of salmon. Pierre Fortin, a fishery magistrate who visited the region in the summer of 1852, reported that many of the early pioneers did not have the means of procuring the necessary tackle, and as a result, many fisheries yielded no more than a hundred pounds annually.[49]

Who or what was responsible for the decline in the settlers' fortunes? One of the probable causes was the increase in the number of fishing stations in the region. Samuel Robertson, in a paper presented before the Literary and Historical Society of Quebec in 1841, states that "there is now in the first one hundred and fifty miles from the Province line, about fifty establishments, more or less extensive chiefly sedentary seal fisheries."[50] Another cause may have been due to fluctuations in the fishery caused by varying weather conditions. Part of the decline, however, stemmed from the lawlessness that prevailed throughout the region during the fishing season.[51]

MIGHT IS RIGHT

In 1825 the British government had placed the Labrador coast from Blanc-Sablon westward under the governance of Lower Canada. As in former years, the province lacked the resources to provide fishermen under its jurisdiction with adequate law enforcement. Beyond the limits of the Mingan seignieury, from the Itamamiou River to Blanc-Sablon, the local fishermen had no legal means of securing their rights from encroachments, except by resorting to the courts at Quebec City. Furthermore, no one in the area had the authority to enforce civil or criminal laws, and the fishermen were required to rely on the goodwill of their neighbours and the British Admiralty.[52]

The protection provided by the Admiralty was sporadic at the best of times. Admiral Bayfield reports that the British men-of-war confined their visits to Mingan and the open bays in the Strait of

Belle Isle, where there were seldom any fishermen, but never visited the intermediate harbours and bays, where the fishermen gathered in large numbers. [53] Even when a ship was located, there were no assurances that the complaints lodged by the settlers against the interlopers would be dealt with. An observer states, "As long as this vessel is in the jurisdiction of Quebec, her Captain receives the complaints that British subjects have against foreigners such as the Americans who have been there since spring. If the delinquent foreigners are kind enough to wait for the vessel of war, they are obliged to give up all they have taken; but if they have gone away, the complaint is deferred till the next spring, or rather that is the end of the matter." [54]

Interlopers, especially Americans, continually harassed the settlers. Étienne Labadie, a fifteen-year resident of the coast, reported in 1849 that Americans committed outrages and inflicted ill-treatment of all kinds on the inhabitants. Since they were the stronger, the Americans did whatever they wanted. "Being foreigners they care but little about preserving or protecting the fisheries. On the contrary they make use of whatever means destructible or not to profit by them in an illicit manner, unfortunately there is no law or force there to prevent them from doing otherwise." [55] Earlier, Samuel Robertson had informed Audubon in 1833 that the American fisherman often acted as badly as pirates towards the Natives, the white settlers, and the "eggers," who more than once were obliged to retaliate, and bloody encounters had been the result.

Most of the American vessels came from the New England states. As soon as the warmth of spring had freed the gulf of ice, a fleet of schooners from Maine and Massachusetts sailed to the coast to fish for cod, mackerel, halibut, and herring. They began their pursuit of the cod fishery at Little Natashquan, and towards the end of July the fishermen proceeded northeastward, following the fish. On route they stopped at Mistanoque, Rocky Bay, Bonne-Espérance, Five Leagues Harbour, Middle Bay, and Bradore Bay. Audubon, in his journal of 26 July 1833, writes,

Bradore is the grand rendezvous of almost all the fishermen that resort to this coast for codfish. We found here a flotilla of about one hundred and fifty sail, principally fore-and-aft schooners, a few pickaxes, mostly from Halifax and the eastern portions of the United States. There was a life and stir about this harbour which surprised us after so many weeks of wilderness and loneliness

– the boats moving to and from, going after fish, and returning laden to the gunwales, others with seines, others with capelines for bait. A hundred or more were anchored out about a mile from us ... hundreds of men engaged cleaning and salting their low jokes and songs resembling those of the Billingsgate gentry.[56]

The number of vessels and men in the region at any one time varied. Admiral Bayfield, in the summer of 1833, reported that 300 vessels participated in the fisheries on the coast, averaging 75 tons each and manned by 50 men to each six vessels, for a total of 2,500 men. "Of these half were American. Each vessel took away on an average of 1500 quintals of codfish, at 112 pounds per quintal."[57] Seven years later, the Reverend Edward Cusack claimed that it was not unusual to find as many as 1,500 schooners with 15,000 men fishing and trading on the coast during the summer.

The American fishermen and others constantly interfered with the spring sedentary seal fishery. They set shoal nets in front of the settlers' sedentary seal fisheries, thus preventing the seals from entering the passes. The interlopers also shot at seals with guns, which drove the seals into the open rather than into the passes. Furthermore, American schooners frequently entered the sedentary seal fishery, causing a great deal of damage.[58]

As well, the interlopers seized salmon rivers and nets held for long periods of time by the local residents. In a letter to Charles Wood, secretary to the Admiralty, in 1837, Bayfield wrote, "Our people being almost always the minority at the various fishing stations are frequently annoyed by these strangers who not only seize and keep the best spots for taking and drying their fish but occasionally plunder the salmon nets set by the people belonging to the posts ashore."[59]

The migratory fishermen also attacked fishing posts, taking whatever they desired. Michel Blais, a twenty-one-year resident of the coast, reported that during his stay the interlopers committed several depredations, outrages, and robberies in his neighbourhood and at other posts, taking fishing gear, including cables, nets, and anchors. François Blais, a resident for eight years at Itamamiou River, declared that the interlopers had also committed several depredations near his post and that he had had forcibly taken from him six to seven hundred deals as well as other articles. Magloire Gaumont, another coastal resident, reported that one of the inhabitants was violently driven away and dispossessed of his post, and his building materials and other effects were destroyed.[60]

The early pioneers also suffered greatly at the hands of "eggers" from Nova Scotia, who came to the area each spring to collect birds' eggs and eiderdown. Admiral Bayfield notes that in some seasons twenty small schooners or shallops of twenty to thirty tons loaded with eggs from this coast were observed.[61] Halifax was the principal market for the eggs; there they at times fetched a much higher price than hen's eggs. "As soon as one vessel is loaded, she is sent to market, others following in succession, so that the market is always supplied, but never glutted. One vessel of twenty five tons is said to have cleared two hundred pounds by this egging business in a favourable season."[62] The eggers preferred murres' eggs, but they also collected the eggs of puffins, gannets, gulls, eider ducks, and cormorants.

The eggers allowed no one to interfere with their business. Might was right with them, and they had arms and were not afraid to use them. As a result, encounters between eggers and fishermen were commonplace. Audubon in 1833 describes such an event

The fishermen, cleanly clad in Sunday attire, arrived at the desired spot, and at once prepared to ascend the rock. The eggers, now numbering a dozen, all armed with guns and bludgeons, bid defiance to the fishermen. A few angry words passed between the parties. One of the eggers, still under the influence of drink, pulled the trigger, and an unfortunate sailor was seen to reel in agony. Three loud cheers filled the air. All at once rushed on the malefactors; a horrid fight ensued, the result of which was that every egger was left on the rock beaten and bruised.[63]

The early pioneers' situation was further exasperated by quarrels among themselves over fishing berths. During the time of the French, fifteen or more kilometres was considered a reasonable distance between fisheries, but according to Robertson, many of the early pioneers had discarded these rules. In 1841 he wrote, "Now days, there are some who say that a few yards is a sufficient berth. However the old settlers do not choose to submit to these self-made legislators. Here the cause of quarrels. One wishing to retain the profits of his capital and industry, and the other insisting on a part of the harvest, which he neither laboured for nor sowed."[64] He also maintained that the fisheries were so crowded thereabouts as to seriously annoy one another, and endless quarrels were going on. He reported that "so far there has been no blood spilt, but, if the government does not soon interfere and enforce some regulations, there is no saying what may happen in a country where the total absence of every mark of authority had bred a contempt for government and laws, where violence is the best title."[65] The lawlessness that prevailed along the Quebec-Labrador coast from Blanc-Sablon westward during the fishing season was a cause for concern for many of the settlers.

THE QUEST FOR LAW AND ORDER

Various settlers petitioned the government of the province of Lower Canada, praying that the government would provide some form of relief from the continual harassment by interlopers and some of the local fishermen. One of the individuals who attempted to bring law and order to the region during the fishing season was Samuel Robertson, owner of the La Tabatière fishing post. On 26 February 1826 he wrote to John Fraser, a member of the government of Lower Canada, and expressed his concerns about the deplorable conditions on that part of the Labrador coast. Robertson informed Fraser that residents had to rely for protection on warships, which seldom came before the month of September, when the aggressor was quite likely to be on his way home with the product of his unjust activities. According to Robertson, the warships made available by the British government to protect the fisheries and keep the peace were unable to do the job. One of the reasons for their ineffectiveness was the inability of the captains to navigate their vessels close to the shoreline. "From Mingan to Bradore there are approximately four hundred miles and it is hardly possible to find pilots who would undertake to conduct a ship of their size among the numerous shoals and rocks found there and that no prudent captain would risk his ship among them."[66] Furthermore, no one had any knowledge as to when or where the foreign fishermen would strike next. Even when the settlers did catch someone, there was little more they could do. Robertson declared that the depredations would of necessity continue while there were no other checks nearer than Quebec City.[67]

He proposed that a surveyor with a commission of the peace be appointed to survey the region, and that this justice of the peace be provided with a light vessel and a sufficient number of men at his disposal, so that he would be ready to act at the shortest warning either in protecting the inhabitants or in keeping the peace. As he would probably require three or four years to make the survey, the justice of the peace would probably be an effectual check on lawlessness during that time. Should this proposal prove too expensive, Robertson recommended that the government appoint local residents as justices of the peace, assisted by a military officer. He commented,

If either of the fore going can be admitted then one or two militia officers be appointed who would be able to call the assistance of his neighbours on emergency to oppose violence or seize a thief or other disturbance of the peace. Any of the three events proposed would, without doubt, be of great service. The very name of a person having a commission from the Government would go far to preserve peace, by intimidating the lawless with a possibility of apprehension, which at present does not exist."[68]

In the summers of 1833 and 1834, the British Admiralty sent Admiral Bayfield to the area to survey the coastline and its waters. However, he was not commissioned as a justice of the peace, nor was he given a vessel in the way requested by Robertson.

William Buckle, a settler from Middle Bay, in the summer of 1832 wrote to the governor of Newfoundland and complained about the activities of the American fishermen. He informed the governor that the American schooner *James Marrow Capt. Bodie* and the *Admiral Captain Templeton* had entered "my frame although I told them not as they kept me from taking my seals, still they persisted on many days which caused me great loss."[69] Buckles's complaints, however, failed to result in any change in the way the fisheries were supervised along the coast.

Four years later, Admiral Bayfield wrote to the British Admiralty and pleaded with it to take action against the interlopers.[70] He recommended that a small ship that did not draw much water would suffice to protect the settlers from the summer adventurers, stating that "a small man of war would be usefully employed by us to protect our fisheries between Mingan and the Strait of Belle Isle inclusive. From the nature of the navigation a schooner not drawing more than ten to eleven feet of water would be best suited for such a service."[71] Bayfield went so far as to send the Admiralty copies of the new maps that he had drawn of the coast. But his pleading, like that of the settlers, went unanswered.

In the spring of 1837, Étienne Labadie and a number of settlers addressed their complaints to a higher authority. They presented a petition to Governor General Lord Gosford setting forth their concerns about the difficulties they were having with the foreigners. At the same time they solicited the interference of His Majesty's government for the purpose of guarding the rights of the people concerned in the fisheries on the coast and settling disputes among the local fishermen themselves and between themselves and the interloping foreigners. The petitioners requested that the British government station a man-of-war along the coast during the fishing season, and that magistrates be appointed to protect the local residents. The king informed them that steps would be taken to protect them.[72]

Shortly after, a representative of the king wrote to the committee of the Executive Council of Lower Canada and inquired about the conditions of the settlers along the Labrador coast from Itamamiou River to Blanc-Sablon. The committee informed him that it was unable to ascertain whether in the interval between 1809 and 1825 the government of Newfoundland had made any local regulations applicable to these settlements. "It might be susceptible of doubt whether such regulations, if made, could be considered in force since the annexation of that territory to this province."[73] Furthermore, they told the king that they did not believe that His Majesty's government had the right to protect the petitioners other than to appoint a justice of the peace. They declared that even if the regulations could be brought into operation in these settlements, it would not appear to be applicable to the difficulties of which the petitioners complain.[74] They nonetheless informed the king that "they deemed it highly important both to the adjustment of these local difficulties among the resident and transient subjects of His Majesty engaged in these fisheries and also the protection against the encroachments of foreigners to which it appears that they were greatly exposed in violation of public treaties."[75] The committee reported that it could not advise His Majesty to adopt any measure of executive authority. It did state, however, that the subject would be raised before the legislature in order to bring about the adoption of some efficient regulations respecting it.[76] Despite these promises, no action was forthcoming.

Finally, after numerous petitions, the government of the Province of Canada,[77] in the spring of 1849, appointed a select committee to investigate the settlers' complaints. Various individuals from the Quebec-Labrador coast and elsewhere were called upon by the committee to provide information about the conditions that prevailed in the area. All complained that the Americans and other transient fishermen were abusing their rights along the coast.

The committee came forward with a number of recommendations for the gulf and the Labrador coastal fisheries. It declared that countries such as England, France, and the United States which had rights to the Newfoundland fisheries were in the process of developing regulations, and that such measures were of vital importance to the preservation and future value of the fisheries. The committee stated that, in the meantime, the rights of Her Majesty's subjects would be more effectively protected by two or three small vessels of the Royal Navy connected with the Halifax naval establishment. These vessels would cruise along the coast of Labrador, Newfoundland, the Îles de la Madeleine, and other places in the gulf. The commanders and other officers, in addition to the powers they derived from the imperial government, should be invested with a sufficient judiciary and administrative authority, under laws to be passed for the purpose by the colonial legislatures involved. The committee also proposed that the legislatures of Canada and Newfoundland furnish this coast guard with armed schooners, which would serve to maintain the civil organizations and to police acts of violence carried out by British subjects among themselves. With respect to the land under its immediate jurisdiction, the select committee proposed that the authorities in Canada appoint commissioners to examine the claims of the present possessors to prove their claims. They recommended that the subject be taken up immediately.[78]

By the middle of the nineteenth century the Quebec-Labrador coast between the Itamamiou River and Blanc-Sablon had been settled by English- and French-speaking settlers. However, because of wanton destruction by local fishermen and interlopers, the seal and salmon fisheries had been all but been ruined. Many local inhabitants experienced considerable economic hardship as a result.

7

Expansion

Throughout the second half of the nineteenth century there was considerable development along the Quebec-Labrador coast between Kegashka and Blanc-Sablon. Settlers took up residence along the coast west of the Itamamiou River to Kegashka, and various religious denominations established church missions in the region. Regular communication with the outside world was also established. The government introduced fishing regulations, and many of the local inhabitants became involved in the cod fishery. Living conditions, however, continued to be abysmal for many of the local residents

NEW MIGRANTS

Since 1821 the Terre Ferme de Mingan seignieury had been under the auspices of the Hudson's Bay Company. Certainly, it had a right to a monopoly over the trade, but the company further endeavoured to convince any would-be settlers that it was the sole proprietor of this immense domain. Samuel Robertson in 1855 commented that "instead of conceding and peopling the [Mingan] seigniory they [the company] strive by threats and otherwise to keep off all British fishermen and coasters who touched on these inhospitable shores."[1] The Company appears to have been successful in its efforts. Pierre Fortin, stipendiary magistrate, reported that

in 1852 from the Coacoacho River westward, the only resident
fishermen were employees of the HBC, who numbered about 150,
besides the chiefs and clerks who carried on trade with the Montagnais (Innu).[2]

Nevertheless, British subjects involved in the Quebec-Labrador
fishery for a number of years had been pressuring the government
of the Province of Canada to annul the company's monopoly over
the Mingan seignieury. Robert Christie, the member of the legislature for Gaspé, raised the issue with the Canadian government
on more than one occasion. In due course, the government began
to take note of his protestations. In the spring of 1853 the Legislative Assembly of the Province of Canada passed an act allowing all British subjects to participate in the fishery along that
portion of the Labrador coast under the jurisdiction of the
province. The act specifically stated that "any Master and Commander of every vessel fitted out from the United Kingdom or any
of the dominions thereto may take possession of so much of the
uncoded beaches of any of the islands of the Labrador or any
unoccupied beach on the mainland within the limits of the
Province [of Canada] as may be necessary for trying his blubber
and rendering the same to oil, or for curing his fish and preparing
it for exportation."[3]

Furthermore, British subjects were allowed to retain and enjoy
the same beach so long as they did not leave it unoccupied for
twelve calendar months. If it was left unoccupied, another person
could lawfully take possession provided that the beach was not
private property.[4] Basically, this legislation meant that British subjects could now establish themselves along the Quebec-Labrador
coast west of the Itamamiou River to Kegashka and beyond
without fear of reprisal from Hudson's Bay Company or its employees. As a result, HBC activities along the coast from Kegashka to
Blanc-Sablon declined considerably, and most of the company's
posts in the region were either closed or only operated periodically.
For instance, in 1869 the HBC opened a post at St Augustine River,
but a few years later it was closed mainly because of a lack of
business.

Following the implementation of the act of 1853 there was an
influx of settlers to the Labrador coast under the jurisdiction of the
Province of Canada. Geologist and explorer Henry Youle Hind
reported that by 1855 there were 457 settlers along the Quebec-

Labrador coast between Kegashka and Blanc-Sablon.[5] V.A. Huard, another visitor, recorded that the number of permanent settlers along the same coast had increased to 934 by the end of the nineteenth century.[6]

Many of the people who came to the coast in the 1850s and 1860s were French-speaking migrants from the counties of Gaspé, Bonaventure, Rimouski, and the Îles de la Madeleine.[7] How did these people get to the area? Some of the newcomers, such as Acadians from the Îles de la Madeleine, arrived in their own fishing schooners. Others, including those from Gaspé, came initially as employees on some fishing schooner. Why did they choose to settler along this portion of the Labrador coast? An Acadian fisherman, for example, when asked by Abbé Jean-Baptiste-Antoine Ferland in 1858 why he had left the Îles de la Madeleine replied, "The plagues of Egypt have fallen upon us. The first three came with the bad harvests, the seignieurs, and the traders; the remaining four arrived with the gentlemen of the law. The moment lawyers set their feet upon our island there was no longer any hope left of maintaining ourselves there."[8] More specifically, he and his fellow Acadians had left the Îles de la Madeleine to escape the deplorable land tenure conditions introduced by Admiral Isaac Coffin, seigneur of the islands, in 1798 and perpetuated by his heirs. The majority of the French-speaking settlers who arrived at this time, however, came to the region because of the possibility of making a great deal of money from the fishery. Stipendiary magistrate André Lavoie reported that "numerous [French-speaking] fishermen from the Counties of Bonaventure, Gaspe, Rimouski and the Magdalene Islands crossed over to seek their fortunes on these shores. Success having crowned their venture, they decided upon settling there with their families."[9]

Many of the French-speaking newcomers established themselves west of the Itamamiou River at places such as Washecontai Bay, Musquaro River, and Kegashka Bay. In the early part of the 1870s, however, they abandoned these areas. For instance, the Acadians from the Îles de la Madeleine who had settled at Kegashka Bay in the early part of the 1850s left the area twenty years later. First, they moved farther west to Betchuan, then to Havre-Saint-Pierre, and finally to the Beauce, a region in the Eastern Townships of Quebec. Their reasons for leaving included lack of wood for heating and construction, inadequacy of the harbour for their schooners, and consecutive years of poor fish returns.

The French-speaking migrants, however, were not the only ones to migrate to that portion of the Quebec-Labrador coast stretching from Kegashka to Blanc-Sablon. There was also an influx of English-speaking settlers from Newfoundland from the 1870s through to the end of the nineteenth century. The Newfoundlanders came from places such as Bonne Bay, Bay of Islands, Basque Harbour, Heart's Desire, and Trinity Bay. How did these people get to that portion of the Labrador coast? Some of the Newfoundlanders came to the area as employees of William Henry Whiteley, a fisherman who owned a large fishing station on the island of Bonne-Espérance. Whiteley, who hailed from Boston, established a fishing post at Bonne-Espérance around 1855. Throughout the years he managed to augment his business, and at one time he employed as many as 156 people. Each spring Whiteley would hire men, boys, and girls from various parts of Newfoundland and transport them to the coast. For instance, a note in his account book for 1874 reads, "Send to St. John's for eight fishermen, 2 boys for stage, 1 splitter, 1 salter, 1 girl for cook, 1 for stage."[10] Once the fishing season was over, the hired help would return to Newfoundland. The Whiteley family carried on the business at Bonne-Espérance until 1945. At that time it was sold to the Standard Fish Company in Montreal because the Whiteleys were unable to find a family member who was willing to continue the enterprise.

Others arrived as employees of Newfoundland fishing companies such as the Job Brothers, which operated several large fishing firms at various places in the region, including Salmon Bay and Blanc-Sablon, until the late 1920s.[11] Job Brothers and the other Newfoundland companies conducted the business in a manner similar to Whiteley's. Employees were taken to the coast in the spring and returned home in the fall once the fishing season had ended. Some, after several years, found places for themselves on the coast and struck out on their own. Still others came as independent fishermen and stayed.

What was it that attracted Newfoundlanders to the area? Some were drawn to the region because of problems of overpopulation on the east coast of Newfoundland and the availability of land on the Quebec-Labrador coast between Kegashka and Blanc-Sablon. Others were drawn by the bountiful fishery. Lavoie, in his annual report for 1873, states that during the spring forty families migrated from Newfoundland to the coast because of successful fishing in previous years and the ability to carry it on.[12] Some of the Newfoundlanders settled at places such as Blanc-Sablon Bay, Middle Bay, Bradore Bay, the St Paul's River archipelago, Old Fort Bay, the St Augustine River archipelago, La Tabatière, Mutton Bay, and Harrington Harbour. Others settled farther west in regions that had been abandoned by the French-speaking settlers, such as Kegashka Bay.

The original settlers along the coast viewed the arrival of the New-foundlanders with considerable ambivalence. On the one hand, the Newfoundlanders "were reckoned as an enterprising class of fisher-men." On the other, the older settlers complained about the New-foundlanders because "most of the new settlers were of quarrelsome depositions and addicted to stealing."[13]

As a result of the influx of Newfoundlanders, marriages between English- and French-speaking settlers, and the abandonment of the coast by some French-speaking residents, a new pattern of set-tlement gradually emerged. By the end of the nineteenth century there were French-speaking settlers principally in the La Romaine region, Tête-à-la-Baleine archipelago, and Lourdes-de-Blanc-Sablon region. The English-speaking residents, on the other hand, had settled in mainly at Blanc-Sablon, Bradore Bay westward to Mutton Bay, Harrington Harbour to Wolf Bay, and Kegashka Bay. As a result, the French language now became of secondary importance with many of the French-speaking residents capable of speaking English.

Despite the increase in the number of settlers, many of the resi-dents continued, as in earlier times, to live in areas separated by a kilometre or two of coastline or more.[14] Nevertheless, various localities through the region, including St Paul's River, La Tabatière, and Mutton Bay, began to attract a fair number of settlers in the winter months. One of the reasons people were drawn to these winter settlements was because of the availability of firewood, which was quite scarce along other parts of the coast. Another was the presence of church missions. The Reverend Charles Carpenter, for instance, wrote that "the location of the winter station of our Mission at this point on the river [St. Paul's River] is drawing, and will doubtless draw the shore-men more together here to spend the winter."[15]

THE ESTABLISHMENT OF CHURCH MISSIONS

In 1854 Noel H. Bowan reports that there was not a missionary to be seen anywhere along the Quebec-Labrador coast from Kegashka to Blanc-Sablon. He asked, "Could not a missionary be spared to visit this portion of the Province occasionally?"[16] Shortly after, there was a dramatic increase in missionary activity throughout the region. This was mainly the result of the influx of new settlers and an increase in the number of transient fishermen.

One of the first religious denominations to take a more active role in the lives of the inhabitants along this portion of the coast was the Roman Catholic Church. In 1854 the region was placed under the auspices of the Oblates of Mary Immaculate (OMI) order, which immediately began sending an itinerant missionary annually from Quebec City to the area. The missionary would travel to the coast in the summer months only, on a merchant's vessel, stopping over at each post on the way. Seven years later, however, the Catholic Church established a permanent mission at Natashquan and the missionary stationed there became responsible for all the Catholic adherents along the Labrador coast from the present-day town of Havre-Saint-Pierre to Blanc-Sablon.[17]

In 1882 the Catholic Church created the apostolic prefecture of the Gulf of St Lawrence North Shore. Its territory extended from Porteneuf River on the North Shore of the St Lawrence to Blanc-Sablon and in a northerly and westerly direction as far as the Hudson Strait. Havre-Saint-Pierre was designated the headquarters of the new prefecture, and a year later a permanent mission was established at Lourdes-de-Blanc-Sablon, several kilometres west of the Quebec-Labrador border. The mission headquarters was placed at this location because it contained the largest number of Catholic adherents.

Father Pierre Théberge, an OMI missionary, in the fall of 1883 was put in charge of the mission and given responsibility for that portion of the Quebec-Labrador coast from Blanc-Sablon Bay westward to Musquaro. The missionary stationed at Natashquan now became responsible for Catholic adherents west of Musquaro. Ten years later a second permanent mission was established at La Tabatière under the auspices of Father D. Tremblay, another OMI missionary. Following the establishment of the latter mission, the missionary stationed at Lourdes-de-Blanc-Sablon became responsible for the territory between Blanc-Sablon Bay and the St Augustine archipelago, and the missionary stationed at La Tabatière took care of the territory extending from that community westward to Kegashka Bay.[18] The OMI continued to serve the region until the early twentieth century.

The Church of England about this time also became more in-volved in the lives of the coastal residents. In 1849 it established a mission headquarters at Forteau, a community forty kilometres east of the Quebec-Labrador border. The missionary stationed there was made responsible for all Anglican adherents east and west of the Forteau mission. Throughout the 1850s, however, the missionary made annual visits westward along the Labrador coast, seldom extending his journey beyond Bradore Bay.[19]

Twelve years after the mission was established at Forteau, George Mountain, the Anglican bishop of Quebec, travelled along the Quebec-Labrador coast from Kegashka to Blanc-Sablon and met with a number of the local residents. He informed them that a church was needed here and that the Church of England was anxious to supply one. Bishop Mountain told the local inhabitants that a minister had already been sent down and had landed a short while ago at Belles Amours. But the minister, finding the coast not what he had expected, moved on to Gaspé.[20]

In the fall of 1862 the Church of England sent another minis-ter, the Reverend John Frederich Cooksley, to the coast. A short while later Cooksley established a mission headquarters on Old Fort Island, opposite the present-day village of Old Fort Bay.[21] He probably set up the mission on the island because of its cen-tral location between the different settlements and its favourable connection with foreign fishing vessels. In 1863, however, the Reverend Richard Wainwright, Cooksley's replacement, moved the mission headquarters from Old Fort Island to St Augustine River. Wainwright abandoned the Old Fort Island mission because "he could not see any probabilities of a settlement being formed there on account of there being no wood and for 2 or 3 months no safe communication with the mainland."[22] In 1872 the Anglican missionary's territory along the coast was expanded, and Natashquan and Forteau became his responsibility as well. As a result, the mission headquarters was moved from St Augus-tine River to Mutton Bay, the mid-point between the eastern and

western limits of the missionary's route. Mutton Bay continued to
be the mission headquarters well into the twentieth century.

The Church of England and the Roman Catholic Church were
not the only denominations to take an interest in the residents along
the Quebec-Labrador coast between Kegashka and Blanc-Sablon.
The Canada Foreign Missionary Society (CFMS) also became active
in the area. Charles Carpenter, a resident of Camden, New Hamp-
shire, travelled to Salmon Bay, which is several kilometres west of
St. Paul's River, in the summer of 1857, hoping that the clean
Labrador air would improve his ailing health. His visit made him
aware of the region's lack of educational and religious facilities.
After returning home in the fall, Carpenter wrote to the American Board of Missions urging it to establish a mission in the area.
The American society, which had foreign missions outside North
America only, forwarded his appeal to the newly formed CFMS in
Montreal. The CFMS heeded Carpenter's request and prevailed
upon him to go to the coast in the summer of 1858 with a view to
exploring and reporting upon its wants and prospects for a mission
station.[23]

Upon his return to Montreal in that fall, Carpenter recommended
that the CFMS build a summer station on Caribou Island, opposite
Salmon Bay. The island was chosen because of its central position
between the different settlements and its favourable connection
with foreign fishing vessels. Carpenter observed, "Some five or six
American vessels regularly made harbour there and at Bonne Esper-
ence [sic], where often a fleet of 50 to 75 sail from Nova Scotia
came early in the summer."[24] The object of the mission was to carry
the Gospel to the inhabitants of the coast and the sailors who
visited annually. It was later decided that it would be more benefi-
cial for the missionary to spend summers on Caribou Island and
winters on the mainland at St Paul's River. By doing so, the CFMS
missionaries were able to provide church and school services to the
settlers during the summer months, while they were away from
their winter homes.

In 1865 the CFMS ceased its affiliation with the Labrador mission,
but a few gentlemen in Montreal continued to provide the mission
with financial support. Four years later, however, the mission was
turned over to the Ladies Missionary Society of Zion Congregational Church in Montreal, and it remained this organization's
responsibility until the mission was closed in 1880. At that time,

both the CFMS and the Ladies Missionary Society of Zion Congregational Church limited their activities east of the St Augustine River archipelago.

The Presbyterian Church also came to administer to the needs of the early settlers. The Presbyterian Church in Nova Scotia began sending missionaries to the region as early as 1864. For the next twenty-five or so years, these missionaries, mainly theology students, spent several months a year in the area before returning to their studies. Then around 1891 the Presbyterian Church established a mission on the coast at Harrington Harbour. Several years later the church expanded its activities eastward and established churches at Mutton Bay, Rocky Bay, Bonne-Espérance, and Salmon Bay. According to F.W. Thompson, there were twenty to forty members in connection with the Presbyterian Church at this time.[25]

The missionaries had to contact people who lived, for the most part, not in settlements but in houses scattered along the coast for a distance of more than 350 kilometres. To reach all the families two or three times a year was a difficult undertaking because there were no roads on this portion of the coast. In the summer months the missionaries travelled on the government schooner or used their own sailing vessels to visit people at their fishing posts. Throughout the winter months they travelled by komatik and snowshoes, visiting the various winter settlements, individuals, and families who lived in one of the many bays, harbours, coves, and rivers. Therefore it was not unusual for a missionary to travel several thousand kilometres a year. The Reverend Richard Wainwright, the Anglican missionary stationed at St Augustine River, reported that in 1864 alone, he travelled 4,800 kilometres.[26] The missionaries continued to attend to their parishioners in this manner well into the twentieth century.

The missionaries from the Roman Catholic Church, the Church of England, and the CFMS also attended to the educational needs of the inhabitants. This task often proved to be quite difficult. One of their biggest problems was how to provide instruction to a populace that was literally scattered throughout the region from Kegashka to Blanc-Sablon. Each denomination grappled with the educational issue in its own way, with varying results.

During the formative years, the Roman Catholic missionaries provided schooling at the mission station only. For instance, when a mission headquarters was established at Lourdes-de-Blanc-Sablon during the early 1880s the missionary stationed there provided the children in the surrounding area with some formal schooling.[27] Following the establishment of another permanent mission in La Tabatière in 1893, a school was established in that community (1894), and a third was built at La Romaine (1897).[28] The Roman Catholic Church also managed to send several students from the region, from Lourdes-de-Blanc-Sablon in particular, to further their studies at a school in Havre-Saint-Pierre.

The church relied on grants from the Quebec government to fund its educational endeavours. The mission priest, who was also the teacher, held classes several months a year at the mission headquarters and wherever schools were available. The curriculum consisted of the four Rs: reading, writing, arithmetic, and religion. According to Huard, the Catholic Church's educational endeavours along the coast were hindered by the dispersal of their adherents, inadequate government funding, and its inability to find teachers willing to move to the coast. He commented, "Who would volunteer themselves to go live in a country which accommodates to people that are born there but comes across as being very ungrateful to people from outside?"[29]

The Church of England, like the Roman Catholic Church, in the early years provided schooling at the mission headquarters only. When the Reverend John Cooksley established the mission headquarters on Old Fort Island in April 1863, he opened a school there a month later.[30] After the mission headquarters was moved to St Augustine River and later on to Mutton Bay, schools were established at each place. In 1881 the Church of England also opened schools at Harrington Harbour and Cape Whittle. Three years later the Anglican missionaries established schools at Stick Point, Bradore Bay, and St Paul's River.[31] By 1895 there was a school at La Tabatière as well.

The Anglican minister and several itinerant teachers travelled along the coast and held classes for a few months of the year at the different schools, where they taught the four Rs. According to Huard, the Church of England was more successful with its educational pursuits than the Roman Catholic Church because of money made available to it from both Bible societies and the Quebec government.[32]

The CFMS, spearheaded by Charles Carpenter, took a more unorthodox approach to education. Carpenter's primary objective was to establish a boarding school in the area. However, because of adverse circumstances in his first year, he was forced to conduct classes at St Paul's River in a small crude cabin, which had previously been used as a "dry house" by a local fisherman. In the spring of 1861, Carpenter recruited Jane Brodie, a graduate of the Canada Normal School for teachers in Montreal. With her help, he held classes at the recently constructed mission on Caribou Island. The children were boarded at the mission house for three shillings a week. Carpenter reported in 1861, "They are given up eventually to our care; our aim is to keep them busy always in play, work, or study and habits of industry or usefulness."[33]

In the fall of that year the CFMS missionaries were forced to abandon the boarding school on Caribou Island because the people in the region could not afford to pay for the service. As a result, Jane Brodie began conducting classes in a deserted hut in St Paul's River. This building was later expanded and served as the schoolhouse for the mission. Once entrenched in the community the missionaries began holding classes at Old Fort Bay and Bradore Bay as well.[34] These missionaries carried on their educational activities at St. Paul's River, Old Fort Bay, and Bradore Bay until the mission was closed in 1880. As at other church schools, the children were taught the four Rs.

Parents and children alike seemed happy to have access to some form of education. Richard Wainwright, the Church of England minister at St Augustine River, in his report of 2 October 1865, had this to say about some of the parents on the coast: "They are very anxious about the education of their children. I have now 19 at school and expecting several more during the winter." Some of his students travelled forty to fifty miles to attend school; others came upwards of eighty miles.[35] Jane Brodie, the teacher at St Paul's River, reported that the school was opened on 4 November 1861, and she had no difficulty in getting children to come to school: "Nine o'clock is my hour for opening school, but they often come at 8. I thought at first, it might be the novelty of the thing that they made them come; but I am glad to find they show the same interest still."[36] According to Huard, in the winter of 1894–95 there were five students who took French literature and also elementary courses in the school at La Tabatière. He commented, "In the little posts near by there were a dozen honorary students of this institution; but when they had to walk so many miles to study their letters it is not surprising that they were happy to cultivate the language that they spoke."[37]

The missionaries did not limit their activities to the propagation of the gospel and the dissemination of education. On many occasions they were called upon to minister to the sick. For instance, the people of St Augustine River entrusted Wainwright, who had no medical training, with a stock of medical supplies. He observed, "The people at St. Augustine have subscribed to purchase a chest of medicine which they have put in my care and which I accepted only stipulating that in no case could I let it interfere with prior duties. When travelling I carry a small chest with me in case of it being required and it is not an unusual case for persons 40 or 50 miles to come for advise or medicine for their friends or family."[38]

The missionaries were not always able to cure their patients. In December 1868, Wainwright was called away from Christmas celebrations at St Augustine River to attend to a sick parishioner at Belles Amours. In his diary he states, "I was unable to be present at the party myself being called upon in my double duty character of clergy man and physician to see a parishioner 90 miles East who had been ill since October last." The minister and several others started for Belles Amours by komatik on 4 January. After two days of treacherous travel and several harrowing experiences, Wainwright arrived at his destination. In his diary for 6 January, he writes that "without further mishap of consequence we arrived without stopping at Belles Amour at 6 pm and found Mr. Buckle very weak and in great pain. I gave him an anodyne mixture and for the first time for 2 months he slept quietly for four hours. Shortly thereafter Mr. Buckle died."[39] The missionaries continued to provide medical services throughout the region until the arrival of Dr Wilfred Grenfell in the late nineteenth century.

Wilfred Grenfell, the famed British missionary and physician who first arrived on the Labrador in 1892, began making regular trips there from Newfoundland in his schooner throughout the summer months shortly after. He quickly realized that his periodic trips were insufficient and that what the area required was a hospital.

Two years after his arrival on the coast he approached the minister of marine and fisheries in Ottawa for a grant of $5,000 to erect a hospital in the area to minister to the needs of the local inhabitants and the "floating population." His request was referred to Commander William Wakeham, long-time fishery magistrate for the Quebec-Labrador coast between Kegashka and Blanc-Sablon and the Gulf of St Lawrence. Wakeham rejected the proposal outright. He wrote, "I cannot advise you to entertain the prayer of these petitions. Leading the open air and primitive lives that they do there is little sickness among them, now and then of course an epidemic of measles or La Grippe, or something of this kind does extend along the coast, and although these diseases strike at people of this kind more severely than they do the rest of us, yet the death rate is not high, and a hospital along the coast would not in any case be of much use."[40] As a result, the Canadian government refused to provide Dr Grenfell with funding for the establishment of a hospital on the coast.

REGULAR SCHOONER AND MAIL SERVICE

Wilfred Grenfell was not the only person to make regular visits to the coast throughout the summer months. Another individual who travelled to the region on a consistent basis was Captain Narcisse Blais, an experienced navigator and trader from Berthier, Quebec. According to author Louis Garnier, Blais had arrived on the coast in the summer of 1848 on a trading schooner that was headed for Blanc-Sablon. En route the schooner stopped over at La Tabatière where Blais was hired by Samuel Robertson to work in the seal fishery.[41] A year or two later, while preparing seal fat for transportation to the foundry, Blais enthralled by an incoming schooner, supposedly informed Robertson that if he had the money, he would buy such a vessel. Robertson purportedly declared, "I believe you would," and he proceeded to give Blais the money required to invest in a schooner.[42] Shortly after Blais purchased his first schooner and became involved in the trade along the coast from Kegashka to Blanc-Sablon. In 1858 he acquired a second schooner and christened her the *Marie Louise*. Later he acquired a third schooner.

He also used these schooners to provide the people along the coast with regular marine transportation. Dr Lavoie, in his annual report for 1873, wrote, " Two schooners belonging to Captain Narcisse Blais, of Berthier, makes three regular trips between Quebec and Blanc-Sablon, stopping at all the settlements to the great conveyance of everyone."[43] According to Huard, it "was an easy and inexpensive line of communication, with passengers paying ordinarily forty cents a day to ride on the vessel."[44] Blais continued to ply his vessels and provide this type of service until the late nineteenth century, at which time he turned over his business to his son Joseph Blais. Joseph established a store at Mutton Bay and carried on the trade along the coast until 1921, when he lost his last schooner at Bradore Bay.[45]

There was, however, still no regular winter mail service to the region. As a result, the residents along the Quebec-Labrador coast between Kegashka and Blanc-Sablon could go six or seven months during the winter without receiving mail. In 1875 the people residing in the St Paul's River area drew up a petition and forwarded it to the Canadian government requesting that they be provided with winter mail service. Dr Lavoie, the stipendiary magistrate, also urged the government to provide the people with such a service. According to Lavoie, winter mail service would enable the settlers to contact the government when they were in need of assistance. "Whenever necessary, relief might be sent them towards the end of March, as it is about then that their wants are most pressing, their hardships greater and sickness most prevalent. No measure could be more considerate, and no one can form an idea of the hardships, which thereby be spared to a population separated from the rest of the world."[46] The appeal for the establishment of winter mail service went unheeded, however.

In 1876 another petition requesting winter mail service was sent to the Canadian government. This one was signed by all the inhabitants from Kegashka to Blanc-Sablon and merchants and other influential persons in Montreal and Quebec City with a vested interest in the area.[47] It had the desired effect. A year later the Canadian government established a post office at Bonne-Espérance and implemented both winter and summer mail service to the region. Over the next three decades the government also established post offices at Lourdes-de-Blanc-Sablon, St Augustine River, Mutton Bay, Tête-à-la-Baleine, Harrington Harbour, and La Romaine.[48] In each community the local resident who had been contracted by the government to serve as the postmaster provided the service from a room in the house in which he or she lived.

The winter mail would leave Quebec City on 1 February by horse-drawn sleigh and was transported to Bersimis, a small village about 225 kilometres to the east. At Bersimis it was loaded onto a komatik and carried to Havre-Saint-Pierre. Another courier travelled from Bonne-Espérance to Havre-Saint-Pierre, gathering up mail en route from various communities along the coast. The courier from Bersimis returned to that place with the return mail, while the one from Bonne-Espérance, who had disposed of the up mail on its way to Quebec City, returned with the down mail. En route the courier would stop at places such as Mingan, Kegashka, Tête-à-a-Baleine and St Augustine River. The mail usually arrived at Bonne-Espérance at the end of March or the beginning of April. A special carrier was sent from there to Blanc-Sablon.[49] Initially, the mail was delivered only once during the winter. In later years, however, this service was increased to three or four deliveries.

If the weather was clear and cold and the ice firm, the mailman travelled on the frozen bays and rivers. When it was mild and the ice conditions were unstable, he travelled overland, through the valleys and over the hills. The first individual to deliver the winter mail was Jos Hébert, a resident of Mutton Bay, who carried it from 1877 until his death in 1919. According to Louis Garnier nothing could frighten this energetic man. If forced to sleep under the open sky, he would set up camp in a wooded area that provided protection from the wind. The komatik was upturned to keep the mailbags from the snow, and the dogs would lie down in a circle with Jos Hébert and the mail in the middle. If he did not always enjoy a profound slumber, he at least got enough rest to resume his journey at the first sign of dawn.[50] This type of winter mail service remained in effect until the 1940s.

The summer mail, on the other hand, would leave Quebec City, on a vessel contracted by the government, in late May or early June. The mail boat would stop at Sept-Îles, Havre-Saint-Pierre, and Natashquan, where the mail was picked up by a carrier who had been hired by the government to deliver the mail from Kegashka to Blanc-Sablon. The first mailman to transport the summer mail along the coast from Kegashka to Blanc-Sablon was a Captain

Joncas, who considered it a great inconvenience.[51] Initially, the mail was delivered once during the summer months. Eventually the service was increased to three mail runs.[52] This type of summer mail service remained in effect until the early decades of the twentieth century. Summer mail also came from the United States via Newfoundland on a mail steamer that made biweekly trips from St John's to Bonne-Espérance.

THE FISHING INDUSTRY

As it promised, the government of the Province of Canada turned its attention to the lawlessness that prevailed throughout the region in the mid-nineteenth century during the fishing season. Following a commission of inquiry in 1849, meetings were held between the Province of Canada, New Brunswick, Nova Scotia, Prince Edward Island, and Newfoundland. It was agreed by all parties that the system for protecting the fisheries was inadequate. Sailing vessels could not protect the fisheries from encroachment, unless they were three or four in number. The representatives declared, "Were the British Colonies united, or each colony equally interested in the fisheries, and would all come forward to protect the fisheries, it would be of great consequence."[53]

In 1851 an arrangement was made between the Province of Canada and New Brunswick for the protection of the fisheries. At that time Canada also made it clear that it was determined to cooperate with Nova Scotia in the effective protection of the fisheries. Canada stated that it was its intention to provide a steamer or two or more sailing vessels to cruise in the Gulf of St Lawrence and eastward along the Quebec-Labrador coast as far as Blanc-Sablon.

The following year a committee of the Nova Scotia Assembly proposed that four fast sailing ships be used to seize all foreign fishing vessels within five kilometres of the coast. In response to that recommendation, New Brunswick agreed to provide two schooners, and Prince Edward Island and the Province of Canada one schooner each. Great Britain also made it clear that it was willing to make available a small fleet of steamers. It was recommended "that the rights of the Province in reference to the fisheries should be strictly and rigidly enforced and that no participation in them should be conceded to any foreign power; but that the Colonial fishermen should be invested with the exclusive rights in the waters adjacent and belonging to the Province."[54]

Dr Pierre Fortin, a native of Verchères, was appointed stipendiary magistrate on 20 April 1852, at a salary of $600 annually, and placed in charge of the Canadian contingent of the newly created Fishery Protection Service.[55] As stipendiary magistrate, he was given judiciary powers that allowed him to rule on all fishing law infractions and issue orders in situations involving violations of the criminal code. The same summer Fortin was given command of the *Alliance*, an armed schooner chartered by the Canadian government from a Mr Joncas, and sent to patrol the waters of the Gulf of St Lawrence and eastward along the Quebec-Labrador coast to Blanc-Sablon. A few years later *Le Canadienne*, an armed schooner built for the Canadian government, replaced the charted vessel. *Le Canadienne* remained in service until the first decades of the twentieth century.

The measures undertaken by the government of the Province of Canada had the desired effect. Within a short time, law and order prevailed during the fishing season throughout the Gulf of St Lawrence and along the coast to Blanc-Sablon. Fortin, in his annual report for 1862, wrote, "With few exceptions public order and peace have not been troubled on the North and South shore, and there was no renewal of the fights and quarrels which often occurred between our fishermen and strangers, and where the right of possession in seal and salmon fisheries used to give rise to many difficulties, especially between neighbours, to trespass and often to encroachment committed by the strongest to the prejudice of the weakest."[56]

In the summer of 1852, Fortin met with many of the local inhabitants and discussed their immediate concerns. They informed him that they had no titles to their property, and they requested that he intercede on their behalf to get the government to grant them titles, securing them the possession of their posts with the necessary precincts. Upon returning to Quebec City in the fall that year, Fortin met with officials from the government and discussed the concerns of the fishermen. He proposed that two experienced fishermen, aided by a Captain Talbot, visit each post to determine its size. Furthermore, fishing licences should be sold to the occupants at rates proportional to the usual produce of each fishery. According to Fortin, the inhabitants, when assured of permanent possession of their posts, would exert themselves to extend and improve their fishing tackle as much as possible, and their produce in seals and fish would be considerably increased. He estimated that the fisheries, which currently yielded no more than a hundred pounds, if furnished with tackle, would yield two to three hundred pounds. Fortin's recommendations were heeded, and over the next few years, precincts were drawn up and fishing licences allotted.[57]

The measures introduced by Fortin proved to be of little consequence as far as the sedentary seal and salmon fisheries went. By the time the government had decided to address the local fishermen's concerns, the wanton destruction by local and foreign fishermen had already taken its toll upon these forms of fishing. Fortin reported in 1865, "Many of those who held and worked them had suffered serious losses, and in some cases, had been ruined in consequence of the trespassers in question."[58] For that matter, sedentary seal and salmon fishing had already become a secondary concern for many settlers.

Nevertheless, those who could still afford to carry on these types of fisheries continued to do so. The Reverend Charles Carpenter in 1858 reported that salmon and seals, each in their season, were taken in nets by the planters who had the means of procuring them, and favourable localities for spreading the necessary "craft."[59] These types of fishery continued to be pursued because in good seasons they were the most lucrative. The Robertsons of La Tabatière pursued the seal fishery as their chief occupation well into the twentieth century, while the Chevalier family at St Paul's River persisted mainly as salmon fishermen until recently.

Faced with declining seal and salmon fisheries and an erratic fur trade, most of the settlers turned their attention to the inshore cod fishery.[60] Magistrate Lavoie later commented, "It was only in 1850, or rather since that date, that cod fishing was fully developed. Before that period, the cod fishing industry was reckoned very low amongst the revenues of the coast, all the available capital and labour being engaged in other pursuits. But when everything was ruined, owing to inconsiderate fishing, and no other opening was left, people had to fall back on cod that frequented the fishing banks and indeed all the waters of the coast in a marvellous manner."[61]

For many years the inshore cod fishery was pursued mainly with hemp lines and hooks baited with fresh capelin or herring. When the codfish were not biting, the local fishermen sometimes used a jigger, a 2.5 by 10 centimetre piece of lead with two codfish hooks attached to one end and at the other a line held in the fisherman's hand. By constantly moving the jigger up and down, the fishermen succeeded in jigging from two to three quintals of fish per day.[62]

They would set out in their boats for the fishing grounds at two or three o'clock in the morning. If the wind was in their favour, they sailed; if not, they rowed for several hours. On arriving where they expected to find cod, they cast anchor and placed the oars across the boat, baited their hooks with freshly caught herring or capelin, and dropped their lead-laden lines into the water. As soon as the exact depth of water was found, the line was hauled in until the hooks were about two metres from the bottom. If the fishing was poor at the first anchorage, the fishermen would weigh anchor, and the boat was sailed or rowed to another location.

They generally remained on the fishing grounds until four or five o'clock in the afternoon. Then with their catch they hastened to shore, where the cod were pitched from the boat onto the wharf with a two-pronged pitchfork and conveyed to a large box attached to the splitting table. The "cutthroat" reached into the box, retrieved a fish, placed it on the splitting table, cut the throat from gill to gill, and made a longitudinal slit down the belly of the fish, allowing the entrails to fall out. He then passed the fish to the header, who removed the liver and dropped it into a special barrel under the table and tore off the head and tossed it, together with the entrails, over the side of the wharf. The fish was then passed on to the splitter, who ran a square knife under the backbone of the fish, cutting out the bone on the return motion, and dropped the fish into a barrel filled with seawater. The cleaned fish were transported to the stage (a small shed where the cod were stored and salted) by wheelbarrow. There the salter laid the fish belly-up on the floor. He stacked the fish layer upon layer lengthwise, sprinkling each layer with coarse salt.

In mid-August the salted cod were removed from the stage, carried to special puncheons filled with seawater, washed and scrubbed free of salt, and then spread out on flakes to dry in the sun. In the evening the partly dried fish were collected and piled into heaps and covered with sailcloth as a precaution against rain. The next morning the fish were again placed on the flakes to dry. This process was repeated for about a week, at which time the fish were nearly dry. The cod were then stored for a few days and taken out for one final drying. Afterwards they were returned to the stage to await the arrival of the fish buyer. The summer catch was shipped to various foreign countries, including Portugal and Spain. What was taken during the fall fishery, which took place during the months of August and September, was salted and packed in barrels, and shipped to the Montreal and Quebec City markets.[63]

During the latter part of the nineteenth century, the cod trap, a device invented by William H. Whiteley, owner of the post at Bonne-Espérance, supplanted the hook and line. It resembled a large room with twine walls, a floor, and a door. The perimeter of the trap ranged anywhere from 65 to 155 metres, and the walls of the trap were usually designed for 11 to 26 metres of water. The trap was anchored off a reef or island, and a leader run off the door was sloped into the trap. The sides of the door were sloped inwards to the centre at the floor level, and fish were thus discouraged from leaving the trap. When the cod trap was hauled up, the side with the door was raised first by the crew in the boat on that side of the trap, while another boat was positioned on the opposite side. Then the floor was pulled up, and the cod were forced into the back of the trap. After that the fish were bailed out of the trap into the boat and taken to the stage.

When the fish were schooling after capelin, the cod trap proved to be a very effective means of taking them. With this method, dozens and even hundreds of hundredweight of cod could be caught in a single day.[64] However, when the codfish remained offshore, the cod trap, because it was a fixed device that was difficult to move or to anchor at any distance from the mainland without risk of loss, was useless.[65]

Abuses committed by cod-trap owners, especially the foreigners, proved to be a cause of concern for many local inhabitants. On 5 February 1894 George Whiteley, the overseer for the Bonne-Espérance district, wrote to the Department of Fisheries recommending that regulations be adopted to control the use of cod traps. His proposal was accepted, and fishing regulations respecting the cod fishery in the Gulf of St Lawrence and along the Labrador coast eastward to Blanc-Sablon were implemented several months later. As a result of these regulations, all cod traps had to be licensed. There was to be a space of at least 230 metres between each trap, and only one trap per vessel. Each cod leader was to extend from the shore with specified minimum mesh sizes and a 50-cent fee for each 1.8 metres of a leader. Gill nets were prohibited within five kilometres of any island, and jiggers were also prohibited. Cod traps were not to interfere with salmon fishing. Because of the small number of cod-trap berths available, the local residents were given prior claim on the location.[66]

As in former years, most of the local fishermen traded their catch with itinerant traders from Quebec City and Halifax. Trade usually took the form of bartering, and a system of credit was introduced, which became widespread. The fishermen received their fishing gear on credit at the beginning of the season, on the understanding that they would pay for it in codfish once the season was over. The rest of the catch would be used to obtain winter provisions. The ability to pay off one's debt and procure winter supplies depended on the success of the fishery, the cod fishery in particular.

When the cod fishery was good, many itinerant traders were usually available to buy up the catch. Lavoie, for example, in his annual report for 1878, stated, that thirty schooners from Quebec City alone were continuously engaged during the whole season in trading articles required for fishermen's use and taking in exchange their fish, oil, and furs. At such times the local fishermen managed to get a much better price for their catch than others involved in the cod fishery in the Gulf of St Lawrence. "The merchants involved from Natashquan to Blanc-Sablon were more moderate in their desires. No difference is made to the quality of fish; good and indifferent alike sell. They paid this year from sixteen to seventeen shillings cash for cod, and goods were disposed of merely to cover the freight, and at a small advance on commission."[67] On such occasions the fishermen had no difficulty paying off their debts and receiving supplies for the upcoming winter.

However, when the cod fishery failed for several consecutive years, the number of trading schooners along the coast between Kegashka and Blanc-Sablon usually dropped off dramatically. At such times, the itinerant traders, having no competitors, increased the price of their goods and often refused to give supplies on credit to the local fishermen whose fishery had failed for consecutive years. According to author Winfrid Stearns, the people in such circumstances were often forced by hunger to give untrue reports of the work done, since a falling-off in the supply of fish and a little prevarication brought them provisions. "One or two years of scarcity of fish soon left the people no means of paying their old debts, and making promises which they could not perform, the traders began to refuse them credit."[68] In such circumstances the fishermen fell into perpetual debt. Itinerant traders continued to sell their wares along the Quebec-Labrador coast from Kegashka to Blanc-Sablon in this manner until the end of the First World War.

FEAST OR FAMINE

Irregularities in the inshore cod fishery were due mainly to variable climactic conditions. Commander William Wakeham, the fishery magistrate, commented, "If the spring is early and the ice gone, the bait fish, capelin and herring, crowd into every cove and bay, and are soon followed by the cod. When the spring is late, and the coves and bays are full [of ice] well into June, the bait fish, and especially the capelin, strike off shore and remain in deep water, and it is seldom, having been once driven off the coast, returns again during the same season."[69] Hence when the baitfish remained offshore, so did the cod. At such times, the local fishermen outfitted mainly with small sailing craft, were unable to venture out to sea to pursue the cod. Therefore on such occasions the inshore cod fishery usually failed. When, on the other hand, the baitfish came inshore, the cod soon followed and the fishermen usually had a good fishing season.

In the 1850s the local fishermen managed to catch enough cod and other types of fish to pay off their debts and to ensure that they were able to acquire from the itinerant traders the basic essentials, such as flour and lard, which enabled them to get through the winter months. A few managed to do well for themselves. Abbé Ferland, who visited the area in 1858, reported that a Mr Lévesque, owner of the post on Burnt Island, was doing good business and certainly merited the prosperity he had achieved.[70]

Throughout most of the 1860s, however, the cod remained off-shore, and many of the local fishermen experienced one bad cod-fishing season after another. Consequently, there was a great deal of suffering, some years more so than the others. For instance, the Reverend Charles Carpenter in his report for 1862, wrote that "the fisheries of the fall and summer before having failed, and there being an unfortunate scarcity of provisions on the coast, there was much want among the people."[71]

Eighteen sixty-six appears to have been an exceptionally difficult year. Samuel R. Butler, a CFMS missionary stationed at St Paul's River, reported that the summer cod fisheries had failed and the settlers' wants for the long winter were all unmet. "For days and weeks, the people in the vicinity were out with their boats and nets up and down the shore, watching and waiting for the coming of the wherewithal to be fed and clothed. Alas it came not. Large families have for their winter supply, 2 or 3 barrels of flour. One man, father of 8, has nothing but one barrel of flour and no way of getting more."[72] As a result, many families were forced to leave their homes on the coast. Some returned to the North or South shore; others moved to Nova Scotia or the United States.

In the fall of 1866 Butler and Richard Wainwright, the Church of England missionary stationed at St Augustine River, travelled to Quebec City to persuade the Quebec government to send a schooner freighted with provisions. Through mismanagement, the vessel did not arrive on the coast until 2 June the following year. Consequently, in the winter of 1866–67, settlers with supplies were required to share with those who had little.

In that same year the coast was ravaged by sickness. Wainwright stated that the sickness and mortality were unusually great: "My chest of medicine that was will stocked last October presents a beggarly case of empty bases and bottles." He, like others on the coast that year, lost a family member. "I am sorry to say my own family has suffered much and our almighty in his wisdom seen fit to remove one of my own."[73]

According to Richard Wainwright, the summer of 1868 saw the greatest failure of the cod fisheries ever known on the coast. He observed, "Destitution and starvation stared us in the face on every side. At Salmon Bay and its neighbourhood there were nearly 40 families totally without food and the means of procuring it or leaving the coast. Many families are now so poor that they have neither nets nor boats, all being worn out so that should there even be a good fishing season many have not the means to catch a single quintal and many families must leave the coast or starve."[74] When advised by the missionaries and Lavoie, the fishery magistrate, that they should leave and settle on the Baie des Chaleurs or in the Eastern Townships, most people refused to do so. "We have nothing now, how can we leave and settle elsewhere? We are not accustomed to farming, having always fished; how else can we earn a living?" Lavoie held out little hope for the local residents. He commented, "The future looks rather gloomy for the people on the coast. The present state of affairs has lasted for some years now, and I think will last till the inhabitants leave the coast."[75]

In the fall of 1868, J.U. Gregory was commissioned by the Quebec government, given $2,000 to buy supplies for the people in need, and told to remove anyone from the coast who wanted to leave. After placing on board the ss *Napoleon* over three hundred barrels of flour, meal, and other provisions, Gregory set out for the coast on 22 September, distributing food at various places on the way, including St Paul's River, St Augustine River, and Bradore Bay.

Just when all appeared to be lost, the cod returned inshore in the summer of 1869 in abundance, and it continued to do so for the next few years. As a result, there were several years of good cod fishing. Lavoie, in his report for 1872, stated that "the catch of the past three years has been so large that the hardships of the winter of 1865 have been entirely forgotten, and that a sense of carefulness and economy seems now to prevail. Thanks to a succession of remunerative fishing, people now experience some prosperity. Taught by former experience some of the local fishermen put aside money for harder times."[76] Lavoie optimistically commented, "Now that the supply of fish, especially cod, is almost boundless, and the prices rule high; they are generally encouraged, and I am quite sure that they will be prepared for any future emergency."

In 1874 and 1875, however, the cod remained offshore and the inshore cod fishery again failed. Despite Lavoie's optimism, there was considerable privation and suffering. Many families were forced to leave their homes. Some families returned to the South

Shore, and others to Nova Scotia or Newfoundland. Those who remained were compelled to gather and feed upon small dead fish thrown upon the shore. According to Lavoie, some of the men were so weakened by privation that they had hardly enough strength to take seals out of the meshes. In the fall of 1875 the Quebec government was compelled to provide the inhabitants with a few barrels of flour to help get them through the winter.

The following year the cod returned inshore in abundance, and they continued to do so until the end of the decade. Again the local fishermen were blessed with several years of good fishing. Lavoie reported that the fishermen scattered along the coast had very little to complain about: "their labours in the several industries carried on by them were crowded with success and that fish were more than usually plentiful and that vegetables, which are more or less cultivated in every place where sufficient land can be found to use a spade or hoe, yielded one hundred percent."[77]

From 1880 to 1886, however, the cod remained offshore, and the local fishermen experienced one bad cod-fishing season after another. As in former years, there was considerable suffering and distress throughout the region. Stearns in 1882 reported that many of the poorer families were feeding on cornmeal, which was generally refused until the last extremity, since most people regard it as hardly fit to feed the dogs with. Whole families were obliged to separate and hire themselves out to their more fortunate neighbours for the winter for their board alone, in order to escape poverty and destitution.[78] Others were forced to leave the region. Kegashka and the surrounding area were abandoned, some of the residents moving to Ontario and others to Prince Edward Island. The destitute inhabitants living at St. Augustine River were moved either to the west or to Newfoundland. Those families that remained behind on the coast were furnished with supplies by the Quebec government.

In 1887 the cod returned inshore once again; they continued to do so until the end of the nineteenth century. Many of the local fishermen took advantage of this new state of affairs. Commander William Wakeham, in a letter to William Smith, deputy minister of marine and fisheries, on 8 January 1894, reported that most of the local inhabitants were very well lodged in fairly comfortable homes, and that many of them were quite well off. "Dry codfish met with ready sale, and with the exception of the usual drones all the families are well off for the winter, in fact many have a year's supply of provisions ahead."[79]

By the end of the nineteenth century, permanent residences had been established along the Labrador coast west of the Itamamiou River to Kegashka. The inhabitants had intermittent access to religious instruction, schools, medical services, mail, and marine transportation. The local fishermen were able to pursue the cod fishery without any major inconveniences. However, fluctuations in the cod fishery caused considerable privation and suffering at times.

8

For Better or for Worse

Between 1900 and 1960 growth and consolidation characterized the Quebec-Labrador coast from Kegashka to Blanc-Sablon. The population increased threefold, outlying regions were abandoned, and medical facilities and schools were established. Telegraph, steamship, and airline services were also introduced to the area. Local fishermen were provided access to bait and storage depots and a codfish-processing plant. Some of the resident fishermen also experimented with offshore fishing. Economic uncertainty, however, continued to prevail throughout the region.

ABANDONMENT OF THE OUTLYING WINTER RESIDENCE

Throughout this period the number of people residing on the coast between Kegashka and Blanc-Sablon increased at a relatively regular rate. In 1900 there were 934 inhabitants in the region. Twenty-six years later that number had increased to 1,280. By the late 1950s there were approximately 3,100 people living in the area.[1] The population growth was the result principally of a high birth rate. Families of eight to ten children or more were not uncommon.

There was also a change in the pattern of settlement. Many of the winter places in the outlying bays, harbours, and coves were gradually abandoned, and the residents spent the winter months at places such as Bradore Plain, Belles Amours, Salmon Bay, St Paul's River, Old Fort Bay, Checatica, St Augustine River, Lac Salle, Baie de la Terre, La Tabatière, Otterbrook, Mainland, Barachoix, Harrington Harbour, Tête-à-la-Baleine, and Wolf Bay.[2] Occasionally, a winter home from one of the outlying regions would be transported to a winter settlement by dog team or trapboat (motorboat).

The transition from the more remote harbours, bays, and coves was facilitated by the increasing use after 1910 of the marine engine, which provided the local fishermen with easier access to their fishing grounds. These people were attracted to the winter settlements primarily because of the availability of various amenities, such as hospitals and clinics, stores, communication and transportation services, and churches and schools.

HOSPITALS AND CLINICS

The Canadian government's refusal in 1894 to provide money for the construction of a hospital on the Quebec-Labrador coast west of the Strait of Belle Isle did not deter Dr Wilfred Grenfell, founder of the Grenfell Mission, or the local inhabitants from pursuing their objective. The coastal residents continued to petition Grenfell about the need for a hospital, and he in turn solicited various individuals for financial assistance. His persistence eventually produced the desired results.

During the winter of 1904–5 Grenfell managed to secure $5,000 towards the construction of a small hospital from the philanthropists Mary and Jessie Dow, daughters of an eminent Montreal lawyer.[3] The following spring, he travelled to Ottawa with the intention of obtaining a maintenance grant for the hospital from the Canadian government. Grenfell met with several members of Parliament, including Prime Minister Sir Wilfrid Laurier, Robert Borden, William Lyon Mackenzie King, and Raymond Préfontaine, and he informed them of his intentions of establishing a hospital at Harrington Harbour and his interest in obtaining some form of assistance. All expressed interest in Grenfell's work. Préfontaine, the minister of marine and fisheries, for instance, informed Grenfell that he would bring the matter before Cabinet and that he would recommend a grant of $2,000 to be placed in the supplementary estimates for the current year.[4] Sir Wilfrid Laurier said that in the event of the minister of marine recommending the grant, it would have his support.

Commander William Wakeham, the fishery magistrate, when consulted by Préfontaine about financial assistance for the construction of a hospital at Harrington Harbour to be placed in the charge of Dr Grenfell, declared that there was much good to be done by cottage hospitals in isolated communities. However, he was of the impression that these types of hospitals were a matter of private charity, and he knew of no reason why any exception should be made for the Labrador.[5] Préfontaine, undoubtedly influenced by Wakeham's response, wrote to Mackenzie King, the minister of labour, on 30 May 1905 and made him aware that he was opposed to the project. King appears to have not been surprised at Préfontaine's decision. He responded, "The truth is that one or two of the officers connected with the Department of Marine and Fisheries including the Deputy Minister and Commander Wakeham are opposed to Grenfell, and anything that is done against their own wishes ... I have no doubt that the report to which Prefontaine refers was made by the Deputy Minister at the insistence of Dr. Wakeham."[6]

Six weeks later King wrote to Grenfell and informed him that the Canadian government had refused the request for a grant. King told Grenfell, "There was a very strong feeling of sympathy expressed, but it was feared that the precedent might be a dangerous one." Grenfell appears not to have been overly distraught at the news. He told King that "we must bow before the inevitable but I don't think this is any reason why we should abandon the project. I am now steaming down full tilt to Harrington and Mutton Bay to see what the people themselves are willing to do in the matter."[7] He further stated that he had already written to the Montreal Committee and suggested that it provide $2,000. In November 1905 Grenfell wrote to King and informed him that the Montreal Committee had agreed to give him the money he had requested.[8]

Meanwhile, Grenfell had convinced Dr Mather Hare, a Halifax surgeon two years his senior with seven years' experience at the Canadian Methodist Mission in West China, to go to Harrington Harbour and begin work as the resident physician. Hare remained in the area until 1916. Following his departure, over the next nine years a new doctor was sent annually to Harrington to take care of the hospital. In 1926, however, Dr Donald G. Hodd, a resident of Hamilton, Ontario, who had received his medical degree from the University of Toronto, was hired by the International Grenfell Association and sent to Harrington Harbour to take charge of the

Grenfell Hospital. Over the next forty plus years, Dr Hodd, a tireless worker and a caring and loving physician, tended to the medical needs of many of the people in the region. He was greatly admired, respected, and appreciated by all the people along the coast. Following his retirement in 1970, Dr Hodd was made a member of the Order of Canada for his work.

By December 1905 construction of the hospital at Harrington Harbour was well underway, the local people having already laid the foundation. It was completed and in operation by 1908. Charles Wendell Townsend, an American naturalist who visited the Grenfell Mission hospital in 1915, observed that "the hospital itself was neat, well arranged, and thoroughly modern in its equipment. The operating room had a good light, and contained modern tables, sterilizers, and so forth. The wards were bright and cheerful, and each bed was marked with the name of the generous supporter."[9] Supporters from Montreal and Toronto supplied the hospital with its own launch, the *Northern Messenger*, while the *Montreal Weekly Witness*, a Montreal-based newspaper, donated dog teams and komatiks.

The doctor stationed at Harrington Harbour usually made three trips a year along the coast from Natashquan to Blanc-Sablon, once in the winter and twice during the summer. In the winter months the physician travelled by komatik, stopping over at each winter settlement and many of the houses in between, tending to various ailments, and dispensing medicines. During the summer the doctor travelled along the coast in the Grenfell Mission launch.

In 1926 Grenfell also opened a clinic at Mutton Bay. One of the first nurses stationed there was Agnes Murray, who was affectionately known throughout the region as Sister Murray.[10] The nurse stationed in Mutton Bay, like the physician at Harrington Harbour, usually made three trips annually along the coast, once in the winter and twice in the summer, visiting many of the local residents en route. Like the doctor, the nurse travelled by komatik in the winter and by boat in the summer, usually in a vessel owned by one of the local residents. Until 1950 the Grenfell physician and the nurse were the only medical personnel to service the region.

According to Oscar Junek, an American anthropologist who visited the area in the mid-1930s, the medical services offered by the Grenfell Mission were meagre, sporadic, and ephemeral. He writes, "First of all, the mission and its Sub stations – one at Harrington and the other at St Anthony were located a fair distance from each village. There was not adequate transportation to or from those places save by slow watercraft in the summer and a dogteam in the winter. The visits made by the travelling doctor or nurse was insufficient perforce, not only in number but in quantity."[11]

Grenfell did not limit his activities to providing medical services. He also encouraged many women to hook rugs, which were sold to travellers to the area and people living in Montreal and elsewhere. Grenfell also operated several clothing stores in the region, including ones at Harrington Harbour and Mutton Bay. Benefactors from Montreal, Quebec City, and various cities throughout New England donated the clothing. More often than not, it was given to local residents.

During the late 1940s, Lionel Scheffer, the newly appointed Catholic bishop of Labrador, attempted to address some of the concerns raised by Junek. In the summer of 1946 Bishop Scheffer travelled to Quebec City and approached Dr Paquet, the provincial minister of health, about the possibility of building a hospital at Lourdes-de-Blanc-Sablon. After considerable deliberation, the minister agreed that the Quebec government would provide funding for the hospital. Shortly after, building supplies were imported, men were hired, and the construction began in earnest.

The undertaking, however, was not without hurdles. For instance, during the construction of the hospital, the Quebec government decided to reduce its grants. As a result, Bishop Scheffer had to make several more trips to ensure that enough money was provided to complete the project. Finally, on 11 August 1950, a twenty-five-bed hospital was opened at Lourdes-de-Blanc-Sablon.[12] Bishop Scheffer persuaded the Sisters of the Holy Family, from Bordeaux, France, to come and work at the hospital. He also managed to recruit Dr Jean-Marie Bélanger of Quebec City as the resident physician. In the late 1950s Dr Camille Marcoux, a resident of Tête-à-la-Baleine and a graduate of the University of Sherbrooke, was placed in charge of the hospital at Lourdes.

A few years after the hospital was constructed at Lourdes-de-Blanc-Sablon, the Quebec government erected clinics at St Augustine River and Tête-à-la-Baleine. The new clinics were small, two-storey houses with an office and several small rooms with beds for patients on the ground floor and a nurses' apartment on the second level.[13] However, because of the low salary and the isolation, the Quebec government had a great deal of difficulty recruiting and keeping nurses at its clinics on the coast.[14] Therefore, more often than not, no nurses were stationed at the newly constructed clinics.

In the formative years, the local residents were required to pay a $5 annual subscription for medical services. Because most people in the region could not afford the subscription, it was eventually abandoned and replaced with a 25–cent visitation fee. In the ensuing years the cost of a visit to a hospital or a clinic increased from 25 to 50 cents and then to a dollar. The fee for delivering a baby was $20. Other procedures, such as appendectomies, cost $25.[15] Those who were unable to pay the fee were usually provided free medical service.

With the establishment of the hospital at Lourdes-de-Blanc-Sablon, there was a dramatic decrease in the number of patients at the Grenfell Mission hospital at Harrington Harbour. For instance, between 1950 and 1959 the population at that facility fell to less than 50 per cent of the bed capacity. Dr Hodd, the resident physician, claimed that the change in fortunes of the Harrington Hospital was due in large part to the influence of the Catholic clergy. He commented in 1960, "Notwithstanding the fact that we still admit a large number of Roman Catholic patients, we are frequently made aware of the fact that priests in Romaine, Whale-Head, Tabatière and St Augustine use their influence to send patients to Roman Catholic hospitals than to our hospital."[16]

The travel itinerary for the doctors and nurses was also rearranged. The Grenfell Mission medical staff became responsible for the people along the coast from St Augustine River westward to Kegashka. Those employed with the hospital at Lourdes-de-Blanc-Sablon served the residents east of the St Augustine River to Blanc-Sablon. The komatik and the motorboat, however, continued to be the main means of transportation for both doctors and nurses until the 1960s. As a result, immediate medical care for many residents remained an issue, especially during fall freeze-ups (November and December) and spring breakups (April to June).[17] At those times of the year, because of the poor ice conditions, travel by komatik or motorboat was all but impossible. On such occasions it was not unusual for someone in a community to contact a doctor or nurse by telegraph for medical advice.

The people who benefited most from the improved medical services were those living near the facilities. In the absence of immediate medical care, many residents along the coast continued to rely on various local remedies. Contusions and lacerations were often bathed in cold salted water and then bandaged with rags. Bread poultices consisting of bread soaked in water or milk, were applied to infected areas. The people often drank tea or homemade cod-liver oil to rid themselves of a severe cold. Midwives continued to play a crucial role, and local residents such as Uncle Jimmy Monger from Tête-à-la-Baleine, Aunt Emily Belvin from St Augustine, Aunt Carrie Fequet from Old Fort Bay, and Mrs. Sam Thomas from St Paul's River were often called upon to deliver babies.

COMMUNICATIONS AND TRANSPORTATION

According to Junek, when telegraph services first became available along the coast between Kegashka and Blanc-Sablon, the local residents viewed it with a great deal of suspicion. He writes, "When Alfred Cormier, one of the region's first telegraph operators, gave out the news of the Boer War as it was coming in, the local people refused to believe that a device such as a meagre, tenuous wire stretched over wooden poles, could possibly be responsible. Later they attributed its magic to the devil, and fulminated heatedly against it, but gradually, however, they became used to it."[18]

The Canadian government introduced telegraph service to the Quebec-Labrador coast east of the Natashquan River around 1900. The cable extended for 2,400 kilometres, from Quebec City to Forteau, 40 kilometres east of the Quebec-Labrador boundary, on short poles along the coast, often in rocky terrain. It was established so that shipping reports could be made by land line to Quebec City.[19]

In many places along the line, there was no separate office, and a room in a local house was rented for the telegraph equipment. Usually one person in each community was trained by the Canadian government to operate the equipment and to test the line daily. Messages were relayed 160 kilometres at a time. The telegraph served not only the families that lived in the area through which the wires passed but also families that lived several kilometres from the stations. But more importantly, it provided the people along the coast with year-round communication with the outside word.

In the mid-1930s the Canadian government supplemented its

telegraph service with a telephone service. Alphonse Blais, a Bradore Bay merchant, in June 1935 petitioned H.A. Stewart, the minister of public works in the federal government, and asked if it would be possible to have a telephone line installed from Bradore Bay to Lourdes-de-Blanc-Sablon.[20] Stewart agreed to set up a long-distance Bridge Bell Telephone Apparatus 1317 G telephone in both the Lourdes-de Blanc-Sablon and Bradore Bay telegraph offices. These magneto sets were connected through a condenser to the telegraph line and were used at night only, when the telegraph operators were not available.[21] Similar types of telephones were later installed in most of the telegraph offices along the Labrador coast between Kegashka and Blanc-Sablon.

The Telephone Company of the Gulf of St Lawrence Limited, a Rimouski-based firm, in the mid-1940s acquired the telegraph and telephone service rights along the coast from the Canadian government. Shortly after, there was a dramatic decline in the quality of service. For instance, the telegraph offices at St Paul's River and Checatica Bay were opened for only a few minutes at eight in the morning and eight in the evening.[22] Eventually the Quebec Telephone Company, a Quebec City–based operation, purchased the telegraph and telephone services from the Telephone Company of the Gulf of St Lawrence Limited, but the service continued to be abysmal.[23]

The decrease in service was alleviated to some extent by the arrival of the radio telephone. Roman Catholic missionaries in the late 1940s purchased radiotelephones from army surplus and installed these devices in various communities throughout the region. The radio signal was transmitted on a semi-private commercial band, and at a set hour every day, the missionaries contacted each other, exchanging pastoral consultations, local news, and information about emergencies.[24]

The Catholic clergy at Lourdes-de-Blanc-Sablon in January 1955 also began a newspaper, the *Coaster*. It was published on a monthly basis with both an English and a French edition and was made available free of charge to local residents. The paper covered various regional issues such as fisheries, employment, education, transportation, and communication.

In addition to the changes in communication, there were a number of transportation initiatives at this time. Some of these were brought to fruition by the governments of Canada and

Quebec. Others were undertaken by private enterprise. In 1901 the Parliament of Canada voted a subsidy to provide regular steamship service to that portion of the Quebec-Labrador coast from Kegashka to Blanc-Sablon. Shortly after, steamships were sent to the area but never on a regular basis. Frustrated with the irregular service, several Roman Catholic missionaries met with Pierre Casgrain, the region's member of the Quebec Legislative Assembly, in 1920 and discussed the possibility of providing a bimonthly steamer service from Quebec City to Blanc-Sablon. Plans were also made to obtain smaller vessels to distribute mail along the coast.

As well, the missionaries discussed the matter with Mr Girard, the federal member of Parliament for the region, who in turn raised the issue with Sir George Foster, the federal minister of commerce. Foster met with Desmond Clarke, an entrepreneur from Clarke City, Quebec, and persuaded him to form a maritime company that would provide transportation service from Quebec City along the North Shore to Blanc-Sablon.[25] In 1921 the Canadian government awarded the Clarke Steamship Company a contract to provide steamer service on a subsidized basis from Quebec City to Blanc-Sablon every two weeks during the navigation season, between 20 June and 15 November, to transport freight, mail, and passengers. In the ensuing years the schedule was revamped, and the steamer made the trip between April and December. The government also contracted local boat owners, such as Sammy Robertson from La Tabatière and Uncle Norman Bobbitt from Harrington Harbour, to supplement the mail service provided by the Clarke Steamship Company. The first Clarke steamship to travel to the area was the *Labrador* under Captain Brie; it was followed by the *Sable 1* under Captain Antoine Fournier and the *Gaspesia* under Captain Garon. The ss *North Voyageur* of 600-tons freight capacity eventually replaced the *Gaspesia*.[26]

The ports of call included Kegashka, La Romaine, Harrington Harbour, Tête-à-la-Baleine, Mutton Bay, La Tabatière, St Augustine River, Bonne-Espérance, St Paul's River, Bradore Bay, and Lourdes-de-Blanc-Sablon.[27] The steamship stopped at these ports on the way down only. Hence an individual wanting to travel up the coast had to board the steamer on the way down, and the travel time was increased considerably. For example, a person commuting from Kegashka to Quebec City had to get on the vessel at Kegashka and travel to Lourdes-de-Blanc-Sablon and from there on to Quebec

City, adding an extra 400 kilometres and thus extending his or her trip by four or five days. The passenger also had to pay the additional expenses incurred by this extended voyage.[28]

Despite the fact that the steamer only travelled to the region once every two weeks, the mail was delivered on a weekly basis along the coast between Kegashka and Blanc-Sablon. During its biweekly voyage, it would deliver the mail at every port of call throughout the region. On an alternate week a Clarke steamer would drop off mail at Natashquan. The local mailman would travel to Natashquan by boat, pick up the mail, and deliver it to all the settlements from Kegashka eastward to Blanc-Sablon.[29] This type of mail service was maintained until the early 1960s.

Most of the ports lacked adequate docking facilities such as wharves and storage sheds. Therefore the steamship usually anchored offshore, and passengers, freight, and mail were offloaded in slings onto local vessels anchored nearby.[30] Accidents were not uncommon, and on many occasions cargo was dumped into the sea. In the early 1950s, however, the Canadian government built much-needed wharves and storage sheds in many of the communities, including Harrington Harbour, Bradore Bay, St Augustine River, Blanc-Sablon, St Paul's River, and Tête-à-la-Baleine.[31] These new facilities helped to ease many of the difficulties encountered by the Clarke Steamship Company and the local residents during the summer navigation season.

Transportation was further facilitated with the introduction of the airplane to the coast. In 1938 Quebec Airways, a Baie Comeau–based airline, later supplanted by Northern Wings Limited, extended winter airline services to Harrington Harbour and then to some of the larger villages, including Lourdes-de-Blanc-Sablon and St Augustine River. Mail and passengers were carried weekly, weather permitting, between December and April, by a Norseman, a single-engine plane equipped with skis. Throughout most of the winter the plane would land on a frozen lake, river, or bay near a village. During the fall freeze-up and the spring breakup, however, the ice conditions were not suitable for landing, and at such times the pilot was required to parachute the mail bags at a designated spot in the community. The pilot would circle the village once to ensure that the drop zone was clear of onlookers, and he then dropped the mail and it was collected by the postmaster and taken to the postal station.[32] Air transportation was further improved with the construction of a landing strip at Lourdes-de-Blanc-Sablon in the early 1950s. With the introduction of the airplane, the winter komatik mail service was gradually phased out.

Furthermore, the Quebec government, encouraged by the Roman Catholic clergy, provided funding for road construction at various places on the Quebec-Labrador coast from Kegashka to Blanc-Sablon. A five-kilometre road was built linking Blanc-Sablon to Lourdes-de-Blanc-Sablon and an eight-kilometre road linking the latter community to a harbour where a new wharf had been established. Roads were also built in various villages, including Harrington Harbour, Tête-à-la-Baleine, La Tabatière, St Augustine River, and St Paul's River. Some of the roads were comprised of crushed rock or hard-packed sand. Others, such the one at Harrington Harbour, consisted of a combination of wooden bridges and stones.[33]

CHURCHES AND SCHOOLS

About this time the Roman Catholic Church also gradually expanded its endeavours along the coast between Kegashka and Blanc-Sablon. To a great extent it did so to accommodate the increasing numbers of Catholic adherents in the region. In the summer of 1903, the Catholic missions in the region were placed under the care of French-speaking Eudist missionaries from France. Initially, a Eudist missionary was stationed at Lourdes-de-Blanc-Sablon only and given the responsibility of tending to the needs of Catholic residents between Kegashka and Blanc-Sablon. In 1932 a second Eudist missionary was stationed at Red Bay, a village five kilometres west of La Tabatière. As a result, the missionary at Lourdes was made responsible for the inhabitants from Blanc-Sablon to the St Augustine archipelago, and the one at Red Bay attended to the people west of the St Augustine archipelago to Kegashka.[34] This missionary order, however, was recalled to France in the summer of 1945.

Following the departure of the Eudist missionaries, the Church on 13 July 1945 created the Apostolic Vicariate of Labrador, which encompassed most of the Labrador Peninsula, including that portion extending from Kegashka to Blanc-Sablon Bay. The following year the vicariate was conferred to Bishop Lionel Scheffer, who established his headquarters at Lourdes-de-Blanc-Sablon. In

1957 the headquarters was transferred from Lourdes-de-Blanc-Sablon to Shefferville and then to Labrador City, in the province of Newfoundland and Labrador.

One of the first things that Bishop Scheffer did was to bring back missionaries from the Oblates of Mary Immaculate (OMI) order. He also established the parishes of Notre-Dame-de-Lourdes, Saint-Augustin, Sainte-Anne-de-Tête-à-la-Baleine, Marie-Reine-des-Indiens, and Sacré-Coeur de La Romaine. Each parish was assigned one missionary and at least one Oblate brother. Furthermore, the OMI established new churches and a sawmill in each of the newly created parishes.[35]

The Catholic missionaries were also required, as in former years, to serve other Catholic adherents in the region. As a result, they carried out their religious duties in a manner similar to their predecessors, visiting their parishioners in the summer by boat and in the winter by komatik. The OMI order continues to minister to the spiritual needs of the Catholic community along the coast.

The Church of England, not to be outdone by its Catholic counterpart, also upgraded its services throughout the region. For the first decades of the twentieth century, Anglican clergy continued to minister to their parishioners between Kegashka and Blanc-Sablon in the same manner as they had done in the second half of the previous century. A missionary stationed at Mutton Bay was made responsible for the territory from Mutton Bay westward to Kegashka, and another missionary at St Paul's River was given the region east of Mutton Bay to Blanc-Sablon. By the third or fourth decade of the twentieth century, however, because of an increase in the number of Anglican adherents, a third missionary was appointed to Harrington Harbour.

The Church of England also built new churches in the larger communities, including Old Fort Bay and St Augustine River. The Anglican missionaries were required, as in former years, to serve other Anglican adherents in the region. Thus they carried out their religious duties in a similar manner to their predecessors, visiting their parishioners by komatik in winter and by boat in summer. The Church of England continues to minister to the needs of its adherents on the coast.

Unlike the Church of England and the Roman Catholic Church, the Presbyterian Church (and after 1925 the United Church) decreased its missionary activity in the region. Places such as Bonne-

Espérance, Salmon Bay, and Rocky Bay were eventually abandoned. One probable cause for the decline in services was a lack of adherents. However, a permanent missionary was stationed at Harrington Harbour, and that locality and Mutton Bay became the focus of the Presbyterian Church.

As in earlier times, both the Roman Catholic Church and the Church of England also continued to take care of the educational needs of the inhabitants. Neither denomination appears to have made a great deal of headway during the first decades of the twentieth century. Both, however, managed to erect a few more schools in the region at that time. The Catholic Church, for example, established a school at St Paul's River, and the Anglican Church erected schools at Old Fort Bay and St Augustine River. And as in earlier times the schools were open for a few months of the year in the more populated regions and usually managed by an itinerant teacher, lay reader, or clergyman. Carl Mayhew, a teacher from McGill University who taught school on Old Fort Island in the summer of 1927, recalled some fifty years later, "Many in the outlying districts had no chance at any schooling. They were scattered for hundreds of miles along the coast just a few families together."[36]

From the 1930s onwards, however, there was a marked improvement in the availability of education throughout the region. This was the result mainly of an increase in funding provided by the Quebec Department of Public Instruction. Both the Church of England and the Roman Catholic Church, aided by the increased funding, throughout the 1930s and 1940s built primary schools in the many winter communities along the Quebec-Labrador coast between Kegashka and Blanc-Sablon.[37] As a result, many people throughout the region were able to pursue their studies up to grade six or seven.

The primary schools were very small, comprised of one or two classrooms only. None had electricity, indoor plumbing, sinks, sources of drinking water, or playgrounds, and they were usually heated with wood stoves. Every family who had a child attending school had to supply one cord of wood each term. If more firewood was needed, it was provided by the fathers of the larger families. The students or one of the men from the village usually lit the stove. Women from the village were responsible for keeping the school clean.[38] The schools were inspected several times a year by the school inspector, usually the Catholic or Anglican missionary. School trustees and teacher-parent committees were created to inform parents of what was expected of them and their children.

Both the Church of England and the Roman Catholic Church attempted to get qualified teachers from outside the region to teach at the newly erected schools. Their solicitations, for the most part, proved to be in vain. Most of the individuals they approached refused outright to come to the area, and those who came only remained for a brief period. One of the reasons that qualified teachers declined to come to the area was the low salaries. In 1948, for example, some teachers in the region were receiving $25 per month for their services.[39] Another reason was the isolation. As a result, local residents were usually hired to provide instruction at the primary schools. Most of these people were not certified teachers, and it was not unusual to have someone teaching with only two or three more years of schooling than his or her pupils.[40] Consequently, the quality of education was usually very poor.

In the 1950s, however, both denominations took further measures to improve education throughout the region. The Church of England built a one-room high school at Harrington Harbour, where courses were provided for students along the coast who were interested in pursuing their studies through to the eighth and ninth grades.[41] Furthermore, a rooming house was erected to board the students from other villages in the region. Anglican students from several villages, such as Mutton Bay and St Augustine River, took advantage of the opportunity and attended the high school at Harrington Harbour. The Quebec government paid $200 for the lodging of every child who left his or her village to pursue high school studies at Harrington,[42] but the parents were required to pay the student's travel expenses.

The Catholic Church, on the other hand, erected multiple-classroom schools in several of the more populated communities. For instance, a five-classroom school was established at Tête-à-la-Baleine, and a six-classroom school in St Augustine River.[43] These schools also provide the students with access to grades eight and nine. As well, the Catholic Church established a trade school at Tête-à-la-Baleine. Further the Catholic Church continued to encourage students to purse their studies beyond what was available on the coast. Every year several students from various villages, including Lourdes-de-Blanc-Sablon, St Paul's River, and Tête-à-la-

Baleine, would leave the coast to attend school at places such as Mont-Joli, Rimouski, Havre-Saint-Pierre, and Montreal.[44]

The Catholic Church also recruited nuns who had been trained as teachers to take responsibility for some of its schools. In 1953 the Sisters of Hope from Bordeaux, France, took charge of the school at Lourdes-de-Blanc-Sablon, and several years later they opened a school at La Romaine. On 3 May 1955 the Sisters of the Holy Rosary, a Rimouski-based order, arrived in St Augustine River to manage that school, and over the next few years they also agreed to take care of the schools at Tête-à-la-Baleine and La Tabatière.[45] According to Dr Hodd, Catholic communities benefited considerably from the nuns' presence. He reported in 1965, "In nearly all of the Roman Catholic villages of this area we have schools that are managed by groups of nuns who are doing an excellent job of training the Roman Catholic children ... This progress is in marked contrast to what has been happening in the [Anglican] schools where there has been a lowering in the qualifications of the teachers who have been engaged to teach the children."[46] Both the Church of England and the Roman Catholic Church continued to minister to the educational needs of the residents on the coast until the mid-1960s.

The schools, however, were perceived as a nuisance by many local residents. Parents often refused to send their children to school in the spring and fall because it interfered with their ability to move to and from their summer places. Even when the children did attend school, there was a high absentee rate throughout the year.[47] As a result, many children did not attend school beyond grade four or five, and a seventh-grade graduate was considered very well educated.[48] Most parents believed that a formal education was unnecessary. After all, their parents and grandparents, who had had little or no schooling, had managed to make a living from the fishery, the cod fishery in particular.

WHEN COD WAS KING

Throughout this period, the cod fishery continued to be the chief source of employment for the residents of the Quebec-Labrador coast between Kegashka and Blanc-Sablon, and the cod trap remained the principal means of procuring the cod. Seal and salmon fishing and the fur trade, as in former times, were pursued as secondary activities.[49] There were, nonetheless, modifications in the cod-fishing industry.

Commander William Wakeham, fishery magistrate for the region, in his annual report for 1912, noted that coastal fishermen had begun installing marine engines in their fishing vessels. He commented that "the introduction of motor power means a great advance; the fishermen will build larger and better boats, and they will go further out to sea."[50] The introduction of the marine engine resulted in the appearance of the trapboat (motorboat).

The first trapboats were fitted with a mast and sail, usually a sloop rig, and a gasoline engine. An adjustable centreboard fitted into the keel made them better under sail and adaptable when motor-driven. Later the masts, sails, and centreboard were abandoned, and the trapboats were "lap seamed" or clinker-built with a square counter or transom. These boats were usually seven to eight metres in length and two to three metres wide and were powered by single-stroke and double-stroke, make-and-break Acadia or Atlantic gasoline engines, which could achieve speeds of six to twelve kilometres per hour.[51] The new trapboats were very seaworthy and manoeuvrable and good for fishing with the cod trap. They also facilitated the movement of the local fishermen and reduced the time spent travelling on the sea, but the vessels did not allow them to venture out to sea to new fishing grounds.

Ten years after the make-and-break made its appearance on the coast, the Quebec government entered into an administrative agreement with the Canadian government which provided for the sharing of jurisdiction over the inshore fishery throughout the Gulf of St Lawrence region and along the coast between Kegashka and Blanc-Sablon. Shortly after, the Quebec government introduced a number of measures to help the inshore fishermen. For instance, it began providing the local fishermen with free salt, a commodity essential for the curing and drying of cod. In the 1930s the Quebec government also built cold storage sheds and bait depots at Kegashka, La Romaine, Harrington Harbour, Mutton Bay, La Tabatière, St Augustine River, Old Fort Bay, St Paul's River, Bradore Bay, and Lourdes-de-Blanc-Sablon. As well, a refrigeration plant was installed at St Paul's River.[52] The cold-storage sheds and the refrigeration plant allowed the local fishermen to refrigerate their freshly caught salmon and other fish until they were able to sell it locally. The bait depots, which were used to store fish bait, provided the local fishermen with bait for their hooks when it was not readily available from the sea.

Furthermore, the Labrador Fish Company, an enterprise owned by the Clarke Steamship Company, during the late 1920s installed a salmon-processing plant and an agent on Bonne-Espérance Island and soon became one of the principal buyers of local salmon, paying for it in cash or cheques.[53] The establishment at Bonne-Espérance remained in service until the 1960s.

About the time that the Quebec government became involved in the development of the inshore fishery, there was a dramatic decrease in the number of itinerant traders travelling to the area to do business. One of the few traders who continued to visit the coast after the First World War was Louis-Télesphore Blais, the son of Joseph Blais and grandson of Captain Narcisse Blais. L.T. Blais inherited the business from his father sometime in 1921.[54] Shortly after, he established stores or local agents at various places along the coast, including Mutton Bay, St Augustine River, Checatica, and St Paul's River.[55]

Throughout the better part of the 1920s and the 1930s Blais carried on his trade from Quebec City on board one of the vessels owned by the Clarke Steamship Company. He would travel along the coast and take orders from his representatives, who had received requests for food, supplies and fishing gear from the local fishermen. Blais would then have the Clarke Steamship Company deliver the merchandise to his establishments and representatives, who would make them available to the local fishermen. He would hire a vessel to collect the salt cod, seal pelts, and seal oil from the local fishermen in return for the food, supplies, and fishing gear. Blais also provided supplies to many of the local merchants who had established small stores at various places throughout the region including Kegashka, Mutton Bay, La Tabatière, St Augustine River, Old Fort Bay, and Lourdes-de-Blanc-Sablon.[56]

In the late 1930s, however, Blais moved to La Tabatière, created St Lawrence Seaway Products Limited, and established a fish-processing plant at La Tabatière for the refining of cod, herring, seal, and dogfish oils and the transformation of seal, dogfish, and spring herring into meal. He built his plant there because La Tabatière was the best area for seals. The plant provided permanent employment for five or six men and part-time work for thirty others.[57] Whole seals were now purchased from the local inhabitants and transported to his plant, where they were processed. St Lawrence Seaway Products Limited carried on this type of activity until the mid-1950s and the salt cod trade until the early 1970s.

L.T. Blais was not the only one to take an interest in the salt cod trade along the coast. In 1929 the Hudson's Bay Company purchased from Job Brothers, a Newfoundland-based fishing company, all of its fishing properties in the Blanc-Sablon Bay area and established a large store halfway between Blanc-Sablon and Lourdes-de-Blanc-Sablon.[58] For a time, the establishment at Blanc-Sablon was involved with the cod fishery, and the HBC hired crews from the Blanc-Sablon Bay area and Newfoundland to carry on the cod fishery. This type of activity was maintained until the end of the Second World War.[59]

More important, the Hudson's Bay Company establishment encouraged local fishermen along the coast from Middle Bay, Bradore Bay, Lourdes-de-Blanc-Sablon, and Blanc-Sablon to trade their salt cod catch at the company's depot at Blanc-Sablon. Once the cod-fishing season was over, the local fishermen from the various localities would load their trapboats with the season's catch and travel to Blanc-Sablon in groups, weather permitting and sell their dried fish to the HBC. Upon their arrival at the depot, each man took his turn unloading his salt cod. Usually the fishermen helped one another to speed up the weighing and storing, because all the dried cod had to be weighed, graded, and stored before the sunset.[60] In return for their salt cod, the fishermen received food, supplies, salt, and fishing gear. The HBC carried on the salt cod trade until the early 1960s.

Both Blais and the HBC conducted this trade in a similar manner to that of the itinerant traders in earlier times. The local fishermen received their fishing gear on credit at the beginning of the season, on the understanding that they would pay for it in fish once the season was over. The rest of the catch would be used to obtain winter provisions, but more often than not, a portion of these supplies were also obtained on credit. Money rarely, if ever, was exchanged between buyer and seller. Given that Blais and the HBC were the principal salt cod buyers, for a number of years they profited considerably from the goods they received in trade, at figures dictated by themselves, and the merchandise they provided in trade, upon which they placed their own value.[61] The fishermen, being almost entirely powerless, and with no way of controlling their commercial affairs, were forced to submit to such terms. As a result, fishermen, unlike in former years, were often kept in perpetual debt to the two buyers. St Lawrence Seaway Products Limited and the HBC were able to perpetuate this situation until the late 1950s.[62]

At that time, fish buyers from Newfoundland, including S.W. Mifflin, began making trips to the coast and buying up the local fishermen's salt cod. The Newfoundland fish buyers, unlike Blais and the HBC, provided the local fishermen with cash or cheques for their salt cod. The increase in competition led to a rise in prices for salt cod purchased from the fishermen along the coast between Kegashka and Blanc-Sablon. It was not uncommon for the fishermen to play off one buyer against the other, ensuring that they got the best possible price for their dried cod. The Newfoundland fish buyers continued to buy salt cod from the local fishermen until the early 1970s.

Meanwhile, Clive Planta, manager of the Fisheries Council of Canada, who had been to the region in the summer of 1949, wrote to Dr A. Labrie, deputy minister of fisheries for the province of Quebec, and the Honourable R.W. Mayhew, minister of fisheries in Ottawa, and described the predicament of the local fishermen. He informed them that both levels of government had neglected the region and that research and aids in new types of gear and equipment should be considered. Planta proposed that efforts should be made to determine whether deep-sea boats could operate from the fishing ports of the area to offshore waters and return with large catches of cod that would employ people in the region in splitting, salting, and drying.[63]

Shortly after, René Savoie, an employee with the Quebec Department of Game and Fisheries, was sent to the region to examine the state of the fisheries. He informed the Quebec government that no fish-processing plant was buying fresh fish (cod) every day and that the fishing gear used was the cod trap and the handline, the latter used infrequently. He wrote, "The fishermen are not rigged to follow the fish so, as soon as it moves away, at the beginning of August the fishing season is over."[64] As a result, many of the local fishermen were making little or no money from the cod fishery and were doing very poorly. He reported that under the current conditions the fishermen could not lead a proper life if they were not helped in some way.

Savoie informed the Quebec government that there were several things that could be done to help improve the coastal fishermen's lot. One of the options, if the Quebec government wanted to keep the existing fishing methods, was to lower the cost of fishing gear either by giving fishing bounties or by some other kind of direct aid. Another was to provide the fishermen with some form of financial assistance so that they could invest in properly rigged vessels, which would enable them to follow the codfish. He reported, "The fishermen do not have the means to involve themselves in such an undertaking and that they would need help of some kind to build and rig a fishing boat and buy gear."[65] The latter solution would have a twofold effect: it would lengthen the fishing season and it would lower the cost of fishing by producing higher yields.

Both the Quebec and Canadian governments heeded Planta's and Savoie's advice. The Quebec government established a research station at La Tabatière to examine the behaviour of the cod along the coast. Through its agency, the Maritime Credit Service, it also agreed to pay 4 per cent interest on loans that were granted to fishermen for the purchase of fishing boats and gear. The maximum loan for the acquisition of a boat varied according to the size of the vessel. For the purchase of machines, equipment, rigging, and tackle, each loan could not exceed $1,500. Boat loans were refundable within four years in payments of one-quarter of the loan a year. Loans provided for other purposes were repayable in two equal payments.[66] The Canadian government, agreed to provide a subsidy of $250,000 a ton for the construction of wooden boats longer than 12 metres and to pay 50 per cent of the approved cost for steel boats. Grants were also made available for the construction or transformation of fish factories.[67]

One of the first people to take advantage of the government subsidies was L.T. Blais, owner of St Lawrence Seaway Products Limited, who was well aware of the abundance of cod offshore. In 1954, with grants from the Canadian government, he converted his seal-oil factory into a fresh cod-processing factory. With the help of federal government grants, Blais also invested in two small wooden trawlers which were later replaced with three deep-sea iron trawlers, with a combined capacity of 700,000 pounds. The large trawlers would strike out to sea and fish for a week or so and then return to the factory with large quantities of fish. One trawler was used to collect fresh cod and dried salt cod from the local fishermen along the coast. The fishermen refused to work the trawlers, and as a result, Blais was required to man them with Newfoundlanders. Most of the factory workers, however, were local residents, women in particular. The operation proved to be a boon for St Lawrence Seaway Products Limited, and thus the company managed to maintain a monopoly on the fresh cod market along the coast until the early 1980s.

Blais was not the only person to make use of the Quebec government subsidy program. During the later 1950s, ten or so fishermen from Tête-à-la-Baleine took advantage of the government's offer to pay 4 per cent interest on loans. With interest-free money that they borrowed from the Caisse Populaire, they purchased eight government-built Gaspésiennes. These fifteen-metre-long vessels, with their double-mast sails and powerful diesel motors, were fitted with sonar, which enabled the fishermen to spot schools of codfish in the deep waters. The boat also came with lines 4,000 metres long and 6,000 hooks. This type of vessel allowed the fishermen to engage in offshore fishing, fish for longer periods, travel long distances and follow the cod along the coast, and cope with heavy fall winds that were too strong for the smaller trapboats.[68]

The owners of the Gaspésiennes did quite well for themselves, and it was not unusual for them to return from a fishing venture with 1,140 kilograms of freshly caught cod. Given that Blais was the only fresh-cod buyer in the region, the fishermen from Tête-à-la-Baleine had no choice but to sell him their catch. According to Pierre Perrault, the factory owner took advantage of his situation. He writes, "When the catch is good the Gaspesiennes line up at Tabatière wharf, where they are unloaded after the plant's trawlers and draggers; a Gaspesienne could loose its entire catch because of the plant's inability to process so much fish. Ironically, when a catch is good, the price goes down; when the catch is meagre, the price goes up."[69]

Within a few years, however, the owners of the Gaspésiennes abandoned this type of fishery. One of the reasons was because they did not have the technical expertise to properly operate the vessels. Another was the poor quality of the boats. Blais' unfair treatment of the fishermen undoubtedly also played a role in their decision to abandon this type of fishery. The majority of the local fishermen along the coast did not participate in the government initiatives, primarily because they did not have the capital and the knowledge required to purchase, operate, and service such vessels and equipment.

PRIVATION AND PROSPERITY

Despite the innovations in the cod-fishing industry, periods of prosperity were followed by spells of privation and want along the Quebec-Labrador coast between Kegashka and Blanc-Sablon. These ups and downs were due in part to fluctuations in the inshore cod fishery brought about by the varying climactic conditions, in part to oscillations in the price of cod on the international markets, and in part to the fact that Blais and the Hudson's Bay Company monopolized the industry on the coast. Therefore, when the demand for cod was high on the international fish markets and cod catches were good, the people benefited considerably from the cod fishery. When the prices were low and the cod catch was poor for several consecutive years, they suffered greatly.

Prior to the outbreak of the First World War, the cod remained offshore, and one bad cod-fishing season followed another. Commander William Wakeham, fishery magistrate for the region, in his annual report for 1907 commented, "For several years past, the summer cod fishing has been below average – so that many of the people have been getting behind. It is perfectly certain that sooner or later we will have serious distress on this coast." He informed W.A. Found, superintendent of fisheries for the Department of Marine and Fisheries in Ottawa, that all possible efforts should be made to induce the young people to leave the coast and settle where they could obtain profitable and steady employment. Wakeham observed, "I can see no hope for the people if they remain here. The fishery is certain to fail them and there is nothing else to turn to."[70] Some of the people heeded Wakeham's call to leave the coast. In a letter to the minister of marine on 29 September 1910, Wakeham reported that a number of young men had left the coast to seek winter employment at Sydney, Halifax, Clarke City, and Anticosti Island.[71]

In the spring of 1911, because of the repeated failures of the fisheries and the abysmal living conditions of many of the local inhabitants, Dr Grenfell travelled to Ottawa and met with Superintendent Found. They discussed the possibility of sending several hundred families along the coast between Kegashka and Blanc-Sablon to the West Coast. Grenfell pointed out that in recent years there had been failure after failure and now many people were in a serious condition. He was informed that it was quite possible there might be immediate openings for the fishermen on the West Coast if reasonable arrangements could be made.[72]

Immediately after, the superintendent of fisheries wrote to E.H. Cunningham, chief inspector of fisheries in New Westminster, British Columbia, and had him contact various companies, whom he believed might be interested in obtaining the services of fishermen from the area between Kegashka and Blanc-Sablon. On 28 June 1911 Cunningham informed the superintendent of fisheries that he had approached several West Coast fishing companies about Grenfell's plan and that the idea was greeted with little or no enthusiasm.[73]

H.A. Stevens, an employee with the Department of Fisheries in Ottawa, undeterred by Cunningham's findings, contacted the Vancouver Board of Trade and made it aware of Grenfell's proposal. He informed the board that the fishermen were "men of the highest type morally and physically and come from Devonshire stock chiefly, are strictly temperate and will make good citizens."[74] A little while later the Vancouver Board of Trade contacted the minister of marine and fisheries in Ottawa and informed him that it had endorsed Grenfell's proposal. When residents along the Labrador coast between Kegashka and Blanc-Sablon were approached about moving to the West Coast, however, they refused to go. Charles Wendel Townsend observed, "It has even been urged that the people be all transported to more favourable regions. The fact is, there is poverty everywhere especially among the ignorant, but after all there is no place like home, and a love of one's native land is possessed by all."[75]

The outbreak of the First World War brought considerable relief for many of the local fishermen. Dried cod, which had been selling for about $6 per quintal in 1914, rose approximately by $1 per quintal each year of the war and was approaching $10 at the time of the Armistice in 1918.[76] Cod catches along the coast from Kegashka to Blanc-Sablon increased accordingly. The consecutive years of good cod fishing appear to have been enjoyed by all. Commander William Wakeham reported in 1920 that "a spirit of emulation and interest has prevailed among the fishermen, as a consequence of the high prices offered for fish, which have been realised

... They show more attention and more activity in their work. At the same time, they manifest a disposition to abandon certain old methods, and to follow more modern processes, which they try to adapt to the conditions in which they find themselves."[77]

Following the war, however, there was a dramatic decrease in the demand and price for dried salted cod on the international market. The price fell to $4.80 a quintal in 1920 and to $4.50 two years later, and it continued at that level throughout most of the 1920s.[78] The number of cod taken by the local fishermen also declined considerably. This turn of events proved to be quite devastating. Commander Wakeham, in his annual report for 1922, noted, "The fishing industry that had regained a little activity during the period extending from 1914 to 1919 has fallen again into a lamentable condition. Many fishermen have all but given up on the cod fishery. Practising their trade as a last resort until they can find less trying and more lucrative occupations are moving in a body to some other fields of activity."[79] This trend continued throughout the better part of the 1920s.

As a result, many of the people who remained along the coast from Kegashka to Blanc-Sablon had to be assisted continually by both the Canadian and Quebec governments. For instance, in the fall of 1923, the inhabitants of Old Fort Bay and the surrounding area wrote to the federal Department of Fisheries requesting immediate assistance. "Owing to ice coming up the first part of the summer and the failure of fish in our harbour after the ice went away, it leaves us in a critical condition for food for the winter, as we had to live through the summer from hand to mouth ... Some of us are moving into our winter quarters with a barrel of flour and some with only half a barrel. Starvation is looking us in the face. We ask you in God's Holy Name to help us and send us food for the winter."[80] Shortly after, the Canadian government provided a number of families in need at Old Fort Bay, St Paul's River, Bradore Bay, and Lourdes-de-Blanc-Sablon with assistance.

Several Roman Catholic missionaries in 1925 met with J.E. Perrault, the Quebec minister of fisheries, and his superintendent, F.M. Gibaut, and discussed the fishermen's difficulties. They were able to persuade the minister and the superintendent to provide a grant of $12,000 to help buy food, fishing equipment, and vessels. Accordingly, every needy fisherman was granted between $50 and $100. In exchange for the scrips, the people were required to do a variety of tasks, including repairing telegraph lines and cutting logs.

The following year a meeting was held between the Catholic missionaries, Wilfred Clarke, owner of the Clarke Steamship Company, and several others, and the fishery issue was discussed again. By mutual consent, a telegram was sent to Perrault, requesting him to come and see for himself the gravity of the situation on the coast. A boat was immediately put at the minister's disposal, and he travelled all along the coast and listened to the local fishermen. Perrault concluded that since inshore fishing was a thing of the past, the Quebec government should help in the building of more spacious and safer vessels. After lengthy negotiations, a grant for this purpose was fixed at $100 per boat. But the money was at best a temporary measure.[81]

In 1929 the stock market crashed. As a result, virtually all countries retreated from competition in international trade, tariffs were introduced, and cod prices dropped off considerably. The price for dried salt cod, which was selling for about $6 per quintal in 1930, fell to $2 in 1931 and 1932, and it continued at that level throughout most of the 1930s.[82] At the same time cod catches along the coast between Kegashka and Blanc-Sablon continued to fluctuate, with good fishing seasons followed by poor ones. The fluctuating cod returns, combined with the decline in cod prices, proved devastating for the local fishermen. Many of them, having little or no fish to trade, were at times unable to obtain credit from their suppliers. On such occasions they could not make the necessary repairs and replacement of equipment to enable them to continue in the cod-fishing industry. As a result, hunger and privation became commonplace. Some people, in their attempt to obtain essentials, had to go from house to house begging for flour and other necessities. Others were forced to abandon the area and move wherever employment was available.

Both the Canadian and Quebec governments once again were called upon to provide local inhabitants with some form of relief. The Quebec government gave out sums of $10 to $35 annually to people in need of assistance,[83] while the minister of fisheries in Ottawa arranged to have grants of $40 or less given to those in real need. John Wilcott, a resident of La Tabatière, who had been appointed to distribute money to the local fishermen, in a letter to MLA Pierre Casgrain on 12 November 1938, wrote, "It is very difficult to say just how many needy fishermen or how much each would need to get them fairly equipped for fishing anyway, there are about 700 fishermen and about five hundred boats, the big

majority are all in need to some extent, some of course are in worse
circumstances than others and some have no boats at all and very
little fishing gear of any kind."[84] As in earlier years, the people were
required to do a variety of tasks, including repairing telegraph lines
and cutting logs, in exchange for the relif payments.

In 1939 the codfish once again returned inshore, and it continued
to do so for the next five or six years. As a result, the local fishermen had several consecutive years of good fishing. Furthermore,
the outbreak of the Second World War led to an increase in the
demand for dried salt cod, which in turn resulted in high prices on
the local and international markets. The fishermen along the coast
made substantial earnings, for all the codfish they could produce.
Their situation was further improved by the availability of family
allowances, old age pensions, and government jobs, such as sur-
veyors, game wardens, and bird and fish inspectors. Therefore
many of the people were able to clear off their debts with local merchants, improve their houses, buy new furniture, build better boats,
and equip themselves with new engines and fishing gear.[85] They
also managed to enlarge their customary diet of bread, potatoes,
cabbage, salt beef, pork, tea, sugar, and molasses with jams, break-
fast foods, and canned vegetables, fruit, and meat.[86]

B.J. Banfill, a Grenfell Mission nurse stationed at Mutton Bay, in
1942 reported that some of the local residents between Kegashka
and Blanc-Sablon were able to afford a few pleasures. One of the
luxuries enjoyed by the women and young girls during the war
years was the annual visit of a beauty specialist, who travelled from
one place to another by fishing vessel providing the women and
young girls with a permanent.

Men, women and children flock to this amateur beauty parlour and stand or
sit about. At first, too loyal to tradition to openly show any interest, the older
fishermen seek some excuse to stroll in, sit or stand and stare at the customer
being transformed, while they mutter comments, under their breath, about this
young generation and frivolities. The middle-aged women stare with longing
eyes, while the young folk giggle and laugh, as they nudge each other and with
eager, bright eyes watch the suffering victims, while they wait their turn. Some
wistfully gaze wishing they could raise a few dollars in a short time.[87]

Banfill also noted that many of the young men from the region
were called up for the army, navy, or air force. Young recruits from

various parts of the coast, including Blanc-Sablon, St Paul's River, Old Fort Bay, and Alymer Sound reported to Quebec City for basic training and were then sent overseas, where they distinguished themselves on the battlefields of Italy, Belgium, Holland, Germany, and France.[88] Most of these young men returned to their respective homes on the coast after the war and turned their attention to the fishery.

Following the war, the demand for dried salt cod remained high, but the codfish, which had been so abundant inshore during the war years, all but disappeared, and within a few years, conditions throughout the region degenerated to the pre–Second World War level. Clive Planta, in a report to the Fisheries Prices Board on 26 August 1949, stated that many of the local fishermen had already fallen several years behind in their payment to the local merchants. Furthermore, the merchants were unable to extend the credit required to sustain the fishermen on the assumption that the cod would return to the inshore fishery the following year. Planta commented, "The most efficient, industrious and thrifty to the lowliest fisherman on the coast are equally affected. Neither cash nor credit will be available to purchase supplies to tide them over the long winter until late May when transportation opens out next year."[89]

He informed the Fisheries Prices Board that something had to be done immediately to ensure that the people had enough supplies to get them through the upcoming winter. The board recommended that a solution to the problem be sought in conjunction with the appropriate departments of the Canadian and Quebec governments. Both governments acted upon the recommendation. A meeting was held in Montreal, on 30 September 1949 to discuss the situation. The Quebec government issued relief cheques totalling $80,000 to enable the needy to buy their requirements of the goods already ordered by the merchants. The federal government donated $35,000 in butter, cheese, powdered milk, and honey.[90] The Clarke Steamship Company delivered the supplies to the region at cost. As in former years, the people were required to do various types work in exchange for the relief.

Throughout most of the 1950s, the inshore fishery along the Quebec-Labrador coast between Kegashka and Blanc-Sablon continued to fluctuate. Furthermore, international restrictions on the free flow of salt fish lead to a decrease in prices for the grade of codfish caught along the coast. As a result, it was not unusual for fishermen to sell their salt cod for one and a half cents a pound.[91] Within a few years, many of the people fell behind in their payments to the local merchants, who in turn refused to provide the people with credit and supplies. The Quebec government once again was required to provide many of the local fishermen with some form of social assistance.

Faced with unpredictable returns and low prices from the cod fishery, many young men in the area during the 1950s began to abandon the cod-fishing industry in the summer months, seeking employment elsewhere. Dr Hodd reports that it was not uncommon for each village to loose from twelve to twenty men during peak fishing season. Initially, some of these men went to Havre-Saint-Pierre to work in the recently opened titanium mines. Following layoffs there in 1953, they travelled to Sept-Îles, Knob Lake, Port-Cartier, and Baie-Comeau, where mining and other industrial developments were in progress.[92] Many of the men found employment as labourers with the Iron Ore Company of Canada, earning a wage that was well beyond what someone could make fishing for cod. As a result, in the ensuing years many young men continued to leave the cod-fishing industry during the peak fishing season, preferring to work elsewhere as migratory seasonal workers.

By the middle of the twentieth century, the people along the Quebec-Labrador coast between Kegashka and Blanc-Sablon had regular access to medical facilities, telegraph service, steamship and air transportation, schools, and churches. Several advances had also been made in the fishing industry, including the construction of a fresh cod-filleting plant. Economic uncertainty, however, still persisted, and poverty was common.

9

Local and Government Initiatives

From the 1960s onwards there were significant political, social, and economic changes along the Quebec-Labrador coast between Kegashka and Blanc-Sablon. The local residents began to take a greater interest in the development of the region, and educational and health facilities, transport and communication services, and fishing methods were modernized. For the first time ever, many of the residents in the region experienced some form of continued economic prosperity.

POPULATION TRENDS

Throughout the 1960s and 1970s the number of people living along the coast continued to increase, but at a much slower pace than in earlier times. In 1968, 4,505 people lived in the region. Ten years later the number of people in the area had increased only to 5,888.[1] This lower growth was due mainly to the fact that families were now having no more than four to six children. From the 1980s onwards, population gradually declined, and by 1995 only 5,150 people were living along the coast.[2] One of the probable causes of the decrease was a drop in the birth rate. Many families were now having no more than two children. Another was the complete collapse of the cod fishery. As a result, some people abandoned the area, taking up residence wherever employment was available.

Furthermore, there was a decrease in the number of winter settlements throughout the region. Winter communities such as Belles
Amours, Salmon Bay, Checatica, Lac Salle, Kecarpoui, Baie de la
Terre, Otterbrook, Mainland, Barachoix, Wolf Bay, and Musquaro
were abandoned in the 1960s and 1970s, many of the residents
moving to one of the larger nearby villages. For example, the people
from Salmon Bay moved to St Paul's River, and those from Checatica took up residence at St Augustine River. Wolf Bay residents
settled in Harrington Harbour, whereas inhabitants from Musquaro
migrated to La Romaine. The Old Post and Red Bay hamlets were
made part of La Tabatière. A new village, Chevery, comprised
mainly of residents from Cross River, Gull Cliff Island, and Mainland, was also founded.

The people moved to the larger villages for a variety of reasons.
Some relocated because they were encouraged to do so by the clergy.
Others moved because the schools in their communities were
closed. Such was the case, for example, with the people wintering
in Checatica, Cross River, Gull Cliff Island, and Mainland. Still
others were enticed to relocate because of the availability of various
amenities, including electricity.[3]

As a result, by the late 1970s there were three French-speaking
villages (Lourdes-de-Blanc-Sablon, Tête-à-la-Baleine, and La Romaine) and twelve English-speaking villages (Blanc-Sablon, Bradore
Bay, Middle Bay, St Paul's River, Old Fort Bay, St Augustine, La
Tabatière, Mutton Bay, Aylmer Sound, Harrington Harbour,
Chevery, and Kegashka) in the region with fairly large year-round
populations.

THE LOWER NORTH SHORE ECONOMIC COUNCIL

For many years, however, there was little or no cooperation among
the villages along the coast on matters of common concern. According to Dr Donald G. Hodd, long-time physician at Harrington
Harbour, "Each village, on its own, would get a hold of their politician and attempt to get something for their individual village. There
was no unity between the villages, each one was asking at
random."[4]

One of the causes for the lack of cooperation was geography. Ten
or more kilometres of rugged coastline separated many of the villages. As a result, the people living in one community were often

unaware of what was going on in a nearby village, let alone in the other villages throughout the region. Another cause stemmed from the many petty rivalries and jealousies that existed among people from the different localities.[5] For example, the residents of La Tabatière and St Augustine River were frequently at odds with one another over various issues, as were those in St Paul's River and Old Fort Bay, and fights were not uncommon. Squabbles over religion, perpetuated throughout the years by both the Roman Catholic Church and the Church of England clergy and many of the local residents, further exacerbated the situation. For instance, in areas where both denominations were active, such as St Augustine River and St Paul's River, it was not uncommon for parents to encourage their children not to associate with children who belonged to a different religious denomination. Over the years, the petty rivalries and jealousies and the differences about religion gradually dissipated.

In recent years, however, language has become an increasing concern for the English-speaking and French-speaking residents in the region. Factors such as Bill 101 (the Charter of the French Language, 1977) and the 1980 and 1995 referendums, in particular, have done much to create tension and distrust between residents. The anglophones believe that there is a deliberate attempt by the government in Quebec, whether Liberal or Parti Québécois, to eradicate their language and force them into becoming francophones. An increase in Quebec nationalism among the French-speaking residents in the area has done little to quell the fears of the English-speaking residents. In Lourdes-de-Blanc-Sablon, for example, the French-speaking residents have fostered a local pride in being francophone, and as such, they often demand that they be addressed in French. This attitude has antagonized many English-speaking residents, who view this as the first step towards the loss of their language and culture.[6]

Nevertheless, there were those in the region who believed that there was much to be gained from a unified front. One of the people at the forefront of this movement was Father Gabriel Dionne, a graduate of the University of St Paul in Ottawa and a member of the Oblate order who arrived on the coast in 1948 and was given charge of the Sainte-Anne-de-Tête-à-la-Baleine parish, which included Tête-à-la-Baleine and the surrounding area. His travels throughout the region and his discussions with the local residents made him well aware of their many trials and tribulations, especially in the areas of transportation, communication, education, medicine, and the fishing industry. After considerable contemplation, he decided that something should be done about these issues. Father Dionne concluded that the best way to tackle the problems was through the creation of a union or an organization that represented the concerns of all of the people along the coast between Kegashka and Blanc-Sablon. In the fall of 1960 he travelled to Montreal and met with Bishop Lionel Scheffer.

As indicated earlier, Bishop Scheffer, had been appointed to the Apostolic Vicariate of Labrador in 1946, and the following year he had established his headquarters at Lourdes-de-Blanc-Sablon, where he remained for the next ten years. In this position, he had spent considerable time in the region, visiting with the local people and discussing their concerns. Like Father Dionne, Bishop Scheffer for a number of years had also been contemplating the possibility of forming a union of some kind. During the meeting, Father Dionne proposed that during the coming winter an assembly, comprising the villages from Kegashka to Blanc-Sablon, be held in St Augustine River. The assembly would serve a twofold purpose: it would bring together the principal representatives of the communities and enable them to discuss subjects of common interest such as fishing, hunting, mail, transportation, and roads; and it would allow the residents to form a common front, a kind of chamber of commerce, to obtain from the authorities improvements and developments that would benefit everyone.[7] Bishop Scheffer agreed with Father Dionne's plan.

At the end of November, Father Dionne contacted clergymen from the Roman Catholic Church and the Church of England along the coast. He informed them of his and Bishop Scheffer's intentions and asked for their cooperation in selecting representatives from each village to the proposed gathering at St Augustine River. Shortly after, he was provided with the names of forty individuals, who were invited to attend a meeting to be held at St Augustine River under Bishop Scheffer's auspices on 15–16 February 1961. Father Dionne, worried about the difficulties that could possibly arise because of denominational differences, informed the participants that no religious matters would be discussed at the upcoming meeting.[8] He was not alone in expressing his concerns about this problem. Other clergymen along the coast made a point of consulting with members of the different denominations about the matter. The Reverend J.E. Burke, a Church of England minister at St Paul's River, in a letter to Father Dionne on 27 January 1961, wrote, "In view of the coming meeting at St Augustine, I had as many as possible of the men, both Anglican and Roman Catholic, meet together to discuss what is needed at St Paul's River and adjoining areas. This was done so that our representatives, when they attend the St Augustine meeting, may give not just their own views but the views of all the families here."[9]

The delegates arrived in St Augustine River on 14 February 1961, and the following day at nine in the morning, they met in the basement of the local church. Father Dionne opened the assembly by declaring, "For the first time in the history of the Lower North Shore, we will have the opportunity to study together our problems; not the problems of one village in particular."[10] He stated, "This Assembly will be the medical doctor. Our sick patient badly needs an operation, but having been ill for so long a time, his constitution is so weak that we will have to start by the beginning and try to improve his general condition first." He concluded his address by announcing, "We hope that these contacts among people of different villages of the Lower North Shore will be the beginning of a positive Union."[11]

Over the next few days a number of issues were discussed, and all the participants agreed that there were many problems and that something had to be done especially in the areas of transportation, communication, education, medicine, and the fishing industry. Everyone concurred that a permanent organization should be formed to study the best means of promoting the social and economic progress of all the villages from Kegashka to Blanc-Sablon.[12] After considerable deliberation, it was decided that the organization would be comprised of a permanent committee, an executive committee, and a general assembly, and it would be called the Lower North Shore Economic Council (LNSEC).[13] Dr Hodd was elected president, Patrick Maurice from St Augustine River and Leon Jones of Lourdes-de-Blanc-Sablon were chosen first and second vice-presidents, and Father Dionne was made secretary-treasurer of the executive committee. One member from each village was also voted to the permanent committee. Shortly thereafter, the LNSEC set about implementing its plans for the improvement of the political, social, and economic conditions along the coast.

THE QUEST FOR MUNICIPAL GOVERNMENT

One of the first undertakings of the Lower North Shore Economic Council was the achievement of municipal government. On 11 April 1961, the executive committee of the LNSEC met at Dr Hodd's home in Harrington Harbour to determine a means of finding members from each village for the general assembly. It was decided that the best way to fulfill this obligation was by organizing a local council in each village. The decision to create village councils for each community was ratified on 19 September 1961 at Lourdes-de-Blanc-Sablon by the permanent and executive committees of the LNSEC. At that time, it was also declared that elections were to be held for positions on the village councils before Christmas, 1961.[14] In December that year each of the villages began preparing for the upcoming village council elections. Meetings were held, delegates were nominated, and ballots were casts. By the beginning of January 1962, each community had a village council and a representative on the general assembly of the LNSEC.

During the third week of January 1962 the LNSEC met at Lourdes-de-Blanc-Sablon to define the structures of the newly formed village councils and to devise a plan to obtain legal status for the councils from the Quebec Department of Municipal Affairs. The delegates on 22 January 1962 formally petitioned that "the Village Councils already established be recognized as having the rights and privileges of Municipal Councils ... a representative from the Economic Council ... be appointed and reside in the territory to maintain continual contact with the Village Councils, to assure their development, stabilization and normal functioning, and to represent the Economic Council and the Village Councils in their relations with governmental or other authority, under supervision of the Executive Committee of the Lower North Shore Economic Council."[15] Copies of the proposal were forwarded to Henri L. Coiteau, member of the Legislative Assembly of Quebec for the region, who passed it on to Pierre Laporte, minister of municipal affairs in the Quebec government.

Jean-Charles Bigonesse, a legal adviser, met with Laporte in April 1962 to discuss the LNSEC's proposal. Laporte requested that Bigonesse prepare a memorandum outlining the difficulties that the region was experiencing. Bigonesse, in his memorandum to the minister of municipal affairs, wrote that "this region is very underdeveloped; in some localities the annual family income does not exceed four hundred dollars. At this stage, however, it would be of little value to proceed with a systematic development of the economy without first preparing the people there to assume community responsibility."[16]

His assessment of the situation appears to have caught Laporte's attention. Bigonesse informed Father Dionne that the proposal was being given serious consideration. "While it is accepted in principle, it must be given further consideration. It is too much to expect that to be done during the current session."[17] Throughout the remainder of the year Bigonesse and members of the Department of Municipal Affairs met and reworked what eventually became Bill 23. Finally, in the winter of 1962 there was an agreement on what should be included in the bill.

In mid-February 1963 the LNSEC met with Bigonesse at Harrington Harbour and discussed Bill 23. He informed the attendants that the bill would unite thirty-six townships as one municipality, and simultaneously the villages on the Labrador coast from Kegashka to Blanc-Sablon would be assigned to these townships. The municipality would be governed by the municipal code, but with one major exception. Its management would be entrusted to an administrator appointed by the lieutenant-governor in council, who would act in place of the municipal council and the secretary-treasurer and would exercise the powers of the municipal council through bylaws that would have to be posted in a public place.

Bill 23 also provided for the establishment of a Municipal Board of Directors comprised of five or more members appointed or elected for a three-year period. The members of the board were to be selected from a local committee from each village. The representatives from the local committees would meet annually to read the administrator's report and to make their comments and suggestions to the minister of municipal affairs. The board's role nonetheless would be advisory.[18]

Many of the delegates were not pleased with portions of Bill 23. Some were upset over the notion that the village councils, though elected, would have only an advisory role. Others were unhappy that authority was to be placed in the hands of an administrator who was not an elected official. Most, however, were consoled by the fact that Bill 23 recognized the area as a municipality, with all its various advantages. The bill was put to a vote before the delegates, and it was accepted unanimously.

On 1 March 1963 Pierre Laporte brought Bill 23 before the Quebec Legislative Assembly. It called for a law allowing for the creation of the Municipality of the North Coast of the Gulf of St Lawrence, extending from the 57th to the 62nd parallel and encompassing an area approximately 400 kilometres long by 80 kilometres wide, from Blanc-Sablon to Vieux-Poste facing Natashquan. Laporte emphasized that Bill 23 was the first of its kind and had been requested by the local authorities, and that with certain exceptions, it would allow the municipal code to apply to this region. After considerable discussion the Legislative Assembly on 4 April 1963 passed Bill 23, and that portion of the Quebec-Labrador coast extending from Kegashka to Blanc-Sablon became a legal municipality.

Soon after, the Department of Municipal Affairs appointed Lawrence Gaston Bergeron, a former professor at the classical college in Matane, administrator of the new municipality. Initially, the administrator resided in Quebec City and made annual visits to the villages along the coast. In later years, however, the administrator's office was relocated to Chevery, and Richmond Monger, a lawyer from Tête-à-la-Baleine, succeeded Bergeron as the municipality's administrator.

Following the appointment of the administrator, local committees were formed in each village with a population of a hundred or more residents. These committees were typically comprised of three to five members, who were elected for a three-year period. One representative from each local committee was selected to sit on the Municipal Board of Directors. This board, in conjunction with the administrator, was responsible for making recommendations related to improvement of various public and private services in the municipality.

Dr Hodd, one of the chief architects of the LNSEC, had reservations about the newly created municipality and the direction in which things were headed. One of his concerns was that the Quebec government and not the people would end up taking responsibility for the development of the region. He commented,

It seems that self government is gradually coming to the people but unfortunately the trend in politics here seems to be in the direction of forming a power group that will be able to make demands on the provincial government for more financial assistance. To date there has been no organisation of a system of taxation whereby the people contribute to their own welfare. This will probably come in time but many of us who were in on the founding of this new composite municipality had hoped that this side of self-government would have received more emphasis than it has.[19]

Despite considerable protest from many of the local inhabitants, the Municipality of the North Coast of the Gulf of St Lawrence introduced a system of taxation in the mid-1970s.

In 1989 the Quebec government divided the region into three municipalities: the Municipality of the North Coast of the Gulf of St Lawrence, the Municipality of Bonne-Espérance, and the Municipality of Blanc-Sablon. The first included the villages between Kegashka and St Augustine River, the second was comprised of the communities from Old Fort Bay to Middle Bay, and the last included the villages from Bradore Bay to Blanc-Sablon. Several years later two more new municipalities were created: the Municipality of Gros Mecatina, which consisted of the villages of Mutton Bay and La Tabatière, and the Municipality of St Augustine, which included the village of St Augustine River.

TRANSPORTATION SERVICES

While working on the municipal council project, the Lower North Shore Economic Council was also involved in a quest for better transportation services for the region. In the spring of 1961 members of the LNSEC approached the owners of the Clarke Steamship Company about the possibility of it upgrading its marine services. After several meetings, the company agreed to provide regular boat runs from Sept-Îles to Blanc-Sablon with a fixed fare, which included passage, room, and meals. In the fall of the following year the company agreed to make stops en route to Quebec, instead of only on the way down.[20] A year later it declared that the *Jean Brilliant* would provide a weekly service from Rimouski to Blanc-Sablon and that the *North Pioneer* would provide twice-a-month service from Montreal to Blanc-Sablon.[21] The former vessel transported cargo and passengers, whereas the latter carried freight only.

In 1970 the Clarke Steamship Company lost its marine transportation contract to Maritime Agency Inc., a Rimouski-based company, and the *Jean Brilliant* and the *North Pioneer* were replaced with two new vessels, the *Fort Mingan* and the *Fort Lauzon*. The *Fort Mingan* carried passengers and freight and travelled to the coast once a week, and the *Fort Lauzon*, a freighter, made a ten-day cycle. Both vessels provided service from 1 April to 20 December, with the *Fort Lauzon* travelling to the coast on the 1st and 20th January as well.[22] During the late 1980s the *Nordic Express* replaced the *Fort Mingan*. Marine transportation was further improved with the initiation of a summer ferry link between Blanc-Sablon and St Barbes, Newfoundland. This service allowed residents from the region to travel to and from Newfoundland.

Members from the LNSEC also met with representatives from Northern Wings Limited in the summer of 1961 and discussed the need for better air transport. After several meetings, they were able to persuade the company to expand its air services to include every community on the coast and to transport mail and passengers twice a week year-round.[23] Air transportation was further facilitated with the construction of airports at Chevery in the mid-1960s and St Augustine River a decade later. Along with the new airports came the Twin Otter, the DC-3, and the 748; the last was capable of transporting forty-eight passengers. In the late 1970s Northern Wings Limited was replaced by Inter-Canadian, a Toronto-based company, Trans-Côte, and Regionair, which was owned and operated by local residents. Both Trans-Côte and Regionair were eventually replaced by Air Labrador, an airline operated from the Province of Newfoundland and Labrador. Small single-engine planes, such as the Beaver and the Otter, provided access to communities that were not directly tied in with the three larger airports. Air transport schedules were increased so that there was at least one flight a day to the region. With the arrival of summer air service, the summer mail boat run was phased out.

In the early 1960s, members of the LNSEC had also met with representatives from the Quebec government and demanded that the road linking Blanc-Sablon to Lourdes-de-Blanc-Sablon be extended westward to Old Fort Bay. After considerable discussion, the Quebec government agreed to provide funding for the construction of the road, and in the mid-1960s work on the highway began in earnest. By 1969 there was a road from Lourdes-de-Blanc-Sablon to Salmon Bay, and six years later it was extended to St Paul's River. Finally, after countless delays, Old Fort Bay during the late 1970s was linked directly by road to Blanc-Sablon.[24] At this time the villages of Mutton Bay and La Tabatière were linked by road as well. Along with the roads came cars, trucks, motorcycles, and all-terrain vehicles.

While pursuing funding for the extension of the highway from Lourdes-de-Blanc-Sablon to Old Fort Bay, the LNSEC carried on negotiations with the Quebec government for a winter road to link all the villages along the coast from Kegashka to Blanc-Sablon. Work on the winter highway began in the winter of 1963 and continued throughout the better part of the 1960s. A trail marked by trees with cabins at intervals, it provided people with safer and easier access to the surrounding communities in the winter months. This road was eventually linked to snowmobile trails maintained by the Quebec Department of Transportation. As a result, local inhabitants now have access to snowmobile trails throughout the province of Quebec.

Winter transportation along the coast was further facilitated with the advent of the snowmobile, a vehicle invented by Armand Bombardier. In the summer of 1959, Bombardier informed Father Dionne that the Ski-Doo, a snowmobile powered by a single-cylinder gasoline engine, would change the lifestyle of the residents living on the coast. But despite Bombardier's optimism, the Ski-Doo was not well received by coastal residents during its first few years of production. One of the reasons for the poor reception was cost. Ski-Doos were selling for $500, a huge sum considering that the annual salary of some people on the coast was only $400.[25] Another had to do with the people's attachment to their dogs. Most of the residents agreed, "The best way is still with our dogs; we can always count on them."[26] By the winter of 1964, however, many local residents had changed their attitude, and two hundred snowmobiles, mostly Ski-Doos and Snow Cruisers, had been acquired. Shortly after, many of the dog teams were destroyed.

COMMUNICATIONS

In addition to its involvement in the development of marine, air, and land transportation services, the Lower North Shore Economic Council sought to ameliorate communication links to the Quebec-Labrador coast between Kegashka and Blanc-Sablon. In the fall of 1961 the LNSEC approached the Quebec Telephone Company about the quality of telephone service it provided in the region. Initially, the company ignored the concerns raised by the council. But finally, after several years of lobbying and threats to bring in another company, the Quebec Telephone Company in February 1964 agreed to send several delegates to meet with the LNSEC to discuss the possibility of providing residents in the region with private telephone service. The company informed the LNSEC that it was its intention to install a new telephone system based on voice transmission on the Hertzian wavelength.[27] Three years later communications towers were erected at St Paul's River and Blanc-Sablon, and over the next decade telephone service was made available to all residents living along the coast. This development heralded the end of the telegraph system, which became unnecessary with instantaneous telephone communication.

Seven years after the communications towers were erected, the Canadian Broadcasting Corporation (CBC) established a repeater station at Mount St Margaret, Newfoundland, which is directly across the gulf from the Labrador coast. As a result, residents living on the coast between St Augustine River and Blanc-Sablon were provided access to CJON, an English-language CBC television station in St John's, Newfoundland. In 1978, with the implementation of microwave transmitters in the region, television reception was made available to everyone on the coast from Kegashka to Blanc-Sablon. CBMT Montreal provided English-language television programming, while CBGAT Matane provided French-language service.[28] Therefore people in the region began to spend considerable time watching various television shows such as *Hockey Night in Canada*, *The Tommy Hunter Show*, and *The Beachcombers*. During the early 1980s some people invested in satellite dishes, which provided them with access to numerous television channels. Later on, cable service was made available throughout the region.

The CBC in the late 1970s also began providing the area with FM radio broadcasts. Initially, English-language (CBC Montreal) and French-language (CBC Matane) service was made available to the villages from Kegashka to Tête-à-la-Baleine. Early in the next decade this service was extended to the other villages in the region.[29] In addition to carrying international and national news, both radio stations broadcast live reports from the different villages along the coast from Kegashka to Blanc-Sablon.

While the CBC was introducing television and radio services, some of the local people lobbied the Canadian government to establish community radio stations in the region. In the 1980s it agreed to establish such stations at Lourdes-de-Blanc-Sablon (CBFS), St Augustine River (CJAS), and Harrington Harbour (CFTH).[30] These government-funded community stations provide local, national, and international news as well as airtime for local entertainers and entertainment such as bingo.

The Canadian government also granted funding for the publication of the *Sextant,* a bilingual newspaper. This newspaper, established in 1969 and managed by the Commission Scolaire du Littoral, was made available to everyone on the coast from Kegashka to Blanc-Sablon twice a month free of charge.[31] It dealt with a range of local issues, including the fishery, transportation, and communications. In 1989, however, the *Sextant* went out of circulation because the government was no longer willing to provide the necessary funding to keep it afloat. Three years later the Coasters' Association, a non-profit organization created to promote the interest of the region and funded mainly by federal government grants, began publishing the *Coastar* a newsletter, which was eventually turned into a full-fledged newspaper. Unlike the *Sextant,* it is published six times a year, with the readers paying for the service. Much like its predecessor, it deals with a range of local issues, including the fishery, transportation, employment, education, and health.

HEALTH SERVICES

The Lower North Shore Economic Council did not limit its activities to the quest for better communications to the region. This organization also sought to improve the quality of health-care services along the Quebec-Labrador coast between Kegashka and Blanc-Sablon. In the spring of 1961 LNSEC representatives met with Northern Wings Limited and convinced the company to station a helicopter at St Augustine River, the halfway point between the two hospitals in the region, for the purpose of transporting patients during fall freeze-ups and spring breakups. Several years later the Quebec government replaced the seasonal helicopter air-ambulatory service with a year-round helicopter fleet, which was stationed at Lourdes-de-Blanc-Sablon. This service was later supplemented with Aero Commander aircraft.[32] As a result, the people along the coast were provided with daily access to and from the hospitals year-round.

In addition, the Quebec government in the 1960s built outpatient clinics in many of the villages. Nurses were recruited and given salaries that were equivalent to their city counterparts, as well as isolation bonuses. In the following decade the Quebec Department of Health designated the hospital at Lourdes-de-Blanc-Sablon the region's primary medical facility, and it purchased the Grenfell Mission hospital at Harrington Harbour and the nursing station at Mutton Bay, placing both under the supervision of the hospital at Lourdes-de-Blanc-Sablon. The hospital at Harrington Harbour was made into a community and chronic care centre.[33] In the 1980s a floor at the Lourdes-de-Blanc-Sablon hospital was designated a residence for the elderly, and a home for the elderly was also built in St Augustine River. Moreover, health-care counsellors and services were made available throughout the region.

Three doctors and one dentist were stationed at the Lourdes-de-Blanc-Sablon hospital; one of the physicians took on the role of a travelling doctor, visiting all of the other villages periodically. Patients with major medical complications were referred to the Grenfell Mission hospital at St Anthony's, Newfoundland, or the Hôtel Dieu-in Sept-Îles or elsewhere.[34]

NON-DENOMINATIONAL SCHOOLS

Not only did the Lower North Shore Economic Council concern itself with a campaign for better health-care services; it also launched an initiative for the improvement of education along the Quebec-Labrador coast from Kegashka to Blanc-Sablon. In 1961 members of the LNSEC declared that it was their intention to establish an education committee, which, with the assistance of the different Boards of Education, would examine some of the region's educational problems. Two years later Anglican teachers convened at Harrington Harbour and Catholic teachers assembled at St Augustine River to discuss the difficulties that they were having providing adequate education in the region.[35] Each group drew up a report about its needs and the many difficulties it was experiencing. The two groups gave their reports to the LNSEC, which endorsed a resolution in February 1964 stating that "an education committee of the Lower North Shore be formed, comprised of an equal number of Protestant and Catholic delegates, to deal with educational projects, with personnel, and with maintenance in the LNSEC territory, and to serve as official liaison between the Lower North Shore and the Department of Education of the Province of Quebec."[36] The reports were then sent to the Quebec Ministry of Education, which by now had taken responsibility for education throughout the province of Quebec.

Shortly after, pressure was brought to bear upon the Quebec government by the LNSEC, the municipal government, and various individuals. As a result, Bill 41 was formulated and passed by the Quebec legislature on 14 April 1967, creating the Commission Scolaire de la Côte-Nord du Golfe St Laurent. This educational body (later renamed the Commission Scolaire du Littoral) became responsible for schools along the coast from Kegashka to Blanc-Sablon. It was the first school board in the province of Quebec to minister to the needs of both Roman Catholics and Protestants.[37] The headquarters for the newly created school board was established at Sept-Îles, five hundred kilometres from its nearest constituents, and a subsidiary office was established on the coast at Chevery. Father Arthur Poisson, an OMI priest responsible for the Immaculate Conception parish at Sept-Îles, was appointed the chief administrator of the school board and Hélène Joncas, a resident of Lourdes-de-Blanc-Sablon, was hired as the director of teaching.[38]

Following the appointment of Father Poisson, the school board implemented a number of changes. One of the first things that it did was to build new schools in all the villages along the Quebec-Labrador coast. Some of the schools were quite large, with ten or more classrooms. All were equipped with running water, flush toilets, electricity, and schoolyards, and a few also had gymnasiums. Education was made available from kindergarten to Secondary I in all the schools, while others included Secondary II as well. During the late 1970s, Secondary III was introduced in nine schools along the coast between Kegashka and Blanc-Sablon.[39] From the mid-1980s onward, Secondary IV and V were implemented in some of the larger villages, including Lourdes-de-Blanc-Sablon and St Augustine River.

Children of both denominations, Anglican and Catholic, were now required to attend the same schools. Initially, some parents in the various villages, especially those with a large Anglican or Catholic community, such as St Augustine River and St Paul's

River, for a time objected to this notion. The Catholic parents were concerned about their children's exposure to Anglican doctrine, whereas the Anglican parents were worried about the effects that the Catholic doctrine would have on their children. Over time this attitude changed. Furthermore, the school board got rid of all the local teachers who were not certified to teach. Qualified teachers from urban areas in the province of Quebec and from the Maritime provinces were recruited to fill the vacant teaching positions. Eventually, this change brought to an end the role of nuns as educators on the coast.

The school board also implemented a special program for students interested in pursuing their secondary studies beyond what was available in the region. It paid all travelling costs, room and board, and school fees, demanding from the parents only a minimum contribution.[40] The students were given access to schools throughout the province of Quebec, including Alexander Galt Regional High School in Lennoxville, the Polyvalent in Gaspé, Queen Elizabeth High School in Sept-Îles, and the Polyvalents in Rimouski, Quebec City, and Mont-Joli. In September, December, January, and June, the school board chartered planes to transport students to or from their schools and their homes, according to the school terms and holidays.

Robert A. Bryan, founder of the Quebec Labrador Foundation, which is dedicated to assisting remote communities and environmental causes in eastern Canada and New England, provided funding to families that were unable to pay for incidental expenses, including clothing.[41] He also paid and arranged for students from the coast to attend various private schools, such as Bishop's College School in Lennoxville, Quebec, and Hebron Academy in Maine.

Initially, many parents expressed grave concerns about this special program. What bothered them most was the uprooting of their children, who found themselves catapulted into new surroundings far from home. But despite their reservations, many parents allowed their children to pursue their secondary studies off the coast. Throughout the 1970s it was not uncommon to see 250 to 300 students leave the coast annually to attend school elsewhere.[42] In the following decade that number decreased to approximately 200 students. By the mid-1990s there were considerably fewer students travelling away from the coast to pursue their secondary studies. The decline in the numbers was due primarily to the introduction of Secondary IV and V classes in the region. Currently, students who do not have access to higher levels of education in their villages now attend a school at a nearby village that provides such a service.

The special program in many respects proved to be unsuccessful. The failure and dropout rates for students from the Quebec-Labrador coast at the various outside schools were considerably higher than those of the rest of the student body. One of the contributing factors was the poor quality of education provided on the coast. Students from the coast, more often than not, were ill-prepared to deal with the rigours and demands of the curriculum at the schools they were attending. Another cause was a lack of involvement and support from the school board. It did a very poor job of informing the students about what life would be like away from the coast at the larger schools and in the towns and cities. Often the students arrived at their destination without any knowledge of where they were going to stay. Upon arrival, they were quickly introduced to the people that they would be boarding with and shuffled off on their own. Many students were billeted with low-income families who cared more for the money they were receiving than for the welfare of the students. The school board, having merely done its duty, made little effort to contact the students to find out how things were going until it was time for them to return home for the Christmas or summer break. Another factor was loneliness. The students, unaccustomed to the hustle and bustle of the larger centres and the rigours and rules of town or city life, often pined for the slow-paced, carefree lifestyle that they had left behind. As a result, it was not uncommon for students to leave school partway throughout the year or not to return after the Christmas break.

COMMUNITY SERVICES

The Lower North Shore Economic Council also helped to lay the groundwork for the establishment of various community services along the coast from Kegashka to Blanc-Sablon. In the summer of 1961 it lobbied the Quebec government about providing the communities in the region with electricity. Two years later, however, the government nationalized hydroelectricity and made it part of its mandate to supply that service to all Quebec residents. As a result, in 1963 diesel plants were installed at Lourdes-de-Blanc-Sablon, St Augustine River, and La Tabatière to provide these communities with electricity. A year later a diesel plant was set up at Mutton Bay. Plants were introduced in Harrington Harbour in 1967 and in La Romaine a year later. Tête-à-la-Baleine, Chevery, and Bradore Bay were provided with diesel plants in 1972, and Kegashka and Middle Bay a year later. Old Fort Bay and St Paul's River did not receive plants until 1974. Two decades later, however, the diesel plants along the coast were closed, and the residents were supplied with electrical power from the recently constructed Hydro-Québec facility at Robertson Lake, several kilometres outside La Tabatière.

Many people quickly took advantage of the availability of electricity. Wax candles and oil lamps, which had been used for many years for lighting, were replaced with electric light bulbs. Wood stoves, employed for both cooking and heating, were often supplanted with electric baseboard heaters and stoves. Cold-storage sheds gave way to deep freezers and upright refrigerators, and the scrubbing board and the wash tub were replaced by the electric washing machine.

In the mid-1960s the LNSEC also lobbied the Quebec government for waterworks systems for the different communities along the coast. The government at that time, however, was not interested in pursuing that objective. The municipal government later took up the quest, and in the 1970s the Quebec government installed waterworks systems in Lourdes-de-Blanc-Sablon, Blanc-Sablon, and La Romaine. In the following decade this service was made available to many other villages in the region.[43] With the implementation of the waterworks systems, the residents invested in flush toilets, bathtubs, and showers. Banks, especially the Caisse Populaire, became common throughout the region.

THE DEMISE OF THE COD FISHING INDUSTRY

The Lower North Shore Economic Council also attempted to bring about improvements in the cod-fishing industry along the Quebec-Labrador coast between Kegashka and Blanc-Sablon. In the early 1960s, members of the LNSEC approached representatives of the Canadian government on a number of occasions and described the plight of the local fishermen. Their solicitation did not go unheeded. The LNSEC managed to persuade the Canadian government to build salt sheds in many places along the coast. As a result, the local fishermen no longer had to worry about having salt readily available for their cod catches. After considerable urging from the LNSEC, the federal government also agreed to build a number of hauling slips throughout the region,[44] which provided the local fishermen with a safe place to store their fishing vessels during the off-season.

About this time the Quebec government made funding available to fishermen throughout the province to purchase gill nets for the pursuit of cod.[45] These are approximately 37 metres in length with a 10-centimetre mesh. Constructed principally of monofilament fibre, they could be either secured to the bottom of the sea with weights or left to drift. Cod are caught as they attempt to swim through the webbing, entangling their gills.

Many of the fishermen along the coast took advantage of the Quebec government's offer and invested in gill nets, and by the end of the 1970s the gill net had supplanted the cod trap as the predominant means of engaging in the cod fishery along the coast.[46] One of the reasons gill nets became so popular was because these nets called for a much lower investment than cod traps. Another was that gill nets were capable of catching more cod with considerably less effort. More important, gill nets, unlike the cod trap, could be set just about anywhere at any time, thereby providing the fishermen with greater access to the cod.

Following the introduction of gill net fishing, many of the local fishermen replaced their trapboats with large outboard boats. These vessels, six to seven metres long and two to three metres wide, were typically lap-seamed and powered by 40- and 50-horsepower Evinrude or Johnston outboard engines. Capable of travelling at speeds in excess of fifteen knots per hour, these boats were ideal for gill net fishing. Eventually, the fishermen abandoned the large outboard boats for smaller outboard boats and engines because they could not afford to pay for the gasoline that was required to keep such vessels in service.

The Canadian government also implemented rules with respect to the purchase of salt cod. In 1967 it took over unsold stocks of dried cod and provided deficiency payments to fishermen. Thus fishermen along the coast now received some kind of compensation for their salt cod, no matter what the circumstances. A few years later, the federal government decided to become more involved in the purchasing and marketing of salt cod. On 25 February 1970 it established the Canadian Saltfish Corporation, which was given the exclusive right to purchase and market salt fish in any province in which the provincial authority might designate it. In March the following year the Quebec government placed that part of the Labrador coast extending from Kegashka to Blanc-Sablon under the jurisdiction of the CSC.[47] As a result, neither Blais nor the fish buyers from Newfoundland were allowed to purchase salt cod from the fishermen along the coast. The local fishermen were now required to sell their salt cod to the CSC, which set the price of cod each spring before the fishery began, and the fishermen for a time benefited considerably from the arrangement.

In the ensuing years, however, the market for salt cod dwindled, and there was a greater demand for fresh cod. Both the Canadian and Quebec governments therefore began to encourage fishermen on the coast to become involved in the fresh cod industry. Aware that the small boats used by the fishermen along the coast were unsuitable for offshore fishing, the Quebec government started to encourage the fishermen to invest in a new type of fishing boat called the longliner. Various types of grants, loans, and subsidies were made available to entice the coastal fishermen to invest in these vessels.

During the late 1970s, fishermen along the coast, especially those living in Kegashka, Harrington Harbour, Mutton Bay, La Tabatière, St Paul's River, and Lourdes-de-Blanc-Sablon, took advantage of the Quebec government's offer and invested in longliners. These vessels, ranging anywhere from eight to nine metres in length and approximately three metres in width, were equipped with diesel engines, radar, fish finders, net finders, and a gurdy, which was used to haul the gill nets up from the sea. Experienced longliner fishermen were sent to the region to instruct the local fishermen on how to use the boats and the new gear. This type of equipment allowed the fishermen to fish with more gear and in other ways to compete with other forms of fishing. It also permitted them to be more selective, landing a higher quality of fish, while using less fuel for the operation. More important, however, was the fact that the longliners allowed the local fishermen to fish offshore, fish for longer periods, travel long distances, follow the migrating codfish, and cope with heavy winds and waves.

The Canadian government also erected fresh fish-processing

plants in a number of places, including Kegashka, Harrington Harbour, St Augustine River, St Paul's River, Old Fort Bay, and Blanc-Sablon. These plants served a twofold purpose: they provided the longliner owners with a market for fresh cod and created seasonal employment for many of the local residents.

The fishermen would head out to sea in their longliners at any time in any type of weather, string out their gill nets, sometimes four or five in a row, and haul them up several hours later. They would continue this process until the vessel was loaded with cod and then head home and deposit their catch at one of the Canadian government's newly constructed fish-processing plants, where the cod was cleaned and filleted. Later various local residents, financed by fish buyers from Newfoundland, also established fish-purchasing companies throughout the region. These new companies created a more competitive market, which meant better prices for fresh cod. At the same time, fishing committees were set up in many of these villages, giving the fishermen more control over the cod fishing industry.

The longliner and the fish-processing plants brought to an end Blais's monopoly over the fresh cod industry along the coast. It also brought to an end the need for fishing posts on the outer islands, bays, and coves along most parts of the coast. Many people, especially those living in St Augustine River, Old Fort Bay, and St Paul's River, continue to use their summer places as cottages.

All this changed in July 1992, when the Canadian government introduced a two-year moratorium on the northern cod fishery, which was later extended indefinitely. The cod fishery, the lifeline of inhabitants along the Labrador coast from Kegashka to Blanc-Sablon, was closed. The demise of the cod fishery was the result of a number of factors, including changes in water temperature and increased salinity, policies of the federal government, and overfishing by offshore draggers.

Faced with the closure of the cod fishery, the people along the Quebec-Labrador coast between Kegashka and Blanc-Sablon turned their attention to other forms of economic activity. Some became involved in the development of mussel and scallop farms, with varying results. For example, Dr Paul-Aimé Joncas, a resident of Lourdes-de-Blanc-Sablon established a scallop farm at Checatica, which provides employment for fifteen to twenty people seven or eight months of the year. Still others shifted to non-conventional economic activities, such as bakeapple picking and tourism. For instance, tourism outfits have been established in various villages throughout the region, including St Augustine River, La Tabatière, Old Fort Bay, and Blanc-Sablon. Some of the fishermen previously involved in the cod fishery took up shrimp and crab fishing. The crab fishery, however, was eventually also closed because of overfishing.

Many residents turned their attention to seasonal employment off the coast, an activity that coasters were often familiar with. Of particular interest has been employment as guides or cooks in fishing camps in northern Quebec and northern Ontario and as construction workers in various provinces across Canada, including Ontario, Alberta, and British Columbia. For seasonal workers, the outward migration usually begins in April or May, and it is not uncommon for a village to lose half or two-thirds of its residents. The exodus involved men and women, young and old alike. Sometimes both parents leave, and their children are placed under the care of an older sibling, aunt, uncle, or grandparents. In October and November the residents return home with savings and enough insurable weeks to get them through to the spring, when the process begins once again.

ECONOMIC PROSPERITY

From the 1960s onwards the residents along the Quebec-Labrador coast between Kegashka and Blanc-Sablon experienced continuous economic prosperity. This was the result primarily of an increase in returns from the cod fishery and financial support from the Canadian and Quebec governments in the form of work programs, welfare, and employment insurance. Economist Marcel Daneau, in a report prepared for the Quebec minister of commerce and fisheries in 1964, stated that the average income along the coast at that time was $2,407. Fifty-five per cent was from the fishery, 25 per cent from transfer payments, 10 per cent from wages and salaries, and 10 per cent from other revenues.[48] Thirty-one years later the average income for residents in the region had increased to $17,275, with government transfer payments (welfare, employment insurance benefits, and government work projects) responsible for approximately 40 per cent of the income.[49]

Throughout most of the 1960s the fishermen along the coast

experienced one good fishing season after another. At the same time there was a continuous increase in salt cod prices, from 2.5 cents per pound in 1960[50] to 8.8 cents per pound in 1969.[51] Furthermore, from 1963 through to 1969 the Canadian government allocated approximately $4.8 million for winter works programs, which involved activities such as brush cutting and construction of penetration roads, winter road beacons, and retaining walls and ditches. A labourer's wage was $1.35 an hour, and a foreman's wage $1.50 an hour.[52] These sources of income, along with the growing prosperity in the fisheries, brought a degree of prosperity hitherto unknown on the coast. The new-found wealth was used to pay for food and clothing, snowmobiles, construction or improvement of houses, and fishing establishments and accessories.[53]

During the first half of the 1970s, however, cod catches along the coast declined considerably, and landings of cod were reduced to almost half those of former years. Salt cod prices, nevertheless, continued to rise, and fishermen in 1973 received 25 cents a pound for their catch.[54] Local fishermen who experienced poor fishing returns were provided with some form of government assistance, through make-work programs, unemployment insurance, or welfare. Some of the younger men abandoned the cod fishery and sought employment elsewhere in places such as Sept-Îles, where they worked for the Iron Ore Company of Canada. Others ventured farther west to Alberta and worked in the construction industry. Still others found work as guides, cooks, or labourers in fishing camps in northern Quebec at such places as Great Whale River.

Between 1975 and 1985, however, there was an increase in the number of cod caught along the coast between Kegashka and Blanc-Sablon, and the residents involved in the cod fishery benefited from several consecutive years of good fishing. Money was invested in a number of items, including fishing gear, longliners, house repairs, and snowmobiles. Some people even began to take regular vacations away from the coast.

In the second half of the 1980s, the cod catches again dwindled, and they continued to do so until the cod fishery was finally closed in July 1992. Once again the Canadian government was called upon to assist the local fishermen. For example, in the fall of 1990 the Lower North Shore Fishermen's Association announced that the Canadian government had approved its project for financial aid to fishermen and plant workers. The main objectives of the project were to provide training and work experience to persons from the fishing sector and to qualify them for unemployment insurance. Slated to last for twelve weeks, the project employed 133 individuals.[55] Two years later a special $300,000 budget was authorized to the Regional Office of Employment and Immigration to support employment projects on the coast.[56] These types of government initiatives continued throughout most of the 1990s.

Following the closure of the cod fishery in 1992, a $1.9 billion program known as the Atlantic GoundFish Strategy (TAGS) was created to provide continuing financial assistance, job training, and licence buyouts from fishermen throughout the Atlantic region and along the Quebec-Labrador coast between Kegashka and Blanc-Sablon. Emergency assistance payments were made to active inshore fishermen, laid-off plant workers, and trawlermen who fished or processed northern cod and who had exhausted their unemployment insurance benefits or lacked sufficient weeks of work to qualify for benefits. This program was maintained until 1998.

By the end of the twentieth century, inhabitants along the coast had access to municipal governments. Advances had also been made in medical, education, transportation, and communication services. However, the cod fishery, the main employer in the region for many years, was closed, and many people are now required to rely on government subsidies and seasonal employment away from the coast.

Conclusion

The one constant for many generations of inhabitants along the Quebec portion of the Labrador coast between Kegashka and Blanc-Sablon has been the sea, with its abundance of marine life, in particular seal and cod. It was these creatures that attracted people to the area, whether they were Maritime Archaic, Dorset, Inuit, Innu, Basque fishermen, French- and English-speaking entrepreneurs, or French- and English-speaking settlers. The seal and the cod helped to shape the lifestyle, living conditions, and economic activities of the region's various cultural groups. Living conditions, however, were not always ideal. When the seal and the cod were in abundance, the inhabitants lived a life of plenty. When they were unavailable for an extended period, it was not unusual for the inhabitants to live a life of privation.

Today, because of years of overfishing and mismanagement, the cod fishery is unavailable to the people living along the coast. Large-scale seal fishing is also off-limits to local residents. Faced with economic uncertainty, many have turned their attention to other types of economic activity. Some have become involved in tourism, berry gathering, or fish farming. Others have established construction companies, sawmill companies, and fishing camps. The majority, however, have turned their attention to seasonal employment off the coast, working as guides or cooks in fishing camps in northern Quebec and northern Ontario and as construction workers in various provinces across Canada. For seasonal workers, the outward migration usually begins in April or May; workers return home in October and November with savings and insurable weeks to get them through to the spring, when the process begins again.

Both the federal and provincial governments continue to have a vested interest in the region. They provide grants to individuals and organizations such as the Coasters' Association to undertake projects that create employment for people long enough for them to gain access to employment benefits. Both governments also continue to provide funding for water, sewage, airports and road construction. There has been much discussion about extending the Trans-Canada Highway from Natashquan to Old Fort Bay. Such a link would provide the local residents with employment for several years, if not more. The road would also give them a quicker and cheaper means of transportation to and from the region. Furthermore, it would provide tourists with easier access to the region, thus potentially boosting the fledgling tourism industry.

The region has many rivers that could be used to generate hydro-electricity. The Quebec government is currently examining such a possibility. It is looking at developing a hydro dam at La Romaine. Such a project would create many short-term economic benefits, including jobs for local residents and possibly cheaper electricity. The area also has an abundance of trees that could be used to produce pulp and paper. What is required to develop such an industry is demand and financing. Companies in Newfoundland are apparently considering such a possibility. If such an enterprise came to fruition, it would lead to a considerable number of jobs for local people.

The people living along the Quebec-Labrador coast between Kegashka and Blanc-Sablon are an adaptable lot, always up to the challenge and ready to do what is necessary to ensure they are able to carry on. No matter what the circumstances, they will undoubtedly find the means to continue living on the coast.

Notes

ABBREVIATIONS USED IN THE NOTES

AD   Archives Deschâtelets
ANQ   Archives nationales du Québec
CO   Colonial Office
LAC   Library and Archives Canada
LNSEC   Lower North Shore Economic Council
PANL   Provincial Archives of Newfoundland and Labrador
SPG   Society for the Propagation of the Gospel

CHAPTER ONE

1 Great Britain, Privy Council, *In the Matter of the Boundary*, 1: 210–11.
2 Bradore Bay was also referred to as the "Baie des Espaniol" and the "Baye de Phelypeau" (Phélypeaux).
3 LAC, MG 40, 12, "St. Lawrence Survey," original directions by Captain W.H. Bayfield, 1828–55, vols. 1–2, reel A-425, pp. 219–20.
4 McKenzie, "Some Account of the King's Posts, the Labrador Coast and the Island of Anticosti," 408.
5 In former years St Paul's River was referred to as Eskimo River.
6 *Fifth Annual Report of the Canada Foreign Missionary Society*, 1862.
7 Audubon, *Audubon and His Journals*, 2: 424.
8 Packard, *The Labrador Coast*, 74–5.

9 Great Britain, Privy Council, *In the Matter of the Boundary*, 8: 3683–9.
10 Ibid.
11 Mutton Bay in former years was also referred to as Baie de Portage.
12 Great Britain, Privy Council, *In the Matter of the Boundary*, 8: 3983–9.
13 McKenzie, "Some Account of the King's Posts, the Labrador Coast and the Island of Anticosti," 408.
14 Great Britain, Privy Council, *In the Matter of the Boundary*, 8: 3683–9.
15 McKenzie, "Some Account of the King's Posts, the Labrador Coast and the Island of Anticosti," 408.
16 Biggar, *The Voyages of Jacques Cartier*, 21–2.

CHAPTER TWO

1 Fitzhugh and Sharp, *The Gateways Project 2003*, 2–15.
2 McGhee and Tuck, *An Archaic Sequence from the Strait of Belle Isle Labrador*, 2–14.
3 Fitzhugh in *Arctic Studies Center News Letter* 11 (December 2003).
4 McGhee and Tuck, *An Archaic Sequence from the Strait of Belle Isle, Labrador*, 16–70.
5 Fitzhugh and Sharp, *The Gateways Project 2003*, 2–15.
6 Ibid.
7 McGhee and Tuck, *An Archaic Sequence from the Strait of Belle Isle, Labrador*, 81–100.
8 Gosling, *Labrador*, 210–12.
9 Bayfield, *The St. Lawrence Pilot*.
10 LAC, MG 17, B1 Series E, SPG, reel A206, pp. 103–4. Rev. Edward Cusack, Gaspé Basin, 27 Oct. 1840.
11 Packard, *The Labrador Coast*, 26.
12 Bowen, "The Social Conditions of the coast of Labrador," 337.
13 Pintal and Martijn, "Early Bird Archaeologists among the Bake Apples," 222–5.

CHAPTER THREE

1 Mowat, *Westviking*, 230–1.
2 Parkman, *Pioneers of France in the New World*, 1: 11.
3 Lanctôt, *Jacques Cartier devant l'histoire*, 157.
4 The exact location of Brest has been the subject of considerable controversy. Some historians maintain that the name referred to a town established at the present day village of Old Fort Bay. Others have claimed

that Brest was located at the present-day village of Bradore. Still others argue that it was located on an island, possibly Bonne-Espérance.

5 Jacques Cartier, on his first voyage to the New World in 1534, referred to Lobster Bay as Port St Servan.

6 Biggar, *The Voyages of Jacques Cartier*, 21.

7 Ibid., 21–4.

8 Innis, *The Cod Fisheries*, 11.

9 Dawson, "Brest on the Quebec Labrador," 23.

10 Biggar, *The Voyages of Jacques Cartier*, 17.

11 Trudel, "Inuit, Amerindians and Europeans," 157–61.

12 Thurston, "The Basque Connection," 53.

13 Trudel, "Inuit, Amerindians and Europeans," 163–164

14 Quoted in Thurston, "The Basque Connection," 53.

15 Great Britain, Privy Council, *In the Matter of the Boundary*, 8: 3686.

16 Barkham, "A Note on the Strait of Belle Isle," 56.

17 Biggar, *The Voyages of Jacques Cartier*, 453.

18 Ibid.

19 Barkham, "A Note on the Strait of Belle Isle," 53–6.

CHAPTER FOUR

1 Great Britain, Privy Council, *In the Matter of the Boundary*, 7: 3143.

2 Roy, "François Bissot, sieur de la Rivière," 34.

3 Quoted in Lunn, "Economic Development in New France," 201.

4 Chambers, *The Fisheries of the Province of Quebec*, 59.

5 Great Britain, Privy Council, *In the Matter of the Boundary*, 7: 3431.

6 Ibid., 3427.

7 Lévesque, *La Seigneurie des Îles et des Îlets de Mingan*, 44–5.

8 Chambers, *The Fisheries of the Province of Quebec*, 60.

9 Lévesque, *La Seigneurie des Îles et des Îlets de Mingan*, 46.

10 Great Britain, Privy Council, *In the Matter of the Boundary*, 7: 3148.

11 Ibid., 3676.

12 Ibid., 3679–80. A league is equivalent to 4.8 kilometres.

13 Ibid., 3680.

14 ANQ, Registers for the Intendants, book 5, folio 39.

15 LAC, RG 1, series B, vol. 29, p. 981.

16 Great Britain, Privy Council, *In the Matter of the Boundary*, 7: 3686.

17 LAC, RG 1, series B, vol. 29-2 p. 303

18 LAC, RG 1, series C 11, VI, vol. 8, p. 151. The concession boundaries were

never clearly defined. Nevertheless, it seems that the Bradore Bay concession began at or near the present-day village of Blanc-Sablon and
extended westward along the Labrador coast, possibly as far as the Bay
of Belles Amours.

19 LAC, RG 1, series B, vol. 29, p. 981.

20 Great Britain, Privy Council, *In the Matter of the Boundary,* 8: 3694.

21 ANQ, Registers of the Conseil souverain, book 5, folio 25 verso.

22 Ibid., folio 50 verso.

23 Great Britain, Privy Council, *In the Matter of the Boundary,* 7: 3170.

24 Ibid., 8: 3520.

25 Ibid., 3521.

26 Ibid.

27 Ibid., 7: 3146.

28 Ibid., 3716–25.

29 ANQ, Register of Ordinances of the Intendants, 30, folio 68.

30 Lunn, "Economic Development in New France," 203.

31 LAC, MG 21, Add. MS. 35915, vol. 107, file 451.

32 LAC, MG 11, CO, 194/18, Case of the Landlords of Canada, 1768.

33 Lunn, "Economic Development in New France," 212.

34 Ibid., 205. It should be noted that the sums given represent the catch
    taken from posts along the Labrador coast from Mingan to Cape
    Charles, Newfoundland-Labrador.

CHAPTER FIVE

1 LAC, MG 11, CO 323/15, Q 31, Murray to Egremont, 5 June 1762.

2 LAC, MG 11, CO 194, vol. 18, pp. 272–3.

3 LAC, MG 11, CO 194/D3, Board of Trade to King, 18 May 1764.

4 Great Britain, Privy Council, *In the Matter of the Boundary,* 7: 3531–2.

5 LAC, MG 11, CO 42, Q2, Murray to Lord Halifax, 24 April 1764.

6 Ibid.

7 LAC, MG 21, Add. MS. 35915, vol. 107, file 451, fol. 318.

8 Ibid.

9 LAC, MG 11, CO 194, vol. 16, pp. 260–4.

10 LAC, MG 11, CO 194/26, Board of Trade to King, 15 March 1763.

11 LAC, MG 11, CO 194/16, Egremont to Board of Trade, 24 March 1763.

12 LAC, MG 11, CO 42, Q2, Complaints of Merchants of Quebec about
    Labrador, 16 February 1764.

13 LAC, MG 11, CO 194/16, Palliser to Board of Trade, 30 March 1765, Reg-
    ulations, 8 April 1765, enclosed.

14 Ibid.

15 Ibid., Regulations, 28 August 1765.

16 Ibid.

17 Innis, *The Cod Fisheries*, 193.

18 Ibid., 193.

19 LAC, MG 11, CO 194/16, 180, Heads of Inquiry and Answers, 19 March 1766.

20 LAC, MG 11, CO 194/16, Merchants of Quebec to Board of Trade, 27 March 1766.

21 LAC, MG 11, CO 194/27, Board of Trade to King, 13 May 1766.

22 Great Britain, Privy Council, *In the Matter of the Boundary*, 7: 3151.

23 LAC, MG 11, CO 42, Q4, Carleton to Lords of Trade, 17 January 1767.

24 LAC, MG 11, CO 194/18, Adventurers in Labrador to Palliser, August 1767.

25 Ibid., Case of the Landlords of Canada, 1768.

26 Ibid., Board of Trade to King, 24 June 1772.

27 LAC, MG 23, A1, John Cartwright to Lord Dartmouth, vol. 8, no. 2408, 13 January 1773.

28 Great Britain, Privy Council, *In the Matter of the Boundary*, 3: 1093.

29 Ibid., 1124–41.

30 LAC, MG 11, CO 43/2, Instructions for Guy Carleton, 3 January 1775.

31 Great Britain, Privy Council, *In the Matter of the Boundary*, 7: 3437–50.

32 LAC, MG 11, CO 42, Q37, Petition of Merchants to Lord Germain, 18 December 1777.

33 Ibid.

34 Great Britain, Privy Council, *In the Matter of the Boundary*, 8: 1174.

35 LAC, MG 21, GII, 22, B, 184–1, 32, Declaration of Simon Boucher about the burning of Posts on the coast of Labrador, 21 November 1778.

36 LAC, MG 12, Admiralty 1/2485, Petition of Merchants from Quebec to the Lord Commissioners of the Admiralty.

37 LAC, MG 21, GII, 22, B, 54, 303, Haldimand to Lord Germain, 18 November 1778.

38 Ibid.

39 LAC, MG 12, Admiralty 1/2485, Petition of Merchants from Quebec to the Lords Commissioners of the Admiralty.

40 LAC, MG 21, GII, 22, B, 54, 141, Haldimand to Lord Germain, 13 September 1779.

41 LAC, MG 12, Admiralty 1/2485, Merchants of Quebec involved in the fisheries along the coast of Labrador.

42 Ibid.

43 Shortt and Doughty, *Relating to the Constitutional History of Canada Documents*, 1: 728.

44 LAC, MG 11, CO 42, Q25, Affidavit of John Ross, 26 September 1785.

45 Ibid., Merchants of Quebec to Henry Hamilton, 13 September 1785.

46 W.H. Whiteley, "Newfoundland, Quebec, and Labrador Merchants, 1783–1809," 23.

47 Great Britain, Privy Council, *In the Matter of the Boundary*, 7: 3447–57.

48 *Quebec Gazette*, 21 June 1804.

49 Great Britain, Privy Council, *In the Matter of the Boundary*, 7: 3473–77.

50 Ibid., 1194.

51 Ibid., 1200.

52 The Province of Quebec, by the Quebec Act of 1791, was divided into the provinces of Upper Canada (Ontario) and Lower Canada (Quebec).

53 LAC, MG 11, CO, W2, Q189, Remarks by James Irvine of Quebec, 1 February 1821.

54 Ibid.

55 Gosling, *Labrador*, 350–61.

56 Great Britain, Privy Council, *In the Matter of the Boundary*, 7: 77–8.

57 Ibid.

58 Gosling, *Labrador*, 371.

59 LAC, MG 11, CO 42, Q189, Remarks of James Irvine of Quebec, 1 February 1821.

60 Chambers, *The Fisheries of the Province of Quebec*, 120–1.

61 LAC, MG 11, CO 42, Q200, Address of Legislative Council of Lower Canada to Lord Dalhousie, 23 February, 1824.

62 Great Britain, Privy Council, *In the Matter of the Boundary*, 1: 210–211.

63 Robertson, "Notes on the Coast of Labrador," 34.

64 *Quebec Gazette*, 15 August 1822.

CHAPTER SIX

1 LAC, MG 11, CO, Q series, vol. 186A, Samuel Robertson to J. Fraser, Berthier, 4 February, 1826.

2 Samuel Robertson, "Notes on the Coast of Labrador," 35.

3 Canada (Province), *Sessional Papers*, 1853, Annual Report of Pierre Fortin, stipendiary magistrate.

4 Audubon, *Audubon and His Journals*, 1: 412–13.

5 Ibid., 2: 410–11. La Tabatière was at one time called Sparr Point.

6 A.S. Whiteley, *Quebec-Labrador Cod Fishery*, 14–15.

7 LAC, MG 24, F28, Henry Wolsey Bayfield, Journal, 1833–36, vol. 5, 94. John Goddard eventually moved to St Paul's River.

8 Audubon, *Audubon and His Journals*, 1: 413.

9 The Jersey firms established large fishing rooms at Blanc-Sablon, Woody Island, and Greenly Island. During the 1880s, the Job Brothers, a fishing company based in Newfoundland, bought them out.

10 LAC, MG 17, B1, Series E, SPG, Report of the Reverend Edward Cusack, 27 October 1840.

11 Bowen, "The Social Conditions of the Coast of Labrador," 330.

12 LAC, MG 17, B1, Series E, SPG, Report of the Reverend Edward Cusack, 27 October 1840.

13 Yvan Breton, *La culture matérielle des Blancs-Sablonais*, 37.

14 Bowen, "The Social Conditions of the Coast of Labrador," 335.

15 *First Annual Report of the Canada Foreign Missionary Society*, 1858.

16 Quoted in the *Fur Trade Journal of Canada*, December 1930.

17 Bowen, "The Social Conditions of the Coast of Labrador," 334.

18 Packard, *The Labrador Coast*, 73.

19 LAC, MG 29, D63, Charles Carpenter, Diary, 2 January, 1863, vol. 9, p. 160.

20 Tucker, *Five Months in Labrador and Newfoundland*, 116.

21 Bowen, "The Social Conditions of the Coast of Labrador," 323.

22 LAC, MG 17, B1, series E, SPG, Report of the Reverend Edward Cusack, 27 October 1840.

23 *First Annual Report of the Canada Foreign Missionary Society*, 1858.

24 Tucker, *Five Months in Labrador and Newfoundland*, 106.

25 Audubon, *Audubon and His Journals*, 1: 415.

26 Tucker, *Five Months in Labrador and Newfoundland*, 106.

27 Stearns, *Labrador*, 175.

28 Bowen, "The Social Conditions of the Coast of Labrador," 337.

29 Quoted in Audubon, *Audubon and His Journals*, 2: 417.

30 Bowen, "The Social Conditions of the Coast of Labrador," 337.

31 LAC, MG 24, F28, Henry Wolsey Bayfield, Correspondence, 1816–39, vol. 1, pp. 39–41, Bayfield to Charles Wood, secretary to the Admiralty.

32 Robertson, "Notes on the Coast of Labrador," 36.

33 Tucker, *Five Months in Labrador and Newfoundland*, 106.

34 Audubon, *Audubon and His Journals*, 2: 408.

35 LAC, MG 11, CO 42, Q, 186A, Samuel Robertson to J. Fraser, 4 February 1826.

36 Some of the local residents also traded their surplus of oils, skins, and

salmon to the Jersey merchants who owned several large fishing rooms in the Blanc-Sablon Bay region.

37 Audubon, *Audubon and His Journals*, 1: 418.

38 "Cronan, Daniel," in *Dictionary of Canadian Biography*, vol. 12.

39 LAC, MG 24, F28, Henry Wolsey Bayfield, Journal, 1833–36, vol. 5, p. 51.

40 Audubon, *Audubon and His Journals*, 1: 15.

41 Ibid., 2: 408–16.

42 Ibid, 1: 416–19.

43 LAC, MG 24, F28, Henry Wolsey Bayfield, Journal, 1833–36, vol. 5, p. 51.

44 Canada (Canada), *Sessional Papers*, 1862, Annual Report of Pierre Fortin, stipendiary magistrate.

45 LAC, MG 24, F28, Henry Wolsey Bayfield, Journal, 1833–36, vol. 5, p. 95.

46 LAC, MG 40, 12, "St. Lawrence Survey," original directions by Captain W.H. Bayfield, 1828–55, vols. 1–2, reel A-425, p. 222.

47 Canada (Province), *Sessional Papers*, 1849, Select Committee's Recommendations on the Report on Petition of Antoine Talbot, 12 April 1849.

48 Ibid.

49 Canada (Province), *Sessional Papers*, 1853, Annual Report of Pierre Fortin, stipendiary magistrate.

50 Robertson, "Notes on the Coast of Labrador," 35.

51 Canada (Province), *Sessional Papers*, 1865, Annual Report of Pierre Fortin, stipendiary magistrate.

52 LAC, MG 11, CO 45, vol. 121, Report of a Committee of the Executive Council, Lower Canada, 10 May 1837.

53 LAC, MG 24, F28, Henry Wolsey Bayfield, Correspondence, 1816–39, Letter from Bayfield, 21 June 1836.

54 Canada (Province), *Sessional Papers*, 1849, Select Committee's Recommendations on the Report on Petition of Antoine Talbot, 12 April 1849.

55 Ibid.

56 Audubon, *Audubon and His Journals*, 1: 413–14.

57 LAC, MG 24, F28, Henry Wolsey Bayfield, Journal, 1831–33, vol. 5, p. 120.

58 A.S. Whiteley, *Quebec-Labrador Cod Fishery*, 15–16.

59 LAC, MG 24, F28, Henry Wolsey Bayfield, Correspondence, 1816–39, vol. 1, pp. 39–41, Bayfield to Charles Wood, secretary to the Admiralty.

60 Canada (Province), *Sessional Papers*, 1849, Select Committee's recommendations on the Report on Petition of Antoine Talbot, 12 April 1849.

61 LAC, MG 24, F28, Henry Wolsey Bayfield, Journals, 1831–33, vol. 4, p. 118

62 Ibid.

63 Audubon, *Audubon and His Journals*, 1: 410.
64 Robertson, "Notes on the Coast of Labrador," 35–6.
65 Ibid.
66 LAC, MG 11, CO, Q series, vol. 186A, Samuel Robertson to J. Fraser, Berthier, 4 February 1826.
67 Ibid.
68 Ibid.
69 A.S. Whiteley, *Quebec-Labrador Cod Fishery*, 14–15.
70 LAC, MG 24, F28, Henry Wolsey Bayfield, Correspondence, 1816–39, vol. 1, pp. 39–41.
71 Ibid.
72 LAC, MG 11, CO 42, Q, 179, Memorial of Etienne Labadie of the Coast of Labrador now at Quebec.
73 Ibid.
74 LAC, MG 11, CO 45, vol. 121, Report of a Committee of the Executive Council, Lower Canada, 10 May 1837.
75 Ibid.
76 Ibid.
77 In 1841 the provinces of Lower Canada (now Quebec) and Upper Canada (now Ontario) were joined to form the Province of Canada. Twenty-six years later, at Confederation, the Province of Canada was divided into the provinces of Ontario and Quebec.
78 Canada (Province), *Sessional Papers*, 1849, Select Committee's Recommendations on the Report on Petition of Antoine Talbot, 12 April 1849.

CHAPTER SEVEN

1 Robertson,"Notes on the Coast of Labrador," 38.
2 Canada (Canada), *Sessional Papers*, 1862, Annual Report of Pierre Fortin, stipendiary magistrate.
3 Canada (Province), *Statutes*, 1853, 331–2.
4 Ibid.
5 Hind, *Exploration in the Interior of the Labrador Peninsula*, 2: 183.
6 Huard, *Labrador et Anticosti*, 471–3.
7 Canada, *Sessional Papers*, 1878, Annual Report of the Department of Fisheries, Appendix I, 85.
8 Ferland, *Le Labrador*, 108–10.
9 Canada, *Sessional Papers*, 1878, Annual Report of the Department of Fisheries, Appendix I, 85.
10 A.S. Whiteley. *Quebec-Labrador Cod Fishery*, 42.

11 During the early 1880s many of the Jersey firms on the coast went bankrupt and were bought out by fishing companies from Newfoundland.

12 Canada, *Sessional Papers*, 1873, Annual Report of the Department of Fisheries, Appendix B, 31.

13 Canada, *Sessional Papers*, 1874, Annual Report of the Department of Fisheries, Appendix B, 35.

14 Stearns, *Labrador*, 126–7.

15 *Sixth Annual Report of the Canada Foreign Missionary Society*, 1863.

16 Bowen, "The Social Conditions of the Coast of Labrador," 332.

17 LAC, RG 13, vol. 895, file 37C, Labrador and Anticosti – Record of Travel, by V.A. Huard, pp. 36–7 and 49–50.

18 Ibid.

19 *First Annual Report of the Canada Foreign Mission Society*, 1858.

20 LAC, MG 29, D63, Charles Carpenter, Diary, July 1861, vol. 18, pp. 101–4.

21 LAC, MG 17, B1, series E, SPG, Report of Rev. John Frederick Cooksley, December 1862.

22 Ibid., Report of Rev. Richard Wainright, 12 May 1865.

23 A.S. Whiteley, *Quebec-Labrador Cod Fishery*, 26–7.

24 *Fourth Annual Report of the Canada Foreign Mission Society*, 1861.

25 *Presbyterian Witness* 46 (29 July 1893): 237.

26 LAC, MG 17, B1, series E, SPG, Report of Reverend Wainwright, 26 May 1866.

27 LAC, RG 3, series B4, vol. 132, file 77/1884, reel T-2401.

28 Huard, *Labrador et Anticosti*, 445–56.

29 Ibid., 487–9.

30 LAC, MG 17, B1, series E, SPG, Report of John Frederick Cooksley, 2 December 1863.

31 Ibid., Report of Joseph Eames, 1885.

32 Huard, *Labrador et Anticosti*, 487–9.

33 *Fourth Annual Report of the Canada Foreign Missionary Society*, 1861.

34 *Fifth Annual Report of the Canada Missionary Foreign Society*, 1862.

35 LAC, MG 17, B1, series E, SPG, Report of Rev. Richard Wainwright, 2 October 1865.

36 *Fourth Annual Report of the Canada Foreign Missionary Society*, 1861.

37 Huard, *Labrador et Anticosti*, 445–6.

38 LAC, MG 17, B1, series E, SPG, Report of Rev. Richard Wainwright, 29 May 1868.

39 Ibid., Report of Rev. Richard Wainwright, 1868–69.

40 LAC, MG 30, B116, William Wakeham to William Smith, deputy minister of marine and fisheries, 8 January 1894.

41 Garnier, *Dog Sled to Airplane*, 160–1.

42 Dionne, *In a Breaking Wave*, 42–3.

43 Canada, *Sessional Papers*, 1875, Annual Report of the Department of Fisheries, Appendix B, 32.

44 Huard, *Labrador et Anticosti*, 473.

45 Garnier, *Dog Sled to Airplane*, 161–2. A Captain Joseph-Elzéar Bernier for a time also purchased salt cod along the coast.

46 Canada, *Sessional Papers*, 1876, Annual Report of the Department of Fisheries, Appendix B, 72.

47 Canada, *Sessional Papers*, 1877, Annual Report of the Department of Fisheries, Appendix B, 41.

48 LAC, RG 3, series B4, vol. 136, file 322/1901, reel T-2401.

49 A.S. Whiteley, "Communications on the Lower North Shore," 44–5.

50 Garnier, *Dog Sled to Airplane*, 103–4.

51 LAC, RG 3, series B4, vol. 131, file 949/1884, reel T-2400.

52 Ibid., vol. 132, file 77/1884, reel T-2401.

53 Innis, *The Cod Fisheries*, 350.

54 Ibid.

55 Chambers, *The Fisheries of the Province of Quebec*, 157–8.

56 Canada (Province), *Sessional Papers*, 1862, Annual Report of Pierre Fortin, stipendiary magistrate.

57 Canada (Province), *Sessional Papers*, 1853, Annual Report of Pierre Fortin, stipendiary magistrate.

58 Canada (Province), *Sessional Papers*, 1865, Annual Report of Pierre Fortin, stipendiary magistrate.

59 *First Annual Report of the Canada Foreign Missionary Society*, 1858.

60 A few of the fishermen were involved in herring, mackerel, trout, and lobster fishing. These types of fishing, according to Lavoie, were of little commercial value.

61 Canada, *Sessional Papers*, 1878, Annual Report of the Department of Fisheries, Appendix I, 87.

62 A quintal of codfish weighs 52 kilograms.

63 Canada (Province), *Sessional Papers*, 1860, Annual Report of Pierre Fortin, stipendiary magistrate.

64 A.S. Whiteley, *Quebec-Labrador Cod Fishery*, 37–8.

65 Canada, *Sessional Papers*, 1893, Annual Report of the Department of Fisheries, Appendix D, 100–1.

66 A.S. Whiteley, *Quebec-Labrador Cod Fishery*, 52–5.

67 Canada, *Sessional Papers*, 1878, Annual Report of the Department of Fisheries, Appendix B.

68 Stearns, *Labrador*, 129.

69 Canada, *Sessional Papers*, 1885, Annual Report of the Department of Fisheries, Appendix no. 5, 175.

70 Ferland, *Le Labrador*, 109.

71 *Fifth Annual Report of the Canada Foreign Missionary Society*, 1862.

72 *Ninth Annual Report of the Canada Foreign Missionary Society*, 1866.

73 LAC, MG 17, B1, series E, SPG, Report of Rev. Wainwright, 24 June 1867.

74 Ibid., Report of Rev. Wainwright, May 1869.

75 Canada, *Sessional Papers*, 1868, Annual Report of the Department of Fisheries, Appendix B, 57–8.

76 Canada, *Sessional Papers*, 1872, Annual Report of the Department of Fisheries, Appendix B, 40–52.

77 Canada. *Sessional Papers*, 1877, Annual Report of the Department of Fisheries, Appendix B, 57–60.

78 Stearns, *Labrador*, 175.

79 LAC, MG 30, B116, Commander W. Wakeham to William Smith, deputy minister of marine and fisheries, 8 January 1894.

CHAPTER EIGHT

1 For further details about the number of inhabitants living in the various villages, see *La Basse-Côte-Nord*, 22.

2 Ibid.

3 Rompkey, *Grenfell of Labrador*, 126–7.

4 LAC, MG 26, J, William Lyon Mackenzie King to Frederick Borden, 10 May 1905.

5 Ibid., W. Wakeham to Minister of Marine and Fisheries, 18 May 1905.

6 Ibid., King to Wrong, 31 May 1905.

7 Ibid., Grenfell to King, 12 July 1905.

8 Ibid., Grenfell to King, 1 November 1905.

9 Townsend, *In Audubon's Labrador*, 144.

10 Hodd, "Mutton Bay Nurses," 8–9.

11 Junek, *Isolated Communities*, 112.

12 Joveneau and Tremblay, *Missionary in Labrador and New Quebec*, 23–5.

13 Carney, *Harrington Harbour*, 93.

14 DA, Personal Archives, Gabriel Dionne, LCB–6055–C75 D1, 13a, LNSEC, Report of the first meeting, held at St Augustine, 15–16 February 1961.

15 *Sextant* 3 (May 1977).

16 LAC, MG 32, B6, volume 10, Grenfell Labrador Missions, 1960–61, Dr Hodd to Dr G. Thomas, 14 May 1960.

17 DA, Personal Archives, Gabriel Dionne, LCB–6055–C75 DI, 13a, LNSEC, Report of the first meeting, held at St Augustine, 15–16 February 1961.

18 Junek, *Isolated Communities*, 96–7.

19 A.S. Whiteley,"Communications on the Lower North Shore," 45–7.

20 LAC, RG 12, Transport Series, A-1, vol. 1693, file 7282, 145, Pierre E. Cosgrain to Honourable H.A. Stewart, Minister of Public Works, 27 June 1935.

21 Ibid., F.G. Sims, General Superintendent, to J.A. Bilodeau, 26 August 1935.

22 DA, Personal Archives, Gabriel Dionne, LCB–6055–C75 DI, 13a, LNSEC, Report of the first meeting, held at St Augustine, 15–16 February 1961.

23 Dionne, *In a Breaking Wave*, 203.

24 Joveneau and Tremblay, *Missionary in Labrador and New Quebec*, 49.

25 Garnier, *Dog Sled to Airplane*, 167–9.

26 LAC, RG 23, vol. 1764, file 795-51-5[1], A Report of the Distressful Conditions Prevailing on the Coast of the Canadian Labrador, 22 August 1949, Clive Planta.

27 Ibid.

28 Dionne, *In a Breaking Wave*, 194.

29 LAC, RG 3, vol. 2279, file 22-2-54, 1957–66.

30 LAC, RG 23, vol. 1764, file 795-51-5[1], A Report of the Distressful Conditions Prevailing on the Coast of the Canadian Labrador, 22 August 1949, Clive Planta.

31 LAC, MG 26, L, F-12-2, vol. 102, Robert H. Winters to Louis St. Laurent, 7 November 1951.

32 Carney, *Harrington Harbour*, 93.

33 Dionne, *In a Breaking Wave*, 91–3.

34 Garnier, *Dog Sled to Airplane*, 245–9.

35 Joveneau and Tremblay, *Missionary in Labrador and New Quebec*, 100–106.

36 *Sextant* 3 (March 1977).

37 *Sextant* 3 (September/October, 1977); *Quebec Diocesan Gazette* 41, no. 4 (July 1934): 28.

38 Banfill, *Labrador Nurse*, 31–5.

39 *Sextant* 3 (September/October 1977).

40 DA, Personal Archives, Gabriel Dionne, LCB–605 –C75M, B.

41 Ibid., LCB–6055–C75D1, 13a, LNSEC, Report of the first meeting, held at St Augustine, 15–16 February 1961.

42 Ibid.

43 *Coaster*, January 1957

44 *Coaster*, April 1957.

45 Joveneau and Tremblay, *Missionary in Labrador and New Quebec*, 100–2.

46 LAC, MG 32, B6, Charles Douglas Abbott Collection, vol. 2, Grenfell Labrador Mission Report, appendix D, 1965.

47 DA, Personal Archives, Gabriel Dionne, LCB–6055–C75M, B.

48 Banfill, *Labrador Nurse*, 31.

49 Activity in the seal, salmon, lobster, herring, and mackerel fisheries and the fur trade usually increased when there was a failure in the cod fishery.

50 Canada, *Sessional Papers*, 1913, Annual Report of the Department of Fisheries, 1911–12, p. 228.

51 Hodd, "Boats on the Labrador," 3–6.

52 Brouillette, "La Côte-Nord du Saint-Laurent," 20–2.

53 Ibid., 25.

54 Garnier, *Dog Sled to Airplane*, 161–2. Captain Joseph-Elzéar Bernier for a time also purchased salt cod along the coast.

55 Brouillette,"La Côte-Nord du Saint-Laurent," 25.

56 Arthur Guillemette (La Romaine), George Court (Kegashka), William Bobbit and Cecil Rousell (Harrington), Jules Boulet (Mutton Bay), Jacques Monger (Tête-à-la-Baleine), Lawrence Organ (La Tabatière), John L. Fequet, John A. Fequet, and Alfred Fequet (Old Fort Bay), L.T. Blais (St Augustine), William Keats (Salmon Bay), Willie Vatcher (Bradore Bay), Alfred Cormier, Johnny Beaudoin, and Napoleon Beaudoin (Lourdes-de-Blanc-Sablon).

57 LAC, RG 23, vol. 1434, file-746-4-5[1], Memorandum to Minister of Fisheries, 7 June 1939.

58 Junek, *Isolated Communities*, 72–3.

59 A.S. Whiteley, *Quebec-Labrador Cod Fishery*, 60.

60 *Beaver*, September 1944, 23.

61 Junek, *Isolated Communities*, 72–3.

62 In the mid-1940s La Cooperative des Pêcheurs-Unis de Québec established a fishing cooperative, Syndicat Belles-Îles, at Lourdes-de-Blanc-Sablon. Various fishermen from that community conducted their business with this organization.

63 LAC, RG 23, vol. 1764, file 795-51-5[1], A Report of the Distressful Con-

ditions Prevailing on the Coast of the Canadian Labrador, 22 August 1949, Clive Planta.

64 Ibid., vol. 1761, file 795-38-6[1], Report of the Fisheries of Quebec, 1949–51.

65 Ibid.

66 Daneau, *Situation économique de la pêche côtière du Québec*, 10–12.

67 Ibid.

68 Perrault, *Toutes isles,* 75.

69 Ibid.

70 Canada, *Sessional Papers,* 1909, no. 22, Annual Report of the Department of Fisheries, 1907, pp. 144–7.

71 LAC, RG 23, vol. 390, file 3633, 1910, pt. 1, file, pp. 299–302.

72 Ibid., vol. 390, file 3633, pt. 2, p. 3, Superintendent of Fisheries to E.H. Cunningham, 17 June 1911.

73 Ibid., p. 4, Cunningham to Superintendent of Fisheries, 28 June 1911.

74 Ibid., H.A. Stevens to the Vancouver Board of Trade.

75 Townsend, *In Audubon's Labrador,* 134.

76 A.S. Whiteley, *Quebec-Labrador Cod Fishery,* 58.

77 Canada, *Sessional Papers,* 1920, no. 40, Annual Report of the Department of Fisheries, pp. 37–8.

78 A.S. Whiteley, *Quebec-Labrador Cod Fishery,* 58–9.

79 Canada, *Sessional Papers,* 1922, no. 40, Annual Report of the Department of Fisheries, 1920, pp. 43–6.

80 LAC, RG 23, vol. 1325, file 729-3-22 [1], Letter from the residents of Old Fort Bay to Minister of Marine and Fisheries.

81 Garnier, *Dog Sled to Airplane,* 59–63.

82 A.S. Whiteley, *Quebec-Labrador Cod Fishery,* 58.

83 LAC, RG 23, vol. 1343, file 729-12-6 [1].

84 Ibid., file 729-12-6 [2], J. Wilcott to Pierre Casgrain, 12 November 1938.

85 Ibid., vol. 1764, file 795-51-5[1], A Report of the Distressful Conditions Prevailing on the Coast of the Canadian Labrador, 22 August 1949, Clive Planta.

86 Ibid.

87 Banfill, *Labrador Nurse,* 134.

88 *Coastar,* December 2003, 14–16.

89 LAC, RG 23, vol. 1764, file 795-51-5[1], A Report of the Distressful Conditions Prevailing on the Coast of the Canadian Labrador, 22 August 1949, Clive Planta.

90 Ibid., file 795-51-3, Memorandum to the Deputy Minister, Relief for the Canadian Labrador, 25 October 1949, Clive Planta.

91 *Coaster*, April 1957.

92 LAC, MG 32, B6, Grenfell Labrador Mission, Dr Donald G. Hodd to Dr G. Thomas, 14 May 1960.

CHAPTER NINE

1 *La Basse-Côte-Nord*, 22.

2 Statistics Canada, *Census of Canada, 1996: Community Profiles.*

3 A.S. Whiteley, "Communications on the Lower North Shore," 47.

4 *Sextant*, May 1977.

5 *Coaster* 2 (1955).

6 Remiggi, "Persistence of Ethnicity," 126–7.

7 DA, Personal Archives, Gabriel Dionne, LCB–6055–C75A, 1a, Father Dionne to Bishop Scheffer, 26 December 1960.

8 Ibid.

9 Ibid.

10 Ibid., LCB–6055–C75 D1, 13a, LNSEC, Report of the first meeting, held at St Augustine, 15–16 February 1961.

11 Ibid.

12 Ibid.

13 Ibid.

14 Ibid., LCB–6055–C75–D5–9, LNSEC, Minutes , 19 September 1961, Blanc-Sablon.

15 Ibid., LCB–6055–C75C, LNSEC, Report of the General Assembly, 1962, Lourdes-de-Blanc-Sablon.

16 Ibid., J.C. Bigonesse to Father Dionne, 5 May 1962.

17 Ibid., J.C. Bigonesse to Father Dionne, 30 November 1962.

18 Quebec, *Statute concerning the Municipality of the North Shore of the Gulf of the St Lawrence* (15–16 Elizabeth II, c.97, 4 April 1963).

19 LAC, MG 32, B6, Grenfell Labrador Mission Reports, vol. 11, appendix B, 1965.

20 DA, Personal Archives, Gabriel Dionne, LCB–6055–C75C, LNSEC, Report of the General Assembly, 1962.

21 *Coaster* 4 (April 1965).

22 *La Basse-Côte-Nord*, 48–9.

23 DA, Personal Archives, Gabriel Dionne, LCB–6055–C75C, Northern Wings, Letter, 19 July 1963.

24 A.S. Whiteley "Communications on the Lower North Shore," 46.

25 Dionne, *In a Breaking Wave*, 177.

26 Hodd, "The Snowmobile Era," 51–2.

27 DA, Personal Archives, Gabriel Dionne, LCB–6055–C75C, LNSEC, Report of the General Assembly, 1964.

28 *La Basse-Côte-Nord*, 72–4.

29 Ibid., 71–2.

30 *A Brief on a Regional Radio Network for the Lower North Shore*, 4–12.

31 *La Basse-Côte-Nord*, 75.

32 LAC, MG 32, B6, Grenfell Labrador Mission, vol. 10, Annual Meetings, 1970–72.

33 Ibid.

34 Ibid.

35 DA, Personal Archives, Gabriel Dionne, LCB–6055–C75C, LNSEC, Minutes of the Executive Committee, pp. 43–5.

36 Ibid., LNSEC, Report of the General Assembly, 1964.

37 Quebec, *Statute concerning the School Commission of the North Shore of the Gulf of the St Lawrence* (15–16, Elizabeth II, c.125, 14 April 1967).

38 Joveneau and Tremblay, *Missionary in Labrador and New Quebec*, 94.

39 *Education on the Lower North Shore Kegashka-Blanc Sablon*, 9.

40 Ibid.

41 LAC, MG 32, B6, Grenfell Labrador Mission Reports, vol. 11, 1971.

42 *La Basse-Côte-Nord*, 60–1.

43 Ibid., 66.

44 Daneau, *Situation économique de la pêche côtière du Québec*, 10–12.

45 Ibid.

46 *La Basse-Côte-Nord*, 30.

47 Ibid., 40–1.

48 Daneau, *Situation économique de la pêche côtière du Québec*, 11.

49 Statistics Canada, *Census of Canada, 1996: Community Profiles*.

50 DA, Personal Archives, Gabriel Dionne, LCB–6055–675D-1, 13 A, LNSEC, Report of the first meeting held at St Augustine, 15–16 February 1961.

51 A.S. Whiteley, *Quebec-Labrador Cod Fishery*, 76

52 *Coaster* 6 (June 1965).

53 Ibid.

54 A.S. Whiteley, *Quebec-Labrador Cod Fishery*, 76

55 *Coastar* 1 (December 1990).

56 *Coastar* 2 (December 1992).

Bibliography

ARCHIVAL SOURCES

ARCHIVES DESCHÂTELETS (OBLATS DE MARIE-IMMACULÉE),
OTTAWA (AD)
Personal Archives, Gabriel Dionne

ARCHIVES NATIONALES DU QUÉBEC (ANQ)
Ordonnances des intendants, 1666–1760
Registres du Conseil souverain, 1663–1758
Registres d'intendance, 1672–1759

LIBRARY AND ARCHIVES CANADA (LAC)
RG 1: Land records for the Province of Quebec
RG 3: Post Office Department fonds
RG 13: Department of Justice fonds
RG 23: Department of Fisheries and Oceans fonds
MG 8, F54: Mingan fonds
MG 11, CO: Colonial Office fonds
MG 12, ADM: Admiralty fonds
MG 17, B1: United Society for the Propagation of the Gospel fonds
MG 21, GII, 22: Sir Frederick Haldimand collection
MG 21, Add. MSS. 35913–15: Hardwicke papers
MG 23, A1: William Legge, 2nd Earl of Dartmouth, fonds
MG 23, 15: Hugh Palliser collection

MG 24, F28: Henry Wolsey Bayfield fonds
MG 24, F33: William Denny fonds
MG 26, J: William Lyon Mackenzie King fonds
MG 26, L: Louis St Laurent fonds
MG 29, D63: Charles Carroll Carpenter fonds
MG 30, B116: Wilfred Thomason Grenfell fonds
MG 30, C244: Henry Mather Hare and family fonds
MG 32, B6: Douglas Charles Abbott fonds
MG 40, I2: Hydrographic Department, Henry Wolsey Bayfield

PROVINCIAL ARCHIVES OF NEWFOUNDLAND AND LABRADOR (PANL)
International Grenfell Assocation (IGA) Collection

PUBLISHED SOURCES

Arnaud, Charles. *Journal des voyages de Charles Arnaud, 1872–1873.* Recherche et transcription, Huguette Tremblay. Montréal: Presses de l'Université de Québec, 1977
Audubon, Maria R. *Audubon and His Journals.* 2 vols. New York: Dover Publications, 1960
Auger, Reginald. *Labrador Inuit and Europeans in the Strait of Belle Isle: From Written Sources to the Archaeological Evidence.* Québec: Centre d'études nordiques, Université Laval, 1991
L'Avenir. Sept-Îles, Qué. 1960–65
Babel, Louis. *Journal des voyages de Louis Babel, 1866–1868.* Recherche et transcription, Huguette Tremblay. Montréal: Presses de l'Université du Québec, 1977
Banfill, Bessie J. *Labrador Nurse.* Toronto: Ryerson Press, 1952
Barbour, Florence G. *Memories of Life on the Labrador and Newfoundland.* New York: Carleton Press 1930
Barkham, S. deL. "A Note on the Strait of Belle Isle during the Period of Basque Contact with Indians and Inuit." *Études/Inuit/Studies* 4, nos 1–2 (1980)
La Basse-Côte-Nord: Perspectives de développement: Rapport de la Mission de la Basse-Côte-Nord au docteur Camille Laurin, ministre d'État au développement culturel. Québec: Gouvernement du Québec, 1979
Bayfield, H.W. *The St Lawrence Pilot: Comprising Sailing Directions for the Gulf and River.* 4th ed. 2 vols. London: Hydrographic Office, 1860
Beck, Brian. "Seal Net Fisheries along the North Shore of the St Lawrence River." *Trade News,* 1965

Bedding, David L. *A Report of the Salmon of the North Shore of the Gulf of St Lawrence and the North Eastern Coast of Newfoundland.* Quebec: Department of Fisheries, 1961

Bélanger, Henri. *Reports on the Scaling of Rivers on the North Shore.* Quebec: Department of Lands and Forests, 1909

Bélanger, René. *Les Basques dans l'estuaire du Saint-Laurent.* Montréal: Presses de l'Université du Québec, 1971

– *De la pointe de tous les diables au Cap Grincedents: Toponymie historique et actuelle de la Côte-Nord.* Québec: Belisle, Éditeur, 1973

Bercher, F.R. "The North Shore." *The Beaver,* Winter 1981

Biggar, Henry Percival, ed. *A Collection of Documents Relating to Jacques Cartier and Sieur Roberval.* Ottawa: Public Archives of Canada, 1930

– ed. *The Voyages of Jacques Cartier.* Ottawa: F.A. Acland, 1924

Blanchard, Raoul. *L'Est du Canada français, "Province de Québec."* Vol. 1. Montréal: Librairie Beauchemin, 1935

Bowen, N.H. "The Social Conditions of the Coast of Labrador." *Literary and Historical Society of Quebec* 4 (February 1855)

Breton, Yvan. *La culture matérielle des Blancs-Sablonnais.* Québec: Centre d'Études nordiques, Université Laval, 1968

– *Étude démographique de la Basse-Côte-Nord de 1900 à 1968.* Québec: Université Laval, Laboratoire d'ethnographie, 1968

– *St. Paul's River: Étude monographique.* Québec: Université Laval, 1968

Breton, Yvan, Marc Adelard, and Paul Charest. *Changement culturel à St. Augustin: Un contribution à l'étude des isolat de la Côte-Nord.* Université Laval, 1965

A Brief on a Regional Radio Network for the Lower North Shore. Coasters' Association, September 1992

Brouillette, B. "La Côte-Nord du Saint-Laurent." *Revue canadienne de géographie* 1, nos. 2, 3, 4 (June–September, December 1947)

Browne, Rev. P.W. *Where the Fishers Go.* Toronto: Musson, 1910

Bussiere, Paul. "La population de la Côte-Nord." *Cahiers de géographie de Québec* 7, no. 14 (1963); 8, no. 15 (1963–64)

Butler, Samuel Russell. *The Labrador Mission.* Montreal: Witness Printing House, 1878

Cabot, William Brooks. *Labrador.* Boston: Small Maynard and Co., 1920

Canada (Province). *Journals of the Legislative Assembly.* 1850–67

– *Statutes of Canada.* 1850–67

Canada. *Sessional Papers.* 1850–1923

Canada Foreign Missionary Society. *Annual Report of the Canada Foreign Missionary Society.* 1st (1858)–9th. Montreal: J. Lovell, 1859–[67?]

Carney, Anne E. *Harrington Harbour: Back Then.* Montreal: Price-Patterson, 1991

Carrière, Gaston. *Les Oblats de M.I. dans le Vicariat apostolique du Labrador, 1844–1956.* Ottawa: Édition des Études oblates 1959

Cartwright, George. *A Journal of Transactions and Events during a Residence of Nearly Sixteen Years on the Coast of Labrador.* London, 1792

Chambers, E.T.D. *The Fisheries of the Province of Quebec.* Quebec: Department of Colonization, Mines and Fisheries of the Province of Quebec 1912

Chappel, Edward. *Voyage of His Majesty's Ship Rosamond to Newfoundland and the Southern Coast of Labrador.* London: J. Mawman, 1818

Charest, Paul. *Écologie culturelle de la Côte-Nord du Golfe Saint-Laurent.* Québec: Université Laval, 1972

– *Histoire, démographie et généalogie des premières populations permanentes de la Basse Côte-Nord (de Kegashka à Blanc-Sablon), 1820–1900.* Québec: Ethnographie de la Côte-Nord du St. Laurent, 1968

– "Le peuplement permanent de la Basse Cote-Nord du Saint Laurent 1820–1900." *Recherches sociographiques* 11, no. 1–2 (1970)

Coaster. 1955–68

Comeau, Napoleon Alexander. *Life and Sport on the North Shore of the St Lawrence and Gulf: Salmon Fishing and Hunting, Legends of the Montagnais.* Quebec: Daily Telegraph Printing House, 1910

Daneau, Marcel. *Le developpement socio-économique des pêcheries de la Côte-Nord du Golfe St-Laurent.* Ottawa: Ministère des pêcheries du Canada, 1968

– *Situation économique de la pêche côtière du Québec.* Québec: Ministère de l'industrie et du commerce, Division des pêcheries 1964

Dawson, S.E. "Brest on the Quebec Labrador." *Transactions of the Royal Society of Canada,* sec. 2, vol. 11 (1905)

– *The St Lawrence Basin and Its Borderlands.* London: Lawrence and Bullen, 1905

De Boilieu, Lambert. *Louis Jolliet, vie et voyages (1645–1700).* Montréal: L'Institute d'Histoire de l'Amérique française 1950

Dictionary of Canadian Biography. Available at www.biographi.ca/index2.html

Dionne, Gabriel. *In a Breaking Wave: Living History of the Lower North Shore.* Trans. Helen Miller and Thelma Marion. Montreal: Missionnaires oblats de Marie Immaculée, 1988

Education on the Lower North Shore, Kegashka–Blanc Sablon. Commission Scolaire du Littoral

Fauteux, Joseph-Noel. *Essai sur l'industrie au Canada sous le régime français.* Québec: Imprimé par L.-A. Proulx, imprimeur du roi, 1927

Feild, Edward. *Newfoundland: Journal of a Voyage of a Visitation in the "Hawk" Church Ship, on the Coast of Labrador, and Round the Whole Island of Newfoundland in the Year 1849.* London: Society for the Propagation of the Gospel, 1850

Ferland, J.-B.-A. *Le Labrador: Notes et récits de voyage.* Montréal: Beauchemin et Valois, 1858

– *Opuscules: Louis-Olivier Gamache et le Labrador.* Nouv. ed. Québec: A. Côté, 1877

Fitzhugh, William, Yves Chretien, and Helena Sharp. *The Gateways Project 2004: Surveys and Excavations from Chevery to Jacques Cartier Bay.* Washington, DC: Arctic Studies Center, National Museum of Natural History, Smithsonian Institution, 2004. Available at http://www.mnh.si.edu/arctic/html/pub-field.html

Fitzhugh, William, and Matthew Gallon. *The Gateways Project 2002: Surveys and Excavations from Petit Mecatina to Belles Amours.* Washington, DC: Arctic Studies Center, National Museum of Natural History, Smithsonian Institution, 2004. Available at http://www.mnh.si.edu/arctic/html/pub-field.html

Fitzhugh, William, and Helena Sharp. *The Gateways Project 2003: Surveys and Excavations from Hare Harbour to Jacques Cartier Bay.* Washington, DC: Arctic Studies Center, National Museum of Natural History, Smithsonian Institution, 2003. Available at http://www.mnh.si.edu/arctic/html/pub-field.html

Fletcher, E.T. "Notes on a Voyage to St. Augustin, Labrador." *Bulletin de la Société de géographie de Québec,* 1881

Galibois, Auguste. "La Côte Nord: Chronique de la mer et des grèves." *Le Terroir* 14, no.7 (December 1932)

Garnier, Louis. *Dog Sled to Airplane: A History of the St Lawrence North Shore.* Trans. Hélène A. Nantais and Robert L. Nantais. Quebec 1949

Gosling, William Gilbert. *Labrador: Its Discovery, Exploration, and Development.* London: Aston Rivers, 1910

Great Britain. Privy Council. *In the Matter of the Boundary between the Dominion of Canada and the Colony of Newfoundland, in the Labrador Peninsula.* 12 vols. London: William Clowes and Sons, 1927

Grégory, J.-U. *En racontrait: Récits de voyages en Floride, au Labrador et sur le fleuve Saint Laurent.* Québec: C. Darveau, 1886

Grenfell, W.T. *Labrador: The Country and the People.* New York: Macmillan, 1910

Hind, Henry Yule. *Exploration in the Interior of the Labrador Peninsula, the Country of the Montagnais and Nasquapie Indian.* 2 vols. London: Longman, 1863

Hodd, D.G. "Boats on the Labrador." *Among the Deep Sea Fishers, International Grenfell Association,* April 1970

– "Mutton Bay Nurses," *Among the Deep Sea Fishers, International Grenfell Association,* April 1966

– "The Snowmobile Era." *Among the Deep Sea Fishers, International Grenfell Association,* April 1969

Howell, R.M. "Summer at Blanc-Sablon." *The Beaver* 275, no. 3 (September 1944)

Huard, V.-A. *Labrador et Anticosti: Journal de voyage, histoire, topographie, pêcheurs canadiens et acadiens, Indiens montagnais.* Montréal: Beauchemin, 1897

Innis, Harold A. *The Cod Fisheries.* Toronto: University of Toronto Press, 1954

Joveneau, Alexis, and Laurent Tremblay. *Missionary in Labrador and New Quebec. Lionel Scheffer, OMI.* Montreal: Fayonnement, 1971

Junek, O.W. *Isolated Communities: A Study of a Labrador Fishing Village.* New York: American Book Company, 1937

Lanctôt, Gustav. *Jacques Cartier devant l'histoire.* Montréal: Lumen, 1947

Lévesque, René. *La Seigneurie des Îles et des Îlets de Mingan.* Archéologie du Québec. Montréal: Lemeac, 1971

Lewis, H.R. "Notes on Some Details of the Explorations of Jacques Cartier in the Gulf of St Lawrence." *Transactions of the Royal Society of Canada* 27, sec. 2

Lunn, A.J.E. "Economic Development in New France." PhD dissertation, McGill University, 1942

McGhee, Robert, and James A. Tuck. *An Archaic Sequence from the Strait of Belle Isle, Labrador.* Ottawa: National Museums of Canada, 1975

McKenzie, James. "Some Account of the King's Posts, the Labrador Coast and the Island of Anticosti, by an Indian Trader Residing There Several Years; with a Description of the Natives, Same." In *Les bourgeois de la Compagnie du Nord-Ouest: Récits de voyages, lettres et rapports inédits relatifs au Nord-Ouest canadien,* ed. L.R. Masson. Québec: A. Coté et Cie, 1889–90

Martijn, C.A. "An Archaeological Research on the Lower St Lawrence North Shore, Quebec." In *Archaeological Salvage Projects 1972, Mercury Series.* Archaeological Survey of Canada Paper no. 15. Ottawa, 1974

Mowat, Farley. *Westviking: The Ancient Norse in Greenland and North America.* Toronto: McClelland and Stewart, 1990

Nobbs, Percy E. *The Salmon Fisheries of the Gulf of the St Lawrence.* Quebec: Department of Fisheries 1948

Packard, A.S. *The Labrador Coast: Journal of Two Summer Cruises to That Region.* New York: N.D.C. Hodges, 1891

Parkman, Francis. *Pioneers of France in the New World.* 2 vols. Toronto: George N. Morang and Co., 1899

Perrault, Pierre. *Toutes isles: Chroniques de terre de mer.* Ottawa: Fides, 1963

Pintal, Jean-Yves, and Charles Martijn. "Early Bird Archaeologists among the Bake Apples: A Quick Swoop along Quebec's Lower North Shore." In *Honoring Our Elders: The History of Eastern Arctic Archaeology,* ed. William W. Fitzhugh, Stephen Loring, and Daniel Odess. Washington, DC: Arctic Studies Center, National Museum of Natural History, 2002

Presbyterian Witness. Halifax, 1864–65, 1888–1900

Proulx, Jean-Pierre. *Basque Whaling in Labrador in the 16th Century.* Studies in Archaeology, Architecture and History. Ottawa: National Historic Sites, Parks Service, 1993

Public Archives of Canada. *Report on Canadian Archives.* 1890–93, 1896–1902, 1921. Ottawa: The Archives

Quebec Gazette. 1764–1822

Remiggi, Frank William. "Persistence of Ethnicity: A Study of the Eastern Lower North Shore, 1820–1970." Master's thesis, Memorial University of Newfoundland, 1975

Robertson, Samuel. "Notes on the Coast of Labrador." *Transactions of the Literary and Historical Society of Quebec* 4, no. 1 (February 1855)

Rochette, E. *Notes sur la Côte-Nord du Bas Saint-Laurent et le Labrador canadien.* Québec: Le Soleil, 1926

Rompkey, Ronald. *Grenfell of Labrador: A Biography.* Toronto: University of Toronto Press, 1991

Rouillard, E. *La Côte-Nord de Saint Laurent et la Labrador canadien.* Québec: Laflame et Proulx, 1908

Roy, J.E. "François Bissot, sieur de la Rivière." *Transactions of the Royal Society of Canada,* ser. 1, vol. 10, section 1 (1892)

Roy, Pierre-Georges, ed. *Inventaire de pièces sur la côte de Labrador conservées aux Archives de la province de Québec.* Québec: Archives de la Province, 1940–42

Sextant. 1970–78

Sharpes, Alice. *Labrador, Newfoundland, Gaspe.* Montreal: Clarke Steamship Co., 1939

Shortt, Adam, and Arthur G. Doughty, eds. *Documents relating to the Constitutional History of Canada, 1759–[1828].* 3 vols. Ottawa: King's Printer, 1918–35

Statistics Canada. *Census of Canada, 1996: Community Profiles*. Available at
www12.statcan.ca/english/Profil/PlaceSearchForm1.cfm

Stearns, W.A. *Labrador: A Sketch of Its People, Its Industries and Its Natural
History*. Boston: Lee and Shepard, 1884

Thurston, Harry. "The Basque Connection." *Equinox*, November/December
1983

Townsend, Charles Wendell. *In Audubon's Labrador*. Boston and New York:
Houghton Mifflin Company; Cambridge: The University Press, 1918

Trudel, François. "Inuit, Amerindians and Europeans: A Study of Interethnic
Economic Relations on the Canadian Southeastern Seaboard, 1500–1800."
PhD dissertation, University of Connecticut, 1981

– "Les Inuit du Labrador méridional face à l'exploitation canadienne et
française des pêcheries (1700–1760)." *Revue d'histoire de l'Amérique
française* 31, no. 4 (1977)

Tuck, James A. *Newfoundland and Labrador Prehistory*. Ottawa: Archaeological Survey of Canada, National Museums of Canada, 1976

Tucker, Ephraim W. *Five Months in Labrador and Newfoundland during the
Summer of 1838*. Concord, NH: I.S. Boyd and W. White, 1839

Tyman, J.L. "Man and the North Shore: A Study in Environmental Response."
MA thesis, Department of Geography, McGill University, 1961

Vigneau, Placide. *Un pied d'ancre: Journal de Placide Vigneau*. Ed. Gérard
Gallienne et René Bélanger. Sillery, Que., 1969

Voorhis, Ernest. *Historic Forts and Trading Posts of the French Regime and of
the English Fur Trading Companies*. Ottawa: Department of the Interior,
1930

White, James. *Forts and Trading Posts in Labrador Peninsula and Adjoining
Territory*. Ottawa: King's Printer, 1926

Whiteley, A.S. "Communications on the Lower North Shore." *Canadian Geo-
graphical Journal*, August/September 1977

– *Quebec-Labrador Cod Fishery: One Hundred Years of Life and Work, the
Story of the Whiteley Family in an Isolated Community*. Ottawa: A.S.
Whiteley, 1975

Whiteley, G.C. "The Pioneers of Labrador." *Maritime Advocate and Busy
East*, October and November 1952

Whiteley, W.H. "Governor Hugh Palliser and the Newfoundland and
Labrador Fishery, 1764–1768." *Canadian Historical Review* 50 (1969)

– "Newfoundland, Quebec, and the Labrador Merchants, 1783–1809." *Newfoundland Quarterly* 73 (1977)

Wright, James. *La préhistoire du Québec*. Ottawa: Musée national de
l'homme, 1980

Index